OCR
Criminal
Law
for A2

Jacqueline Martin

Editor: Chris Turner

HODDER
EDUCATION
AN HACHETTE UK COMPANY

Orders: please contact Bookpoint Ltd, 130 Milton Park, Abingdon, Oxon
OX14 4SB. Telephone: (44) 01235 827720. Fax: (44) 01235 400454. Lines are
open from 9.00 – 5.00, Monday to Saturday, with a 24 hour message
answering service. You can also order through our website
www.hoddereducation.co.uk

If you have any comments to make about this, or any of our other titles,
please send them to educationenquiries@hodder.co.uk

British Library Cataloguing in Publication Data
A catalogue record for this title is available from the British Library

ISBN: 978 0 340 97362 2

First Edition Published 2006
This Edition Published 2009
Impression number 10 9 8 7 6 5 4 3 2 1
Year 2013 2012 2011 2010 2009

Hachette UK's policy is to use papers that are natural, renewable and
recyclable products and made from wood grown in sustainable forests.

The logging and manufacturing processes are expected to conform to the
environmental regulations of the country of origin.

Cover illustration by Peter Gudynas/Zap Art
Illustrations by Barking Dog Art and Ian Foulis
Typeset by Dorchester Typesetting Group Ltd
Printed and bound in Italy for Hodder Education, an Hachette UK company,
338 Euston Road, London NW1 3BH

Contents

Acknowledgements

The publishers wish to thank the following for permission to use copyright material:

Oxford Cambridge and RSA Examinations for OCR examination questions and source material.
Daily Telegraph for extract from 'Mercy for mother who was driven to kill her Down's Syndrome son', page 74.
Kent Messenger Group for extract from 'Thug jailed for stamping on policeman's face', page 115.
Courier Newspapers for extracts from '£2,000 stolen in cash scam', page 150; and 'Armed raid at off-licence', page 154.
Daily Mail for extract from 'Jury in rape trial accepts the defence of sleepwalking', page 176.

Extracts on pp 205–206 and 211–212 from *Criminal Law* by Michael Jefferson by permission of Pearson Education Limited.
Extract on page 207 from 'Consent: Public policy or legal moralism' by Susan Nash, *New Law Journal* and on page 212 from *New Law Journal* Law Reports by permission of LexisNexis Butterworths.
© Crown Copyright Material is reproduced with permission of the Controller of HMSO.

Every effort has been made to trace and acknowledge ownership of copyright. The publishers will be glad to make suitable arrangements with any copyright holders whom it has not been possible to contact.

Preface

This second edition has been updated and also amended to match closely the new specification of the OCR examining board. It covers the general principles of criminal law: *actus reus, mens rea*, strict liability, attempts and general defences. It also covers the law on the offences of murder, voluntary manslaughter, involuntary manslaughter, assaults, theft, robbery and burglary. As well as explaining the present law, the text explores problem areas and proposals for reform in each topic.

As with Criminal Law for A2, the aim has been to explain the topics as clearly as possible. I have built on Criminal Law for A2 by adding more diagrams and charts. The text is broken down with the use of many subheadings, diagrams and activities. There are also key facts charts and key cases charts to help students to revise topics.

After the chapters on substantive law, there are four appendices. The first explains the style of the examination in Unit G153 and gives students help with how to answer examination questions on this Unit. The second contains the source material for Unit G154 and also contains tips on how to answer questions for this Unit. As there may still be students re-sitting the previous G144 Unit of the special study material on duress, this has been included in Appendix 3. The final appendix contains key points from the Law Commission's Report, *Murder, Manslaughter and Infanticide* (Law Com 304) 2006.

The law is stated as I believe it to be on 1st January 2009.

Jacqueline Martin

Table of Acts of Parliament

Table of Cases

Chapter 1

Introduction to criminal law

Murder, manslaughter, robbery, rape and theft

Virtually everyone can identify these as criminal offences. But how many others can you name? There are thousands of different offences. They vary from the most serious, such as murder and manslaughter, to minor breaches of regulations, such as selling a lottery ticket to someone who is under the age of 16.

Fortunately, for A level, you only have to learn about a small number of offences, but you will have to understand the general principles involved in criminal law. This chapter looks at what defines a crime and then gives a brief introduction to:

- the elements of offences
- defences
- standard and burden of proof.

1.1 Defining a crime

With such a wide range, it is difficult to have a general definition covering all offences. The only way in which it is possible to define a crime is to say that it is:

- conduct forbidden by the State
- for which there is a punishment.

Lord Atkin supported this definition when, in the case of *Proprietary Articles Trade Association v Attorney-General for Canada* (1931), he said:

> 'The criminal quality of an act cannot be discerned by intuition (made out by "gut feeling"); nor can it be discovered by reference to any standard but one: is the act prohibited with penal consequences?'

This is the only definition which covers all crimes. However, there have been other definitions. An American legal writer, Herbert Packer, thought that, to be a crime:

- the conduct must be wrongful and
- it must be necessary to condemn or prevent such conduct.

However, what is considered criminal will change over time. This can be caused for example by changing views in society, or changes in technology which lead to the need for new offences to cover new situations.

Changing views on what is criminal can be demonstrated by the changes in the law on consenting homosexual acts. In 1885 the Criminal Law Amendment Act made consenting homosexual acts criminal even if they were in private. This remained as the law until 1967 when the Sexual Offences Act 1967 decriminalised such behaviour between those aged 21 and over. The age was reduced to 18 in 1994 and finally, in 2000, it was further reduced to 16. This age brings the law into line with consenting sexual acts between heterosexuals.

New technology can lead to new areas of criminal law. For example, the invention of the motor car over a hundred years ago led to new road traffic laws. These have been added to over the years so that we now have such offences as driving without a licence, driving while over the legal limit of alcohol, having tyres which do not have the right level of tread, and causing death by dangerous driving.

Computers and the Internet have led to new offences being created, to protect people from Internet fraud and to prevent pornographic material from being viewed or downloaded.

1.1.1 The role of the State

The criminal law is mainly set down by the State. This can be by passing an Act of Parliament such as the Theft Act 1968 or by the issuing of regulations.

A breach of criminal law can lead to a penalty, such as imprisonment or a fine, being imposed on the defendant in the name of the State. Therefore, bringing a prosecution for a criminal offence is usually seen as part of the role of the State. Indeed, the majority of criminal prosecutions are conducted by the Crown Prosecution Service (CPS) which is the State agency for criminal prosecutions.

However, it is also possible for a private individual or business to start a prosecution. For example, organisations such as the RSCPA regularly bring prosecutions. It is, however, very unusual for an individual person to bring a prosecution.

Even where an organisation or an individual brings a prosecution, the State still has control over the case as the Attorney-General can stay (halt) the proceedings at any time. This is done by the Attorney-General entering what is called a *nolle prosequi*. This stops the case from taking place, even if the original prosecutor wants it to continue.

1.1.2 Conduct criminalised by the judges

Although, in the vast majority of offences, the State decides what conduct is considered to be criminal, some conduct is criminalised by judges rather than the State. This occurs where judges create new criminal offences through case law. In modern times this only happens on rare occasions because nearly all law is made by Parliament. An example of conduct criminalised by judges is the offence of conspiracy to corrupt public morals. This offence has never been enacted by Parliament. However, the judges recognised that it existed in *Shaw v DPP* (1962).

Shaw v DPP (1962)

The defendant published a *Ladies Directory* which advertised the names and addresses of prostitutes, with their photographs and details of the 'services' they were prepared to offer. He was charged with conspiracy to corrupt public morals. The House of Lords accepted that there was an offence of conspiracy to corrupt public morals, as there did not appear to be an offence which covered the situation.

Another offence which has been created by the judges in modern times is marital rape. This was declared a crime in *R v R* (1991). Before that case, the law held that a husband could not be guilty of raping his wife, as she was assumed, by the fact of marriage, to consent to sexual intercourse with him. When the Law Lords decided the case of *R v R* they pointed out that society's views on the position of women had changed. The Law Lords said:

> 'The status of women and the status of a married woman in our law have changed quite dramatically. A husband and wife are now for all practical purposes equal partners in marriage.'

The Law Lords ruled that if a wife did not consent to intercourse, then the husband could be guilty of raping her.

1.2 Elements of a crime

There are many offences aimed at different 'wrong' behaviour. The offences you will have to study for OCR A2 are murder, manslaughter, non-fatal offences against the person, theft, burglary and robbery. However, there are general principles which apply to all offences.

The most important principle is that for all crimes, except crimes of strict liability (see Chapter 4), there are two elements which must be proved by the prosecution. These are:

- *actus reus* and
- *mens rea*.

These terms come from a Latin maxim (*actus non facit reum nisi mens sit rea*) which means 'the act itself does not constitute guilt unless done with a guilty mind'. Both an act (or omission) and a guilty mind must be proved for most criminal offences.

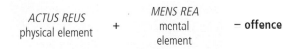

Figure 1.1 The elements of an offence

1.2.1 *Actus reus*

'*Actus reus*' has a wider meaning than 'an act', as it can cover omissions or a state of affairs. The term '*actus reus*' has been criticised as misleading. Lord Diplock in *Miller* (1983) preferred the term 'prohibited conduct', while the Law Commission in the Draft Criminal Code (1989) used the term 'external element'. We will look at the concept of *actus reus* in detail in Chapter 2.

1.2.2 *Mens rea*

'*Mens rea*' translates as 'guilty mind' but this is also misleading. The Law Commission in the Draft Criminal Code (1989) used the term 'fault element'. The levels of 'guilty mind' required for different offences vary from the highest level, which is specific intention for some crimes, to much lower levels, such as negligence or knowledge of a certain fact, for less serious offences. The levels of *mens rea* are explained in detail in Chapter 3.

1.2.3 Examples

The *actus reus* and *mens rea* will be different for different crimes. For example, in murder the *actus reus* is the killing of a human being, and the *mens rea* is causing the death 'with malice aforethought' which means that the killer must have intended to kill or to cause grievous bodily harm. For theft, the *actus reus* is the appropriation of property belonging to another, while the *mens rea* is doing this dishonestly and with the intention permanently to deprive the other of the property.

The *actus reus* and the *mens rea* must be present together, but if there is an ongoing act, then the existence of the necessary *mens rea* at any point during that act is sufficient. This is explained fully in Chapter 3. However, even where the *actus reus* and *mens rea* are present, the defendant may be not guilty if he has a defence (see section 1.3).

1.2.4 Strict liability offences

There are some crimes which are an exception to the general rule that there must be both *actus reus* and *mens rea*. These are crimes of strict liability, where the prosecution need prove only the *actus reus*; no mental element is needed for guilt. (See Chapter 4 for discussion of strict liability.)

1.3 Defences

Although the defendant may have done the required act, there are a number of general defences that may be available which will lead to a 'not guilty' verdict. The general defences you have to study are:

- insanity
- automatism
- intoxication
- duress and
- necessity.

Automatism can be a defence to any offence. Insanity is a defence to all crimes which require *mens rea*; it is not a defence to strict liability offences. Duress and necessity are not defences to a charge of murder.

Intoxication is only a defence where, because of his intoxication, the defendant did not have the required specific intention for the offence charged. If the defendant, even though he was drunk, had the required specific intention, then he cannot use intoxication as a defence. Also intoxication is never a defence to any offence where recklessness is sufficient for the *mens rea*. Each of these defences is considered in detail in Chapter 12.

You will also study two more defences in relation to non-fatal offences against the person. These are:

- self-defence/defence of another/prevention of crime
- consent.

In fact self-defence/defence of another/prevention of crime can be a defence to all offences including murder. There are also two special defences which apply to murder only. These are diminished responsibility and provocation. Both are explained in Chapter 7.

1.4 Standard and burden of proof

The prosecution has to prove the case against the defendant. There are rules on the level to which the case has to be proved. This is referred to as the 'standard of proof'.

1.4.1 Standard of proof

The standard of proof in criminal cases is 'beyond reasonable doubt'. This is usually explained by the judge telling the jury that they should only convict if they are satisfied on the evidence, so that they are sure of the defendant's guilt.

This is a higher standard than the one used in civil cases. Civil cases have to be proved only 'on the balance of probabilities'. The reason that criminal cases require a higher standard of proof is because the defendant is at risk of losing his liberty if he is found guilty.

1.4.2 Presumption of innocence

An accused person is presumed innocent until proven guilty. The burden is on the prosecution to prove the case. This means that it must prove both the required *actus reus* and the required *mens rea*. An important case on these principles is *Woolmington* (1935).

Woolmington v DPP (1935)

D's wife had left him and gone to live with her mother. D went to the mother's house and shot his wife dead. He claimed that he had decided to ask his wife to come back to him and, if she refused, that he would commit suicide. For this reason he was carrying under his coat a loaded sawn-off shotgun. When his wife indicated that she would not return to him, he threatened to shoot himself and brought the gun out to show her he meant it. As he brought it out, it somehow went off, killing his wife. He claimed that this was a pure accident.

The judge at the trial told the jury that the prosecution had to prove beyond reasonable doubt that the defendant killed his wife. He then went on to tell them that, if the prosecution satisfied them of that, the defendant had to show that there were circumstances which made that killing a pure accident. This put the burden of proof on the defendant to prove the defence. In the House of Lords it was held that this was not correct.

The decision in this case made several important points which the House of Lords regarded as fixed matters on English law. These were:

- the prosecution must prove the case
- this rule applies to all criminal cases
- the rule must be applied in any court where there is a criminal trial (currently the Magistrates' Court and the Crown Court)
- guilt must be proved beyond reasonable doubt and
- a reasonable doubt can be raised by evidence from either the prosecution or the defence.

1.4.3 Raising a defence

If the defendant raises a defence then it is for the prosecution to disprove that defence. In *Woolmington v DPP* (1935) the defendant stated that the gun had gone off accidentally, thus raising the defence of accident. The prosecution was obliged to disprove this if the defendant was to be found guilty.

For all common-law defences, except insanity, there must be some evidence of the key points of the defence given at the trial. This can be from evidence given by the defence or by the prosecution. If evidence of a defence is given at the trial then, even where the defendant has not specifically raised the defence, the prosecution must disprove at least one element of that defence. The trial judge must direct the jury to acquit unless they are satisfied that the defence has been disproved by the prosecution.

Reverse onus

For certain defences, the burden of proof is on the defendant. For example, if the defendant claims that he was insane at the time of the crime, the burden of proving this is on the defendant. This shifting of the burden of proof to the defendant is known as the 'reverse onus'. As well as applying to the common-law defence of insanity, it also applies to some defences which have been created by statute. One of these is the defence of diminished responsibility in the Homicide Act 1957 where s 2(2) states:

> 'On a charge of murder, it shall be for the defence to prove that the person charged is, by virtue of this section, not liable to be convicted of murder.'

Where a statute places the burden of proof on the defendant to prove a defence, the standard is the civil one of 'on the balance of probabilities'.

Chapter 2

Actus reus

2.1 What is *actus reus*?

As already stated in Chapter 1, the *actus reus* is the physical element of a crime. It can be:

- an act or
- a failure to act (an omission) or
- a 'state of affairs'.

In most cases the *actus reus* will be something the defendant does, but there are situations in which a failure to act is sufficient for the *actus reus*. These are set out at section 2.2. 'State of affairs' cases are very rare. These are considered at section 2.1.2.

2.1.1 Voluntary nature of *actus reus*

The act or omission must be voluntary on the part of the defendant. If the defendant has no control over his actions then he has not committed the *actus reus*. In *Hill v Baxter* (1958) the court gave examples of where a driver of a vehicle could not be said to be doing the act of driving voluntarily. These included where a driver lost control of his vehicle because he was stung by a swarm of bees, or if he was struck on the head by a stone or had a heart attack while driving.

Other examples of an involuntary act include where the defendant hits another person because of a reflex action or a muscle spasm. Yet another is where one person pushes a second person, causing them to bump into a third person. In this situation the act of the second person who has been pushed is involuntary. Even though he has hit the third person, he has not committed the *actus reus* for any assault offence. This happened in the case of *Mitchell* (1983) (see section 8.1.2).

Of course, the original 'pusher' can be liable.

These examples show that the criminal law is concerned with fault on the part of the defendant. Where there is an absence of fault, then the defendant is usually not liable.

2.1.2 'State of affairs' cases

There are some rare instances in which the defendant has been convicted even though he did not act voluntarily. These situations involve what are known as 'state of affairs' cases. An example of this is the case of *Larsonneur* (1933).

Larsonneur (1933)

The defendant had been ordered to leave the United Kingdom. She decided to go to Eire, but the Irish police deported her and took her back to the UK. She did not wish to go back and was certainly not doing this voluntarily. When she landed in the UK she was immediately arrested and charged that being 'an alien to whom leave to land in the UK had been refused', she had been found in the UK. She was convicted because she was an alien who had been refused leave to land and she had been 'found in the UK'. It did not matter that she had been brought back by the Irish police against her will (see also section 4.1 on strict liability).

2.1.3 Consequence of *actus reus*

For some crimes the *actus reus* must also result in a consequence. This can be seen in the offence of assault occasioning actual bodily harm (s 47 Offences Against the Person Act 1861). There must be an *actus reus* (the application or threat of unlawful force) but there must also be a consequence of 'actual bodily harm', in other words some injury to the victim. This could be just a bruise or it could be a broken nose or broken finger. It could even be psychiatric injury. Without this consequence there cannot be a s 47 offence.

2.2 Omissions as *actus reus*

The normal rule is that an omission cannot make a person guilty of an offence. This was explained by Stephen J, a nineteenth-century judge, in the following way.

> 'A sees B drowning and is able to save him by holding out his hand. A abstains from doing so in order that B may be drowned. A has committed no offence.'

Activity

Read the following scenario and discuss whether you think Zoe should be guilty of an offence.

Scenario

Zoe is sitting by a swimming pool in the grounds of a hotel. Jason is swimming in the pool. He is the only person in the water and there are no other people near the pool. Jason gets out of the pool and while walking around it slips and falls into the water. He is knocked unconscious. Zoe sees this happen but she does nothing. Jason drowns.

Would it make any difference to your answer if Zoe could not swim?

A 'Good Samaritan' law?

Some other countries have a law which is known as a 'Good Samaritan' law. It makes a person responsible for helping other people in an 'emergency situation', even though they are complete strangers. French law has this and an example was seen when Princess Diana's car crashed in Paris in 1997. Journalists who had been following her car took photographs of her, injured, in the car. They did not try to help her, even though she was critically injured. The French authorities threatened to charge these journalists under the French 'Good Samaritan' law.

There are problems in enforcing such a law. What if a 'rogue' pretends to be seriously hurt in order to lure a stranger to his assistance, so that the rogue can then rob the stranger? There is also the risk that an untrained person, by intervening, could do more harm to an injured person. Also, what is an 'emergency situation'? Who decides that there is an emergency so that the 'Good Samaritan' law is operating?

A problem would also arise if several people witnessed the incident. Do all of them have to help? Or is it enough if one of them helps? If one person helps, are the others still under a duty to help?

Finally, there is the question of whether would-be rescuers have to put themselves at risk in order to help. It seems unlikely that the law would require this. In the case of *Miller* (1983) (see section 2.2.1) the House of Lords thought that a defendant who has created the risk would only be expected to take reasonable steps. He would not be expected to put himself at risk. If this is the situation for the person who has caused the problem, then surely the same would have to apply to innocent passers-by?

2.2.1 Exceptions to the rule

There are exceptions to the rule that an omission cannot make a person guilty of an offence. In some cases it is possible for a failure to act (an omission) to be the *actus reus*.

An omission is only sufficient for the *actus reus* where there is a duty to act. There are six ways in which such a duty can exist.

1. A statutory duty.
2. A contractual duty.

3. A duty because of a relationship.
4. A duty which has been taken on voluntarily.
5. A duty through one's official position.
6. A duty which arises because the defendant has set in motion a chain of events.

A statutory duty

An Act of Parliament can create liability for an omission. Examples include the offences of failing to report a road traffic accident and of failing to provide a specimen of breath. In fact, these offences can only be committed by failing to do something. Another example where an Act of Parliament creates a duty is in s 1 of the Children and Young Persons Act 1933. This section puts parents who are legally responsible for a child under a duty for providing food, clothing, medical aid and lodging for their children. If a parent fails (omits) to do this, they can be guilty of the offence of wilful neglect.

A more recent example is the duty of family members to protect a child that they know is being abused.

A contractual duty

In *Pittwood* (1902) a railway-crossing keeper omitted to shut the gates, with the result that a person crossing the line was struck and killed by a train. The keeper was guilty of manslaughter. A more modern example would be of a lifeguard at a pool who leaves his post unattended. His failure to do his duty could make him guilty of an offence if a swimmer were injured or drowned.

A duty because of a relationship

This is usually a parent–child relationship as a parent has a duty to care for young children. A duty can also exist the opposite way round, where a grown-up child is caring for their elderly parent. A case example involving a parent–child duty is *Gibbins and Proctor* (1918).

Gibbins and Proctor (1918)

The father of a seven-year-old girl lived with a partner. The father had several children from an earlier marriage. He and his partner kept the girl separate from the father's other children and deliberately starved her to death. They were both convicted of murder.

The father had a duty to feed her because he was her parent and the mistress was held to have undertaken to look after the children, including the girl, so she was also under a duty to feed the child. The omission or failure to feed her was deliberate with the intention of killing or causing serious harm to her. In these circumstances they were guilty of murder. The failure to feed the girl was enough for the *actus reus* of murder.

A duty which has been undertaken voluntarily

In the above case of *Gibbins and Proctor* (1918) the partner had voluntarily undertaken to look after the girl. She therefore had a duty towards the child. When she failed to feed the child she was guilty of murder because of that omission.

Another example of where a duty had been undertaken voluntarily is *Stone and Dobinson* (1977).

Stone and Dobinson (1977)

Stone's elderly sister, Fanny, came to live with the defendants. Fanny was eccentric and often stayed in her room for several days. She also failed to eat. She eventually became bedridden and incapable of caring for herself. On at least one occasion Dobinson helped to wash Fanny and also occasionally prepared food for her. Fanny died from malnutrition. Both defendants were found guilty of her manslaughter.

As Fanny was Stone's sister, he owed a duty of care to her. Dobinson had undertaken some care of Fanny and so also owed her a duty of care. The duty was either to help her themselves or to summon help from other sources. Their failure to do either of these meant that they were in breach of their duty.

A duty through one's official position

This is very rare but did happen in *Dytham* (1979).

Dytham (1979)

Dytham (D) was a police officer who was on duty. He saw a man (V) being thrown out of a nightclub about 30 yards from where he was standing. Following the throwing out, there was a fight in which three men kicked V to death. D took no steps to intervene or to summon help. When the fight was over, D told a bystander that he was going off-duty and left the scene. He was convicted of misconduct in a public office.

Because Dytham was a police officer, he was guilty of wilfully and without reasonable excuse neglecting to perform his duty.

A duty which arises because the defendant set in motion a chain of events

This concept of owing a duty and being liable through omission was created in the case of *Miller* (1983) where a squatter had accidentally started a fire.

Miller (1983)

D was living in a squat. He fell asleep while smoking a cigarette. He awoke to find his mattress on fire. He did not attempt to put out the fire or to summon help but went into another room and went back to sleep. The house caught fire. He was convicted of arson.

In *Miller* (1983) it was not the setting of the mattress on fire which made him guilty. Instead, it was the fact that he had failed to take reasonable steps to deal with the fire when he discovered that his mattress was on fire. This failure or omission meant that he had committed the *actus reus* for arson. The House of Lords pointed out that Miller was only expected to take reasonable steps. He did not have to put himself at risk. So, if, when he woke and found the fire, it was very small and could easily be put out then he was expected to do that. However, if it was too dangerous for him to deal with it personally then his duty was to summon the fire brigade.

Another case where the defendant knew that there was a dangerous situation but failed to take any steps is *Santana-Bermudez* (2003).

Santana-Bermudez (2003)

A policewoman, before searching the defendant's pockets, asked him if he had any needles or other sharp objects on him. The defendant said 'no', but when the police officer put her hand in his pocket she was injured by a needle which caused bleeding. The defendant was convicted of assault occasioning actual bodily harm under s 47 of the Offences Against the Person Act 1861.

In this case it was the failure to tell the police officer of the needle which made the defendant liable. He knew that there was danger to the police officer but failed to warn her about it. This failure was enough for the *actus reus* for the purposes of an assault causing actual bodily harm.

Key facts

Source	Examples
Statutory duty.	Failing to provide a specimen of breath (s 6 Road Traffic Act 1988). Wilful neglect (s 1 Children and Young Persons Act 1933).
Under a contract, especially of employment.	*Pittwood* (1902)
Because of a relationship such as parent and child.	*Gibbins and Proctor* (1918)
A duty voluntarily undertaken, eg care of an elderly relative.	*Stone and Dobinson* (1977)
Because of a public office, eg police officer.	*Dytham* (1979)
As a result of a dangerous situation created by the defendant.	*Miller* (1983) *Santana-Bermudez* (2003)

Figure 2.1 Key facts chart of when omissions can be *actus reus*

2.2.2 Involuntary manslaughter and omissions

Involuntary manslaughter can be committed in different ways. The two main ways are:

- unlawful act manslaughter and
- gross negligence manslaughter.

Unlawful act manslaughter cannot be committed by an omission. There must be an 'act'. This was decided in *Lowe* (1973).

Lowe (1973)

D was the father of a nine-week-old baby who became ill and died. D, who was of low intelligence, said he had told the baby's mother to take the child to a doctor, but he had not done anything else. The child's mother was of subnormal intelligence. D was convicted of manslaughter of the baby. The Court of Appeal quashed the conviction because there was no unlawful 'act'. A failure to do something could not be an 'act'.

However, gross negligence manslaughter can be committed by an omission. It could be argued that Lowe should have been convicted of this because he owed the child a duty of care and he had failed to get help. This idea was seen in *Stone and Dobinson* (1977) (above).

For gross negligence manslaughter, the defendant must owe the victim a duty of care. If a duty of care exists then the defendant can be liable if an omission or failure to act by him causes the death of the victim.

A full discussion of involuntary manslaughter is contained in Chapter 8.

2.2.3 The duty of doctors

There can be cases where doctors decide to stop treating a patient. If this discontinuance of treatment is in the best interests of the patient then it is *not* an omission which can form the *actus reus*. This was decided in *Airedale NHS Trust v Bland* (1993).

Airedale NHS Trust v Bland (1993)

Bland was a young man who had been crushed by the crowd at the Hillsborough football stadium tragedy in 1989. This had stopped oxygen getting to his brain and left him with severe brain damage. He was in a persistent vegetative state (PVS), unable to do anything for himself and unaware of what was happening around him. He was fed artificially through tubes. He had been in this state for three years and the doctors caring for him asked the court for a ruling that they could stop feeding him.

The court ruled that the doctors could stop artificially feeding Bland even though it was known that he would die as a result. This was held to be in his best interests.

2.2.4 Comment on the law of omissions

There are several issues. These include:

- should there be wider liability for omissions such as the Good Samaritan law discussed in section 2.2
- the problems of deciding when a duty should be imposed so that an omission is sufficient for the *actus reus* of an offence
- should a person be liable for failure to act when they assume a duty
- omissions in medical treatment
- the justification for statutory imposition of liability for an omission.

Good Samaritan law

As already pointed out, other countries have a law that places people under a duty to help. Although there are problems in having such a law (see section 2.2) it can be argued that the modern view of moral responsibility is in favour of such a duty.

What about the situation where it is clear that a child is going very near the edge of a cliff? The child's parents or guardians would be liable for failure to act of they did not warn the child and try to remove them from the danger. However, a stranger would not be liable. In today's society is this acceptable?

Problems of deciding when a duty exists

It not completely certain when a duty to act will exist. The normal way of deciding this is:

1. By the judge at the trial determining whether there is evidence capable of establishing a duty in law
2. The jury then deciding whether the duty does actually exist
3. Finally the jury have to decide if the duty has been broken.

This means that the law is capable of expanding to cover more situations. This was stated in *Khan and Khan* (1998).

Khan and Khan (1998)

The defendants had supplied heroin to a new user who took it in their presence and then collapsed. They left her alone and by the time they returned to the flat she had died. Their conviction for unlawful act manslaughter was quashed but the Court of Appeal thought there could be a duty to summon medical assistance in certain circumstances, so that a defendant could be liable for failing to do so.

The point that the law is capable of expanding to include new duty situations was stressed in *Khan and Khan* when the Court of Appeal stated *obiter* that duty situations could be extended to other areas. However, this could be argued to make the law too uncertain. In what new situations will it be decided that a failure to act can be sufficient for the *mens rea* of an offence?

Assuming a duty

It can seem harsh that someone who accepts an adult into their home can be held to have assumed a duty towards that adult. This was the situation in *Stone and Dobinson*, although there was also a blood relationship to victim in that case. The victim was also a vulnerable person who had become incapable of looking after herself.

An adult is normally held to be responsible for their own life. In fact a mentally capable adult can refuse medical treatment even though this is likely to cause their death.

If the adult is vulnerable, then the argument for imposing a duty is that the person assuming the duty is in the best position to ensure that potential harm is avoided. He or she will know of the vulnerability of the victim when others do not. This is the reason for placing such a person under a duty to act and making them liable for failure to do anything.

Such a duty can be fulfilled by summoning help. It is not necessary for the person to do more than that. In *Stone and Dobinson* the defendants were found guilty because they did not summon help.

Medical treatment

One area where the law seems contradictory is in the duty of doctors. If doctors decide it is for the patient's best interests to withdraw feeding from that patient, then they are not liable for any offence in respect of the patient's death. This was the effect of the judgment in *Airedale NHS Trust v Bland*. Even though by withdrawing feeding from an unconscious patient, the medical staff are aware that this will cause the patient to die, they are not liable for the omission. The key issue being that such a failure to feed has to be in the patient's best interests.

However, the House of Lords in *Bland* emphasised that euthanasia by a positive act terminating the patient's life would remain unlawful.

Statutory duties

Statutes impose duties in a wide variety of situations and make it an offence to fail to do something. Many of these are connected with vehicles and/or driving. Laws in this area often also impose strict liability. This means that not only is the defendant liable because he has failed do to something but, in addition, the prosecution do not have to prove that he had any *mens rea*.

The justification for this is the greater good of society. If a driver fails to get insurance to drive, those injured by him will have difficulty getting compensation for their injuries. The defendant himself is unlikely to be able to pay.

Some of the statutory duties have been imposed because of the difficulty of proving an offence. This was the reason for the introduction of the offence of causing or allowing the death of a child or vulnerable adult under the Domestic Violence, Crime and Victims Act 2004.

Prior to this Act, where a child had died as a result of physical abuse in the home the prosecution used to have difficulty in discovering which member of the household had actually caused the death. For example, if both the mother and the father were charged with murder of the child then each would blame the other so that it could not be proved which one had done it.

Under the 2004 Act all members of the household are liable for failure to protect the child. This makes it much easier to succeed in a prosecution. This is important as the law should provide children and vulnerable adults with as much protection as possible. The law may have the effect of persuading other family members to report the abuse.

2.3 Causation

Where a consequence must be proved, then the prosecution has to show that:

- the defendant's conduct was the factual cause of that consequence, and
- it was the legal cause of that consequence, and

- there was no intervening act which broke the chain of causation.

2.3.1 Factual cause

The defendant can only be guilty if the consequence would not have happened 'but for' the defendant's conduct. This 'but for' test can be seen in operation in the case of *Pagett* (1983).

Pagett (1983)

The defendant took his pregnant girlfriend from her home by force. He then held the girl hostage. Police called on him to surrender. D came out, holding the girl in front of him and firing at the police. The police returned fire and the girl was killed by police bullets. D was convicted of manslaughter.

Pagett was guilty because the girl would not have died 'but for' him using her as a shield in the shoot-out. The opposite situation was seen in *White* (1910) where the defendant put cyanide in his mother's drink, intending to kill her. She died of a heart attack before she could drink it. The defendant was not the factual cause of her death. So, he was not guilty of murder, although he was guilty of attempted murder.

2.3.2 Legal cause

There may be more than one act contributing to the consequence. Some of these acts may be made by people other than the defendant. The rule is that the defendant can be guilty if his conduct was more than a 'minimal' cause of the consequence. But the defendant's conduct need not be a substantial cause. In some cases they have stated that the conduct must be more than *de minimis*. In *Kimsey* (1996) the Court of Appeal held that instead of using this Latin phrase '*de minimis*' it was acceptable to tell the jury it must be 'more than a slight or trifling link'.

Kimsey (1996)

D was involved in a high-speed car chase with a friend. She lost control of her car and the other driver was killed in the crash. The evidence about what happened immediately before D lost control was not very clear. The trial judge directed the jury that D's driving did not have to be 'the principal, or a substantial cause of the death, as long as you are sure that it was a cause and that there was something more than a slight or trifling link'. The Court of Appeal upheld D's conviction for causing death by dangerous driving.

There may be more than one person whose act contributed to the death. The defendant can be guilty even though his conduct was not the only cause of the death. In *Kimsey* both drivers were driving at high speed, but the one driver could be found guilty.

The 'thin-skull' rule

The defendant must also take the victim as he finds him. This is known as the 'thin-skull' rule. It means that if the victim has something unusual about his physical or mental state which makes an injury more serious, then the defendant is liable for the more serious injury. So, if the victim has an unusually thin skull which means that a blow to his head gives him a serious injury, then the defendant is liable for that injury. This is so even though that blow would have only caused bruising in a 'normal' person. An example is the case of *Blaue* (1975).

Blaue (1975)

A young woman was stabbed by the defendant. She was told that she needed a blood transfusion to save her life but she refused to have one as she was a Jehovah's Witness and her religion forbade blood transfusions. She died and the defendant was convicted of her murder.

The fact that the victim was a Jehovah's Witness made the wound fatal, but the defendant was still guilty because he had to take his victim as he found her.

2.3.3 Intervening acts

There must be a direct link from the defendant's conduct to the consequence. This is known as the chain of causation. In some situations something else happens after the defendant's act or omission and, if this is sufficiently separate from the defendant's conduct, it may break the chain of causation.

An example would be where the defendant has stabbed the victim who needs to be taken to hospital for treatment. On the way to hospital, the ambulance carrying the victim is involved in an accident and crashes, causing fatal head injuries to the victim.

Under the 'but for' test it could be argued that the victim would not have been in the ambulance but for the defendant's act in stabbing him. However, the accident is such a major intervening act that the defendant would not be liable for the death of the victim.

Figure 2.2 Breaking the chain of causation

The chain of causation can be broken by:

- an act of a third party or
- the victim's own act or
- a natural but unpredictable event.

In order to break the chain of causation so that the defendant is not responsible for the consequence, the intervening act must be sufficiently independent of the defendant's conduct and sufficiently serious.

Where the defendant's conduct causes a foreseeable action by a third party, then the defendant is likely to be held to have caused the consequence. This principle was applied in *Pagett* (1983) where his girlfriend was shot when he held her as a shield against police bullets (see section 2.3.1).

2.3.4 Medical treatment

Medical treatment is unlikely to break the chain of causation unless it is so independent of the defendant's acts and 'in itself so potent in causing death' that the defendant's acts are insignificant. The following three cases show this.

Smith (1959)

Two soldiers had a fight and one was stabbed in the lung by the other. The victim was carried to a medical centre by other soldiers, but was dropped on the way. At the medical centre the staff gave him artificial respiration by pressing on his chest. This made the injury worse and he died. The poor treatment probably affected his chances of recovery by as much as 75 per cent. However, the original attacker was still guilty of his murder.

In this case it was held that a defendant would be guilty, provided that the injury caused by D was still an 'operating' and 'substantial' cause of death. Smith was guilty because the stab wound to the lung was still 'operating' (it obviously had not healed up) and it was a substantial cause of V's death.

Cheshire (1991)

D shot the victim in the thigh and the stomach. V needed major surgery. He developed breathing problems and was given a tracheotomy (ie a tube was inserted in his throat to help him breathe). Some two months after the shooting, V died from rare complications left by the tracheotomy. These complications were not diagnosed by the doctors. By the time V died, the original wounds had virtually healed and were no longer life-threatening. The defendant was still held to be liable for V's death.

In this case the Court of Appeal held that even though treatment for injuries was 'short of the standard expected of a competent medical practitioner', D could still be criminally responsible for the death. The prosecution had only to prove that D's acts contributed to the death. D's acts need not be the sole cause or even the main cause of death, provided that his acts contributed significantly to the death.

Jordan (1956)

The victim had been stabbed in the stomach. He was treated in hospital and the wounds were healing well. He was given an antibiotic but suffered an allergic reaction to it. One doctor stopped the use of the antibiotic but the next day another doctor ordered that a large dose of it be given. The victim died from the allergic reaction to the drug. In this case the actions of the doctor were held to be an intervening act which caused the death. The defendant was not guilty of murder.

In the first two cases the doctors were carrying out treatment for the injuries in an attempt to save the victim's life. The victims would not have needed treatment if they had not been seriously injured by the defendant. In such situations the attacker is still liable even though the medical treatment was not very good. This was pointed out in *Cheshire* (1991) by Beldam LJ:

> 'Even though negligence in the treatment of the victim was the immediate cause of death, the jury should not regard it as excluding the responsibility of the accused unless the negligent treatment was so

independent of his acts, and in itself so potent in causing death, that they regard the contribution made by his acts as insignificant.'

In the third case of *Jordan* (1956) the fact that the victim was given a large amount of a drug when the doctors knew he was allergic to it was a sufficiently independent act to break the chain of causation. However, if a normal dose of a drug is given as part of emergency treatment and the doctors do not know that the victim is allergic to it, then the giving of the drug would not break the chain of causation.

Life-support machines

Switching off a life-support machine by a doctor when it has been decided that the victim is brain-dead does not break the chain of causation. This was decided in *Malcherek* (1981).

Malcherek (1981)

D stabbed his wife in the stomach. At hospital she was put on a life-support machine. After a number of tests showed that she was brain-dead, the machine was switched off. D was charged with her murder. The trial judge refused to allow the issue of causation to go to the jury. D was convicted and the Court of Appeal upheld his conviction.

2.3.5 Victim's own act

If the defendant causes the victim to react in a foreseeable way, then any injury to the victim will be considered to have been caused by the defendant. This occurred in *Roberts* (1971).

Roberts (1971)

A girl jumped from a car in order to escape from Roberts' sexual advances. The car was travelling at between 20 and 40 mph and the girl was injured by jumping from it. The defendant was held to be liable for her injuries.

Key cases

Case	Facts	Law
Smith (1959)	Soldier stabbed another soldier. V's medical treatment very poor and affected chances of recovery.	D liable if the injuries he caused are still an operating and substantial cause.
Cheshire (1991)	D shot V. V needed a tracheotomy. V died because of complications from the tracheotomy. His wounds were virtually healed.	Medical treatment would only break the chain of causation if it is 'so independent' of D's acts and 'in itself so potent in causing death'.
Jordan (1956)	V was stabbed. When his wounds were almost healed he was given a large dose of a drug to which it was known he was allergic.	The chain of causation was broken in this case.
Malcherek (1981)	D stabbed his wife. She was put on a life-support machine but when tests showed she was brain dead, the machine was switched off.	Switching off a life-support machine does not break the chain of causation.

Figure 2.3 Key case chart on medical intervention and causation

Another case in which it was held that D was liable if V's actions were reasonably foreseeable was *Marjoram* (2000).

Marjoram (2000)

Several people, including D, shouted abuse and kicked the door of V's hostel room. They eventually forced the door open. V then fell (or possibly jumped) from the window of the room and suffered serious injuries. D's conviction for inflicting grievous bodily harm was upheld by the Court of Appeal.

In this situation it was reasonably foreseeable that V would fear that the group were going to use violence against him and that the only escape route for him was the window.

Unreasonable reaction

However, if the victim's reaction is unreasonable, then this may break the chain of causation. In *Williams* (1992) a hitch-hiker jumped from Williams' car and died from head injuries caused by his head hitting the road. The car was travelling at about 30 mph. The prosecution alleged that there had been an attempt to steal the victim's wallet and that was the reason for his jumping from the car. The Court of Appeal said that the victim's act had to be foreseeable and also had to be in proportion to the threat. The question to be asked was whether the victim's conduct was:

> 'within the ambit of reasonableness and not so daft as to make his own voluntary act one which amounted to a *novus actus interveniens* (a new intervening act) and consequently broke the chain of causation.'

This makes it necessary to consider the surrounding circumstances in deciding whether the victim's conduct has broken the chain of causation. Where the threats to the victim are serious, then it is more likely for it to be reasonable for him to jump out of a moving car (or out of a window or into a river etc). Where the threat is very minor and the victim takes drastic action, it is more likely that the courts will hold that it broke the chain of causation.

The main rules on causation are shown in a flowchart in Figure 2.3

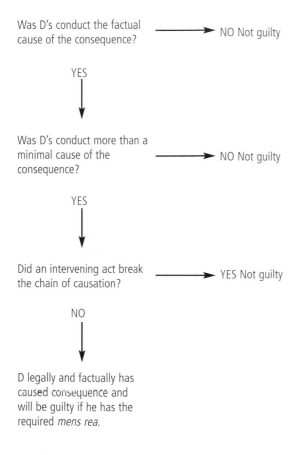

Was D's conduct the factual cause of the consequence? ⟶ NO Not guilty

YES

Was D's conduct more than a minimal cause of the consequence? ⟶ NO Not guilty

YES

Did an intervening act break the chain of causation? ⟶ YES Not guilty

NO

D legally and factually has caused consequence and will be guilty if he has the required *mens rea*.

Figure 2.4 Flowchart of rules on causation

2.3.6 Problems in the law on causation

A major problem in the law on causation is: what is meant by more than a 'slight and trifling link'? This is vague and difficult to define. As a result, it could lead to juries applying different standards in different cases.

Taking your victim as you find him

Where V has a medical condition which makes the injury more serious, should D be liable for the more serious injury? It can be seen as being unjust where D does not know about the medical condition. For example, if a victim has an exceptionally thin skull, so that a blow kills him, is it justified that D should be liable for murder when the blow would not have killed a normal person? D did not intend to kill but if he intended to cause really serious injury then D is guilty of murder. (This is also a criticism of the *mens rea* for murder – see Chapter 6 for more on this.)

Also, should D be liable when V refuses treatment? This was probably justified when medical treatment was very primitive, especially when operations had to be carried out without anaesthetic. In *Holland* (1841), D deliberately cut V's finger. The cut became infected and V was advised that he should have the finger amputated. He refused to have the amputation until it was too late, and he died from the infection. D was liable for his death. In 1841 surgery was very primitive and this decision can be justified, but should D be liable on the same scenario today? D is in any event guilty of an assault causing actual bodily harm, but should he be liable for the death?

In *Blaue* (1975) the victim refused a blood transfusion because of her religious beliefs. Her life could have been saved had she had a transfusion. It can be argued that D should not be liable for her death. He could have been charged with wounding with intent to do so (s 18 Offences Against the Person Act 1961). This offence has a maximum penalty of life imprisonment, so a suitable punishment could have been imposed on D. On the other hand, it is clear that the stab wound was the cause of V's death, so on this basis it can be argued that he should be liable for her death.

What if a victim refused a blood transfusion because of a fear of becoming HIV positive through the transfusion? Is this any different from the situation in *Blaue*? Surely the rule must apply in the same way, regardless of the reason for refusing medical treatment? An even more extreme case is *Dear* (1996).

Dear (1996)

D slashed V several times with a Stanley knife, severing an artery. V did not bother to have the wounds attended to and, possibly, even opened the wounds further, making the bleeding worse. V died from loss of blood. D's conviction for murder was upheld by the Court of Appeal.

The court held that, provided the wounds were an operating and significant cause, the jury was entitled to convict D. Even if V had effectively decided to commit suicide by allowing the wounds to continue to bleed, the wounds were still the cause of death.

If V really had opened up the wounds further, should this be regarded as an intervening act which broke the chain of causation? Or is the court's view justifiable that as the wounds were the cause of death, then D was liable for the death?

Negligent medical treatment

In *Smith* (1959) the court used the test of 'operating and substantial cause'. However, this test might not have led to a conviction in *Cheshire* (1991). In *Cheshire*, V's wounds were virtually healed. Were they an 'operating and substantial cause' of V's death? Probably not.

Yet, V would not have had to have a tracheotomy if he had not been shot by D. So, the medical negligence in failing to notice the complications from the tracheotomy was not 'independent of' D's acts. D's acts were a significant factor in V's death. The test developed in *Cheshire* was more suited to the situation in that case.

Activity

Read the following situations and explain whether causation would be proved.

1. Aled has been threatened by Ben in the past. When Aled sees Ben approaching him in the street, Aled runs across the road without looking and is knocked down and injured by a car. Would Ben be liable for Aled's injuries?
2. Toyah stabs Steve in the arm. His injury is not serious but he needs stitches, so a neighbour takes Steve to hospital in his car. On the way to the hospital, the car crashes and Steve sustains serious head injuries. Would Toyah be liable for the head injuries?
3. Lewis has broken into Katie's third-floor flat. He threatens to rape her and in order to escape from him she jumps from the window and is seriously injured. Would Lewis be liable for her injuries?
4. Ross stabs Panjit in the chest. Panjit is taken to hospital where he is given an emergency blood transfusion. Unfortunately, he is given the wrong type of blood and he dies. Would Ross be liable for Panjit's death?

Examination question

'Law should encourage citizens in their civic duty to do "the right thing" in a moral sense and not to turn a blind eye or fail to act to help someone who is in need.'

Consider to what extent the criminal law relating to omissions (failures to act) reflects this.

(OCR, G143, January 2008)

Chapter 3

Mens rea

Mens rea is the mental element of an offence. Each offence has its own mens rea or mental element. The only exceptions are offences of strict liability. These offences do not require proof of mental element in respect of at least part of the actus reus. In criminal cases it is for the prosecution to prove the required mens rea.

There are different levels of mens rea. To be guilty, the accused must have at least the minimum level of mens rea required for the offence.

The highest level of mens rea is intention. This is also referred to as 'specific intention'. The other main types of mens rea are recklessness, negligence and knowledge.

3.1 Intention (specific intent)

In the case of *Mohan* (1975) the court defined 'intention' as:

> 'a decision to bring about, in so far as it lies within the accused's power, [the prohibited consequence], no matter whether the accused desired that consequence of his act or not'.

This makes it clear that the defendant's motive or reason for doing the act is not relevant. The important point is that the defendant decided to bring about the prohibited consequence.

This can be illustrated by looking at the offence set out in s 18 of the Offences Against the Person Act 1861. For this offence, the defendant must wound or cause grievous bodily harm. The *mens rea* is that the defendant must intend to wound or cause grievous bodily harm or intend to resist arrest. If the defendant did not intend one of these then he cannot be guilty of this offence. For example, if a person opens a door very suddenly and hits and seriously injures someone on the other side of the door who they did not know was there, then they do not intend to 'bring about' the prohibited consequence.

Motive

Mohan (1975) also makes it clear that motive is not the same as intention and is not relevant in deciding whether the defendant had intention. For example, a person may feel very strongly that the banking system in the Western world is causing poverty in poorer nations. That person then steals millions of pounds from a bank so that he can give it to people in poorer nations. His motive is to make sure that the poor receive money. This is irrelevant in deciding whether the defendant has the *mens rea* required for theft.

3.1.1 Direct and oblique intent

In the majority of cases the defendant has what is known as *direct intent*. This means that he intends the specific consequence to occur. For example, D decides to kill V. He aims a gun directly at V's head and pulls the trigger. Here D has the direct intent to kill V.

However, there can be situations where the defendant intends one thing but the actual consequence which occurs is another thing. This is known as *oblique intent* or *indirect intent*.

An example of this is if the defendant intends to frighten someone so as to stop them going to work, but does not intend to kill or seriously injure them. This occurred in the case of *Hancock and Shankland* (1986). The actual consequence was that the driver of the car taking the person to work was killed. This is shown in diagram form in Figure 3.1.

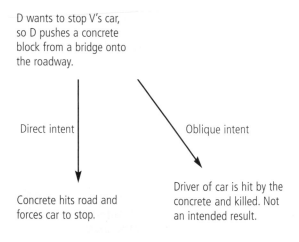

D wants to stop V's car, so D pushes a concrete block from a bridge onto the roadway.

Direct intent

Oblique intent

Concrete hits road and forces car to stop.

Driver of car is hit by the concrete and killed. Not an intended result.

Figure 3.1 Direct intent/oblique intent

3.1.2 Foresight of consequences

The main problem with proving intention is in cases where the defendant's main aim was not the prohibited consequences. He intended something else. If, in achieving the other thing, the defendant foresaw that he would also cause those consequences, then he may be found guilty. This idea is referred to as 'foresight of consequences'.

An example of this type of situation is where the defendant decides to set fire to his shop in order to claim insurance. His main aim is damaging the shop and getting the insurance. Unfortunately, he starts the fire when members of staff are still in the shop and some of them are seriously injured. Has the defendant the intention for the s 18 offence of causing grievous bodily harm?

The starting point for foresight of consequences is s 8 of the Criminal Justice Act 1967 which states that:

> 'A court or jury, in determining whether a person has committed an offence—
>
> (a) shall not be bound in law to infer that he intended or foresaw a result of his actions by reason only of its being a natural and probable consequence of those actions; but
>
> (b) shall decide whether he did intend or foresee that result by reference to all the evidence, drawing such inferences from the evidence as appear proper in the circumstances.'

This wording has been the subject of several cases over the last 20 years or so. These are mainly cases where defendants have been charged with murder. The important point is that the defendant must intend or foresee a result. In a murder case this means that the defendant must foresee that death or really serious injury will be caused. The leading case on this is now *Woollin* (1998), but to understand the law and the problems it is necessary to look at cases which came before *Woollin*. The first of these was *Moloney* (1985).

Moloney (1985)

D and his step-father had drunk a considerable amount of alcohol at a family party. After the party, they were heard talking and laughing. Then there was a shot. D phoned the police, saying that he had just murdered his step-father.

D said that they had been seeing who was the faster at loading and firing a shotgun. He had loaded his gun faster than his step-father. His step-father then said that D hadn't got 'the guts' to pull the trigger. D said 'I didn't aim the gun. I just pulled the trigger and he was dead'. D was convicted of murder but this conviction was quashed on appeal.

In this case the House of Lords ruled that foresight of consequences is only evidence of intention. It is not intention in itself. This part of the House of Lords' judgment is still law.

However, other parts of this judgment have been overruled by later cases. This was because Lord Bridge stated that jurors should be told to consider two questions:

1. Was death or really serious injury a natural consequence of the defendant's act?
2. Did the defendant foresee that consequence as being a natural result of his act?

The problem with these questions (which are often referred to as the *Moloney* guidelines) is that the word 'probable' is not mentioned.

If you look back to s 8 of the Criminal Justice Act 1967, you will see that the section uses the phrase 'natural and probable consequence'. Lord Bridge referred only to a 'natural' result. This omission of the word 'probable' was held in *Hancock and Shankland* (1986) (see below) to make the guidelines defective. The guidelines are therefore no longer law.

Hancock and Shankland (1986)

Ds were miners who were on strike. They tried to prevent another miner from going to work by pushing a concrete block from a bridge onto the road along which he was being driven to work in a taxi. The block struck the windscreen of the taxi and killed the driver. The trial judge used the *Moloney* guidelines to direct the jury, and Ds were convicted of murder. On appeal, the Court of Appeal quashed their convictions. This was upheld by the House of Lords.

The problem with *Moloney* (1985) was explained by Lord Scarman who stated that the guidelines in that case were unsafe and misleading. He said:

> 'In my judgment, therefore, the Moloney guidelines as they stand are unsafe and misleading. They require a reference to probability. They also require an explanation that the greater the probability of a consequence the more likely it is that the consequence was foreseen and that if that consequence was foreseen the greater the probability is that that consequence was also intended.'

The next case was *Nedrick* (1986) where the Court of Appeal thought that the judgments in the two earlier cases of *Moloney* (1985) and *Hancock and Shankland* (1986) needed to be made clearer.

Nedrick (1986)

D had a grudge against a woman. He poured paraffin through the letter box of her house and set it alight. A child died in the fire. D was convicted of murder but the Court of Appeal quashed the conviction and substituted one of manslaughter.

To make the law decided in *Moloney*, *Hancock* and *Nedrick* easier for jurors to understand and apply in murder trials, the Court of Appeal said that it was helpful for a jury to ask themselves two questions:

1. How probable was the consequence which resulted from D's voluntary act?
2. Did D foresee that consequence?

It was necessary for the consequence to be a virtual certainty and for D to have realised that. If this was so then there was evidence from which the jury could infer that D had the necessary intention. Lord Lane CJ put it this way:

" 'The jury should be directed that they are not entitled to infer the necessary intention unless they feel sure that death or serious bodily harm was a virtual certainty (barring some unforeseen intervention) as a result of the defendant's actions and that the defendant appreciated that such was the case.' "

This remained the law until 1998 and the case of *Woollin* (1998). This went to the House of Lords who felt that the Court of Appeal's views in *Nedrick* (1986) were not helpful.

Woollin (1998)

D threw his three-month-old baby towards his pram which was against a wall some three or four feet away. The baby suffered head injuries and died. The court ruled that the consequence must have been a virtual certainty and the defendant must have realised this. Where the jury was satisfied on both these two points, then there was evidence on which the jury could find intention.

The Law Lords thought that the two questions in *Nedrick* were not helpful. They held that the model direction from *Nedrick* should be used, but that the word 'find' should be used rather than the word 'infer'. So the model direction to be given to a jury considering foresight of consequences should now be:

'the jury should be directed that they are not entitled to *find* the necessary intention unless they feel sure that death or serious bodily harm was a virtual certainty (barring some unforeseen intervention) as a result of the defendant's actions and that the defendant appreciated that such was the case.'

Problems with the decision in *Woollin*

The decision in *Woollin* causes some problems. First of all, the word 'infer' is used in s 8 of the Criminal Justice Act 1967 and this is presumably why it was used in *Nedrick*. Does the substitution of the word 'find' improve the clarity of the direction to the jury? Another problem is whether the use of the word 'find' means that foresight of consequence is intention and not merely evidence of it.

In his judgment Lord Steyn also went on to say that the effect of the direction is that 'a result foreseen as virtually certain is an intended result'. He also pointed out that in *Moloney* the House of Lords had said that if a person foresees the probability of a consequence as little short of overwhelming, this 'will suffice to establish the necessary intent'. Lord Steyn emphasised the word 'establish'. This seems to suggest that the House of Lords in *Woollin* regarded foresight of consequences as the same as intention, when *Moloney* had clearly stated that it was not.

In later cases there have been conflicting decisions on this point. In the civil case of *Re A* (2000), doctors asked the courts whether they could operate to separate conjoined twins when they foresaw that this would kill the weaker twin. The Court of Appeal (Civil Division) clearly thought that *Woollin* laid down the rule that foresight of consequences *is* intention.

In the criminal case of *Matthews and Alleyne* (2003) the Court of Appeal held that the judgment in *Woollin* meant that foresight of consequences is *not* intention: it is a rule of evidence. If a jury decides that the defendant foresaw the virtual certainty of death or serious injury, they are entitled to find intention but do not have to do so.

Matthews and Alleyne (2003)

The defendants dropped the victim 25 feet from a bridge, into the middle of a deep, wide river. The victim had told them that he could not swim. They watched him 'dog paddle' towards the bank but left before seeing whether he reached safety. The victim drowned.

The trial judge had directed the jury that the defendants' intention to kill could be proved *either* by direct intention to kill *or* by the defendants' appreciation that V's death was a virtual certainty (barring an attempt to save him) together with the fact that the defendants did not intend to save the victim.

The Court of Appeal stated that the trial judge had been wrong to say that an appreciation of a virtual certainty constituted intention.

However, they upheld the convictions because, if the jury were sure that the defendants appreciated the virtual certainty of death if they did not attempt to save V **and** that at the time of throwing V off the bridge they had no intention of saving him, then it was impossible to see how the jury could not have found that the defendants intended V to die.

A chart of the cases on foresight of consequences is included below to help keep the cases clear.

3.1.3 Comment on intention

It can be seen from the above that the courts have struggled with the concept of intention where foresight of consequences is involved. For example:

Case	Facts	Law
Moloney (1985)	D shot step-father in 'quick on the draw' incident.	Foresight of consequences is *not* intention; it is evidence of intention.
Hancock and Shankland (1986)	Miner dropped lumps of concrete onto road, killing taxi driver.	The greater the probability of a consequence, the more likely it is that the consequence was foreseen and that if that consequence was foreseen the greater the probability is that that consequence was also intended.
Nedrick (1986)	Poured paraffin through letter box, causing fire in the house in which a child died.	Jury not entitled to *infer* the necessary intention unless sure that death or serious bodily harm was a virtual certainty and that the defendant appreciated this.
Woollin (1998)	Threw baby at pram, causing his death.	The direction in *Nedrick* should not use the word 'infer'. Instead, the jury should be told they are entitled to *find* intention.
Re A (2000)	Doctors wanted to operate on conjoined twins but knew this would cause one of them to die.	Court thought that *Woollin* made it law that foresight of consequences *is* intention.
Matthews and Alleyne (2003)	Threw V into river where he drowned.	*Woollin* meant that foresight of consequences is *not* intention. It is a rule of evidence. If a jury decides that the defendant foresaw the virtual certainty of death or serious injury then they are entitled to find intention but they do not have to do so.

Figure 3.2 Case chart on foresight of consequences

Activity

In each of the following situations, explain whether the defendant has the required intention for murder. The *mens rea* for murder is an intention to kill or an intention to cause grievous bodily harm.

1. Geraint dislikes Victor and decides to attack him. Geraint uses an iron bar to hit Victor on the head. Victor dies as a result.
2. Inderpal throws a large stone into a river to see how much of a splash it will make.

Jake is swimming in the river and is hit on the head by the stone and killed.
3. Kylie throws a large stone from a bridge, onto the motorway below. It is rush hour and there is a lot of traffic on the motorway. The stone smashes through the windscreen of Ashley's car and kills his passenger.

● natural and probable consequence
● difficulty for jurors in applying the tests after the cases of *Moloney* and *Hancock and Shankland*
● the change in *Woollin* from *inferring* intention to *finding* intention
● the fact that there are still two interpretations of the judgment in *Woollin*.

Natural and probable consequences

It is necessary to include both words in the test for intention. This is because something can be a natural consequence without being a probable consequence. For example, a natural consequence of sexual intercourse is that the girl becomes pregnant. However, it is not a probable consequence. Pregnancy only occurs in a small percentage of cases.

The difficulty for jurors applying the law

Following the cases of *Moloney* and *Hancock and Shankland* where jurors had to be directed on the level of probability, the law was left in a state which made it difficult for judges to explain it to jurors and for jurors to apply the law. The difficulties it caused were emphasised when the Court of Appeal in *Nedrick* thought it necessary to try to make the law easier for jurors to understand and apply.

Infer or find

The use of the two question test from *Nedrick* operated for some 12 years until the case of *Woollin*. Then the House of Lords said that they thought the two questions from *Nedrick* were not helpful. They also held that the direction to the jury should use the word *find* instead of *infer*. As already discussed in the previous section, the decision in *Woollin* appears to create more problems than it solved.

Two interpretations of *Woollin*

There are still problems in the law on intention as shown by the fact that the Court of Appeal in two different cases has interpreted the decision of the House of Lords in *Woollin* in different ways.

In *Re A* the Court of Appeal thought that *Woollin* meant that foresight of consequences *is* intention, whereas in *Matthews and Alleyne* they stated that foresight of consequences is only *evidence* of intention.

It can be seen from this that the law on intention is still not in a satisfactory state.

3.1.4 Reform of the law

In 1993 the Law Commission, in its report *Offences Against the Person and General Principles*, proposed that 'intentionally' should be defined as follows:

> 'A person acts intentionally with respect to a result when:
> (a) it is his purpose to cause it; or
> (b) although it is not his purpose to cause it, he knows that it would occur in the ordinary course of events if he were to succeed in his purpose of causing some other result.'

This was only in relation to non-fatal offences against the person, but there seems to be no reason why the definition should not be brought to apply to all offences as suggested by the Draft Criminal Code.

However, even this definition could cause problems. What is meant by 'in the ordinary course of events'? The meaning of this phrase appears broader than the test of 'virtual certainty' used in *Nedrick/Woollin*. This could mean that such a change in the law would lead to more people being convicted of offences which they did not directly intend to commit.

3.2 Recklessness

This is a lower level of *mens rea* than intention. Recklessness is where the defendant knows there is a risk of the consequence happening but takes that risk.

3.2.1 The case of *Cunningham*

The explanation of recklessness comes from the case of *Cunningham* (1957).

Cunningham (1957)

D tore a gas meter from the wall of an empty house in order to steal the money in it. This caused gas to seep into the house next-door, where a woman was affected by it. Cunningham was charged with an offence under s 23 of the Offences Against the Person Act 1861, of maliciously administering a noxious thing. It was held that he was not guilty since he did not realise the risk of gas escaping into the next-door house. He had not intended to cause the harm, nor had he taken a risk he knew about.

The offence involved in *Cunningham* uses the word 'maliciously' to indicate the *mens rea* required. The court held that this word meant that to have the necessary *mens rea* the defendant must either intend the consequence or realise that there was a risk of the consequence happening and decide to take that risk. Knowing about a risk and taking it can also be referred to as 'subjective recklessness'. It is subjective because the defendant himself realised the risk.

The case of *Savage* (1992) confirmed that the same principle applies to all offences where the definition in an Act of Parliament uses the word 'maliciously'. The Law Lords said that 'maliciously' was a term of legal art. In other words, it has a special meaning when used in an Act of Parliament, not its normal dictionary definition. It means doing something intentionally or being subjectively reckless about the risk involved.

Do not forget that if the defendant has the higher level of intention he will, of course, be guilty. For example, if the defendant intends to punch the victim in the face, that defendant has the higher level of intention and is guilty of a battery. It is only when the defendant does not have the higher level that recklessness has to be considered.

Offences for which recklessness is sufficient for the *mens rea* include:

- assault and battery
- assault occasioning actual bodily harm (s 47 for the Offences Against the Person Act 1861)
- malicious wounding (s 20 of the Offences Against the Person Act 1861)
- criminal damage.

3.2.2 Past problems in the law

There used to be two levels of recklessness. These were:

- subjective, where the defendant realised the risk, but decided to take it
- objective, where an ordinary prudent person would have realised the risk: the defendant was guilty even if he did not realise the risk.

The first type of recklessness is the only recklessness that the law now recognises as being sufficient to prove a defendant guilty where recklessness is sufficient to make the defendant guilty. However, during the period from 1982 to 2003, it was accepted that a defendant could be guilty of certain offences even though he had not realised that there was a risk. This was decided in the case of *Metropolitan Police Commissioner v Caldwell* (1981).

Metropolitan Police Commissioner v Caldwell (1981)

D had a grievance against the owner of a hotel. He got very drunk and decided to set fire to the hotel. The fire was put out quickly, without serious damage to the hotel. D was charged with arson under s 1(2) of the Criminal Damage Act 1971. This requires that D intended endangerment to life or was reckless as to whether life was endangered. D claimed that he was so drunk he had not realised people's lives might be endangered. His conviction was upheld.

In *Caldwell* the House of Lords held that recklessness covered two situations. The first is where D had realised the risk, and the second is where D had not thought about the possibility of any risk.

This second meaning of 'reckless' caused problems in cases where D was not capable of appreciating the risk involved in his conduct, even though a reasonable person would have realised there was a risk. This occurred in *Elliott v C* (1983) where D was a 14-year-old girl with learning difficulties. She did not appreciate the risk that her act might set a shed on fire. But she was found guilty because ordinary adults would have realised the risk.

This seemed very unfair. The girl was not blameworthy. If she had been judged by the standard of a 14-year-old with learning difficulties then she would not have been convicted. It was absurd to judge her against the standard of ordinary adults. This problem was eventually resolved when the House of Lords overruled *Caldwell* in the case of *G and another* (2003).

G and another (2003)

The defendants were two boys, aged 11 and 12 years, who set fire to some bundles of newspapers in a shop yard. They threw them under a large wheelie bin and left. They thought that the fire would go out by itself. In fact, the bin caught fire and this spread to the shop and other buildings, causing about £1 million worth of damage. The judge directed the jury that they had to decide whether ordinary adults would have realised the risk. The boys were convicted under both ss 1 and 3 of the Criminal Damage Act 1971. On appeal, the House of Lords quashed their conviction.

The House of Lords held that a defendant could not be guilty unless he had realised the risk and decided to take it. The House of Lords overruled the decision in *Caldwell*, holding that in that case the Law Lords had adopted an interpretation of s 1 of the Criminal Damage Act 1971 which was 'beyond the range of feasible meanings'.

In *G and another* the House of Lords approved of the definition of recklessness set out in the draft Criminal Code which states that a person acts:

> 'recklessly with respect to:
> (i) a circumstance when he is aware of a risk that it exists or will exist;
> (ii) a result when he is aware of a risk

that it will occur, and it is, in the circumstances known to him, unreasonable to take the risk.'

The reasons for the defendant taking the risk are not relevant. It does not matter whether it was done because the defendant was in a temper or he chose to disregard the risk or simply did not care about the risk.

The important point is that the defendant must be aware of the risk. This is the subjective aspect of recklessness.

General application of law on recklessness

Initially it was thought that this decision in *G and another* only affected the law on recklessness in relation to criminal damage. However, the *G and another* version of recklessness has since been applied by the Court of Appeal to other areas of law. For example, they applied the subjective recklessness test in the case of *Attorney-General's Reference (No 3 of 2003)* (2004). This case was about a very different area of law as it involved the common law offence of wilful misconduct in a public office.

So now the law is clear. Where recklessness is sufficient for the *mens rea* of an offence, it must be subjective recklessness. The prosecution must prove that the defendant realised the risk and decided to take it.

3.2.3 Recklessness in manslaughter

An area in which subjective recklessness has been re-established is involuntary manslaughter. Following the decision in *Caldwell* there was a brief period when it was held that both subjective and objective recklessness applied to manslaughter.

Objective recklessness was a very harsh test to apply in the case of such a serious offence. This had the effect that a person could be guilty of manslaughter when they had not personally foreseen any risk at all. In addition, the risk which needed to be foreseen by a reasonable person was only the risk of some injury.

The law was re-stated in 1994 in the case of *Adomako* (1994). This case re-introduced a test of gross negligence for manslaughter (see section 8.2), rather than recklessness in any form. Following *Adomako* it was initially thought that recklessness was no longer relevant in the law of manslaughter.

However, in the case of *Lidar* (2000) the Court of Appeal affirmed that involuntary manslaughter could still be based on subjective recklessness.

Lidar (2000)

D and others had been asked to leave a public house in Leicester. They went into the pub car park and got into a Range Rover, with D as driver. One of the passengers shouted something at V, who was the doorman of the pub. V approached the vehicle and put his arms through the open front passenger window. D then drove off, with V half in and half out of the window. After about 225 metres, V was dragged under the rear wheel of the Range Rover and suffered injuries from which he died. D was convicted of manslaughter.

To prove manslaughter, it must be shown that the defendant foresaw there was a highly probable risk of serious injury (or death) to the victim. This test of a highly probable risk is different to the test for risk-taking in relation to other offences for which recklessness is sufficient for the *mens rea*. For other offences the level of risk needed to be foreseen by the defendant is only that there is a possible risk of the consequence or circumstance occurring.

The difference in the level of risk which has to be foreseen can be justified by the seriousness of the offence of manslaughter.

3.3 Negligence

A person is negligent if they fail to meet the standards of the reasonable man. This means it is an objective test. The defendant will be guilty because he did not act as a reasonable man would have done in the circumstances. What the defendant intended or thought is not relevant. This makes it a much lower level of fault to the two levels of fault, intention and recklessness, that we have already looked at.

The concept of negligence making a person liable is well known in the civil law, but it is not widely used in the criminal law. It occurs in some statutory offences, for example s 3 of the Road Traffic Act 1988 which makes it an offence to drive without due care and attention.

The only mainstream offence for which negligence is relevant is manslaughter. One form of manslaughter can be committed by 'gross negligence'. This means there has to be a very high degree of negligence. The leading case is *Adomako* (1994). The level used in civil cases is not enough. Manslaughter is explained in more detail in Chapter 8.

3.4 Knowledge

This type of *mens rea* is the level required by some statutory offences. In some Acts of Parliament, a section will state that the offence is committed where the defendant 'knowingly' does something.

Even where the Act does not actually state that the defendant must have knowledge, it is sometimes inferred that knowledge is required for the defendant to be guilty. This was the position in *Sweet v Parsley* (1969).

Sweet v Parsley (1969)

The defendant was charged with 'being concerned in the management of premises used for the smoking of cannabis resin'. She owned a farmhouse which was let out. She did not know that the tenants in the farmhouse were smoking cannabis there. The House of Lords held that she was not guilty because she did not have knowledge that cannabis was being smoked.

Key facts

Level of *mens rea*	Explanation	Case/example
Intention (specific intent)	'A decision to bring about, in so far as it lies within the accused's power, [the prohibited consequence], no matter whether the accused desired that consequence of his act or not'.	*Mohan* (1975)
Recklessness (basic intent)	The defendant must realise that there is a risk of the consequences occurring and decide to take that risk.	*Cunningham* (1957)
Negligence	A failure to meet the standards of the reasonable man.	*Adomako* (1994)
Knowledge	D must have knowledge of a certain fact in order to be guilty.	*Sweet v Parsley* (1969)

Figure 3.3 Key facts chart on levels of *mens rea*

3.5 Transferred malice

This is the principle that the defendant can be guilty if he intended to commit a similar crime but against a different victim. An example is aiming a blow at one person with the necessary *mens rea* for an assault causing actual bodily harm, but actually hitting another person. This occurred in *Latimer* (1886).

Latimer (1886)

D aimed a blow with a belt at a man in a pub because that man had attacked him. The belt bounced off the man and struck a woman in the face. Latimer was guilty of an assault against the woman, although he had not meant to hit her.

However, where the *mens rea* is for a completely different type of offence, then the defendant may not be guilty. This was the situation in *Pembliton* (1874), where the defendant threw a stone, intending it to hit people with whom he had been fighting. The stone hit and broke a window. The intention to hit people could not be transferred to the window.

The doctrine of transferred malice was confirmed in an *obiter* statement by the House of Lords in the case of *Attorney-General's Reference (No 3 of 1994)* (1997). (See section 6.2.2 for details of the case).

3.5.1 General malice

In some cases the defendant may not have a specific victim in mind: for example, a terrorist who plants a bomb in a pub, intending to kill or injure anyone who happens to be there. In this case the defendant's *mens rea* is held to apply to the actual victim.

3.6 Coincidence of *actus reus* and *mens rea*

In order for an offence to take place, both the *actus reus* and the *mens rea* must be present at the same time. For example, if you decide to go round to your next-door neighbour, intending to assault them, but when you get to their house you change your mind and do not actually assault them, you cannot be guilty of an assault even though you had the *mens rea*.

If, two hours later, you are driving your car out of your driveway and knock down your neighbour because you did not see them, you have now done what could be the *actus reus* for an assault. However, you are not guilty of any criminal offence since at the moment you hit your neighbour you did not have the necessary *mens rea*. The *mens rea* and the *actus reus* were not present at the same time.

In *Thabo Meli v R* (1954) the court had to decide whether the *actus reus* and *mens rea* were present together.

Thabo Meli v R (1954)

Ds attacked a man and believed they had killed him. They then pushed his body over a low cliff. In fact, the man had survived the attack but died of exposure when unconscious at the foot of the cliff. It was held that Ds were guilty of murder.

The defendants in this case were guilty as the required *mens rea* and *actus reus* were combined in a series of acts. A similar situation occurred in *Church* (1965).

Church (1965)

D had a fight with a woman and knocked her out. He tried, unsuccessfully, for about half an hour to bring her round. He thought she was dead and he put her in the river. She drowned. His conviction for manslaughter was upheld.

3.6.1 Continuing act

Where there is a continuing act for the *actus reus* and at some point while that act is still going on the defendant has the necessary *mens rea*, then the two do coincide and the defendant will be guilty. This is illustrated by the case of *Fagan v Metropolitan Police Commissioner* (1986).

Fagan v Metropolitan Police Commissioner (1986)

Fagan was told by a police officer to park by a kerb. In doing this Fagan drove onto the policeman's foot, without realising he had done so. Initially, Fagan refused to move the car. When the policeman pointed out what had happened, he asked Fagan several times to move the car off his foot. Eventually, Fagan did move the car. Fagan was convicted of assaulting the police officer in the execution of his duty.

The Court of Appeal held that once Fagan knew the car was on the police officer's foot he had the required *mens rea*. As the *actus reus* (the car putting force on the foot) was still continuing, the two elements were then present together. The *actus reus* in this case was a continuing act as, so long as the defendant developed the *mens rea* at some time while the act was continuing, then he could be guilty.

Why should I move it?

Activity

Explain in the following situations whether *actus reus* and *mens rea* are present. (Do not forget that there may be transferred malice.)

1. Bart has had an argument with Cara. He aims a punch at her head, but Cara dodges out of the way and Bart hits Homer, who was standing behind Cara.
2. Desmond is sitting in a lecture. He pushes his chair back, but does not realise that one of the chair legs is pressing onto Mark's foot. Mark asks Desmond to move the chair, but Desmond thinks what has happened is funny and does not move but sits there laughing for several minutes.
3. Sian throws a stone at a cat. Her aim is very poor and the stone hits Ratinder who is standing several feet away.

Examination question

'The meaning of intention in criminal law has now been clearly settled by decisions of the courts and there is no longer any need for Parliament to legislate upon the matter.'

Critically consider whether you agree with this statement.

(OCR, Unit 2571, January 2005)

Chapter 4

Strict liability

4.1 The concept of strict liability

The previous chapter explained the different types of *mens rea*. This chapter considers those offences where *mens rea* is not required in respect of at least one aspect of the *actus reus*. Such offences are known as strict liability offences.

An example demonstrating strict liability is *Pharmaceutical Society of Great Britain v Storkwain Ltd* (1986).

Pharmaceutical Society of Great Britain v Storkwain Ltd (1986)

D was charged under s 58(2) of the Medicines Act 1968 which states that no one shall supply certain drugs without a doctor's prescription. D had supplied drugs on prescriptions, but the prescriptions were later found to be forged. There was no finding that D had acted dishonestly, improperly or even negligently. The forgery was sufficient to deceive the pharmacists. Despite this, the House of Lords held that the Divisional Court was right to direct the magistrates to convict D. The pharmacists had supplied the drugs without a genuine prescription and this was enough to make them guilty of the offence.

4.1.1 Requirement of *actus reus*

For nearly all strict liability offences, it must be proved that the defendant did the relevant *actus reus*. For *Storkwain*, this meant proving that the chemist had supplied drugs without a genuine prescription. It also has to be proved that the doing of the *actus reus* was voluntary. If the chemist had been forced at gun-point to provide the drug, then the act would not have been voluntary.

However, there are a few rare cases where the defendant has been found guilty even though they did not do the *actus reus* voluntarily. These are known as crimes of absolute liability.

4.2 Absolute liability

Absolute liability means that no *mens rea* at all is required for the offence. They involve 'status offences', offences where the *actus reus* is a 'state of affairs'. The defendant is liable because they have 'been found' in a certain situation. Such offences are very rare. To be an absolute liability offence, the following conditions must apply:

- the offence does not require any *mens rea* and
- there is no need to prove that the defendant's *actus reus* was voluntary.

The following two cases demonstrate this.

Larsonneur (1933)

The defendant, who was from a foreign country (and was therefore termed an 'alien', in the language of the time), had been ordered to leave the United Kingdom. She decided to go to Eire, but the Irish police deported her and took her in police custody back to the UK, where she was put in a cell in Holyhead police station. She did not want to return to the UK. She had no *mens rea*. Her act in returning was not voluntary. She was taken back to the UK. Despite this, she was found guilty under the Aliens Order 1920 of being 'an alien to whom leave to land in the United Kingdom has been refused … found in the United Kingdom'.

The other case is *Winzar v Chief Constable of Kent* (1983).

Winzar v Chief Constable of Kent (1983)

D was taken to hospital on a stretcher, but when he was examined by doctors they found that he was not ill but was drunk. D was told to leave the hospital, but was later found slumped on a seat in a corridor. The police were called and they took D to the roadway outside the hospital. They formed the opinion that he was drunk so

they put him in the police car, drove him to the police station and charged him with being found drunk in a highway, contrary to s 12 of the Licensing Act 1872. The Divisional Court upheld his conviction.

As in *Larsonneur*, the defendant had not acted voluntarily. He had been taken to the highway by the police. In the Divisional Court Goff LJ justified the conviction, pointing out that the particular offence was designed to deal with the nuisance which can be caused by persons who are drunk in a public place.

It is not known how Winzar came to be taken to the hospital on a stretcher but it is possible that there may have been an element of fault in his conduct. He had become drunk (presumably voluntarily) and must have either been in a public place when the ambulance collected him and took him to hospital, or he must have summoned medical assistance when he was not ill but only drunk.

4.3 Strict liability

For all offences there is a presumption that *mens rea* is required. The courts will always start with this presumption, but if they decide that the offence does not require *mens rea* for at least part of the *actus reus* then the offence is one of strict liability. This idea of not requiring *mens rea* for part of the offence is illustrated by two cases: *Prince* (1875) and *Hibbert* (1869). In both these cases the charge against the defendant was that he had taken an unmarried girl under the age of 16 out of the possession of her father, against his will, contrary to s 55 of the Offences Against the Person Act 1861.

Prince (1875)

Prince knew that the girl he took was in the possession of her father but believed, on reasonable grounds, that she was aged 18. He was convicted as he had the intention to remove the girl from the possession of her father. *Mens rea* was required for this part of the *actus reus* and he had the necessary intention. However, the court held that knowledge of her age was not required. On this aspect of the offence there was strict liability.

Hibbert (1869)

The defendant met a girl aged 14 on the street. He took her to another place where they had sexual intercourse. He was acquitted of the offence as it was not proved that he knew the girl was in the custody of her father. Even though the age aspect of the offence was one of strict liability, *mens rea* was required for the removal aspect and, in this case, the necessary intention was not proved.

4.3.1 No fault

As already stated, the *actus reus* must be proved and the defendant's conduct in doing the *actus reus* must be voluntary. However, a defendant can be convicted if his voluntary act inadvertently caused a prohibited consequence. This is so even though the defendant was totally blameless in respect of the consequence. An example was the case of *Callow v Tillstone* (1900).

Callow v Tillstone (1900)

A butcher asked a vet to examine a carcass to see if it was fit for human consumption. The vet assured him that it was all right to eat and so the butcher offered it for sale. In fact, it was unfit and the butcher was convicted of the offence of exposing unsound meat for sale.

Because it was a strict liability offence the butcher was guilty, even though he had taken reasonable care not to commit the offence. The butcher was not at fault in any way.

4.3.2 No 'due diligence' defence

For some offences the statute provides a defence of 'due diligence'. In other words, the defendant will not be liable if he can show that he did all that was within his power not to commit the offence.

However, there does not seem to be any sensible pattern for when Parliament decides to include a 'due diligence' defence and when it does not. It can be argued that such a defence should always be available for strict liability offences. If it was a defence, then the butcher in *Callow v Tillstone* would not have been guilty. By asking a vet to check the meat, he had clearly done all that he could to make sure that he did not commit the offence.

Another example of where the defendants took all reasonable steps to prevent the offence but were still guilty because there was no 'due diligence' defence available is *Harrow London Borough Council v Shah and Shah* (1999).

Harrow LBC v Shah and Shah (1999)

The defendants owned a newsagents' business where lottery tickets were sold. They had told their staff not to sell tickets to anyone under 16 years old. They frequently reminded their staff that if there was any doubt about a customer's age, the staff should ask for proof of age, and if still in doubt should refer the matter to the defendants. One of their staff sold a lottery ticket to a 13-year-old boy, without asking for proof of age. The salesman mistakenly believed the boy was over 16 years old. D1 was in a back room of the premises at the time: D2 was not on the premises. The defendants were charged with selling a lottery ticket to a person under 16, contrary to s 13(1)(c) of the National Lottery Act 1993. The magistrates dismissed the charges, but the prosecution appealed to the Divisional Court which held that the offence was one of strict liability. This meant that the defendants were guilty.

The Divisional Court held that the offence did not require any *mens rea*. The act of selling the ticket to someone who was actually under 16 was enough to make the defendants guilty, even though they had done their best to prevent this happening in their shop.

4.3.3 No defence of mistake

Another feature of strict liability offences is that the defence of mistake is not available. This is important as, if the defence of mistake is available, the defendant will be acquitted when he made an honest mistake. Two cases which illustrate the difference in liability are *Cundy v Le Cocq* (1884) and *Sherras v De Rutzen* (1895). Both of these involved offences under the Licensing Act 1872.

Cundy v Le Cocq (1884)

D was charged with selling intoxicating liquor to a drunken person. The magistrate trying the case found as a fact that the defendant and his employees had not noticed that the person was drunk. The magistrate also found that while the person was on the licensed premises he had been 'quiet in his demeanour and had done nothing to indicate insobriety; and that there were no apparent indications of intoxication'. However, the magistrate held that the offence was complete on proof that a sale had taken place and that the person served was drunk, and convicted the defendant. The defendant appealed against this but the Divisional Court upheld the conviction.

Sherras v De Rutzen (1895)

D was convicted of supplying alcohol to a constable on duty. Local police, when on duty, wore an armband on their uniform. An on-duty police officer removed his armband before entering the defendant's public house. The officer was served by D's daughter in the presence of D. D thought that the constable was off duty because he was not wearing his armband. D was convicted but the Divisional Court quashed the conviction. It held that the offence was not one of strict liability and accordingly a genuine mistake provided the defendant with a defence.

The judge pointed out that there was nothing the publican could do to prevent the commission of the crime. Even if the publican asked the officer, it would be as easy for the constable to deny that he was on duty as for him to remove his armband before entering the public house. This explains the different decisions in the two cases. The fact of a person being drunk is an observable fact, so the publican should be put on alert and could avoid committing the offence.

4.3.4 Summary of strict liability

So, where an offence is held to be one of strict liability, the following points apply:

- The defendant must be proved to have done the *actus reus*.
- This must be a voluntary act on his part.
- There is no need to prove *mens rea* for at least part of the *actus reus*.
- No 'due diligence' defence will be available.
- The defence of mistake is not available.

These factors are well established. The problem lies in deciding which offences are ones of strict liability. For this, the courts will start with presuming that *mens rea* should apply. This is so for both common-law and statutory offences.

Key facts

Levels of liability	Law	Cases
Absolute liability	These offences do not need proof of *mens rea* or voluntary *actus reus*.	*Larsonneur* (1933) *Winzar* (1983)
Strict liability	*Mens rea* need not be proved. Proof will not be required for one aspect of *mens rea* but may be required for another aspect of *mens rea*.	*Storkwain* (1986) *Prince* (1875) *Hibbert* (1869)
No fault liability	D is liable if he voluntarily did the *actus reus* (eg 'sells') even though he is not blameworthy.	*Callow v Tillstone* (1900)
No 'due diligence' defence	If the Act of Parliament does not allow a 'due diligence' defence, then D will be guilty even though he took all possible care.	*Harrow LBC v Shah and Shah* (1999)
No defence of mistake	D will still be guilty even though he made a genuine mistake.	*Cundy v le Cocq* (1884)

Figure 4.1 Key facts chart on strict liability

4.4 Strict liability at common law

Nearly all strict liability offences have been created by statute. Strict liability is very rare in common-law offences. Only four common-law offences have been held to be ones of strict liability. These are:

- public nuisance
- criminal libel
- blasphemous libel
- criminal contempt of court.

Public nuisance and criminal libel probably do not require *mens rea*, but there are no modern cases. There has been a relatively recent case on blasphemous libel which confirmed that it is a strict liability offence. This was *Lemon and Whitehouse v Gay News* (1979).

Lemon and Whitehouse v Gay News (1979)

A poem was published in *Gay News*, describing homosexual acts done to the body of Christ after his crucifixion and also describing his alleged homosexual practices during his lifetime. The editor and publishers were convicted of blasphemy. On appeal to the House of Lords, the Law Lords held that it was not necessary to prove that the defendants intended to blaspheme.

The common law offence of blasphemous libel has now been abolished by Parliament.

Criminal contempt of court was a strict liability offence at common law. It is now a statutory offence and Parliament has continued it as a strict liability offence.

4.5 Strict liability in statute law

The surprising fact is that about half of all statutory offences are ones of strict liability. This amounts to over 3,500 offences. Most strict liability offences are regulatory in nature. This may involve such matters as regulating the sale of food, alcohol and gaming tickets, the prevention of pollution and the safe use of vehicles.

Strict liability offences created by an Act of Parliament will not contain any words requiring *mens rea* in their definition. However, the courts will still look at a number of factors before deciding that a statutory offence is one of strict liability.

4.6 Interpretation by the courts

Statutory interpretation of Acts of Parliament is an important role of the courts. You will have studied the different rules and approaches to interpretation. Strict liability is an area of law where the courts will use statutory interpretation. The starting point is one of the presumptions of statutory interpretation – the presumption of *mens rea*.

4.6.1 Presumption of *mens rea*

In order to decide whether an offence is one of strict liability, the courts start by assuming that *mens rea* is required, but they are prepared to interpret the offence as one of strict liability if Parliament has expressly or by implication indicated this in the relevant statute.

The judges often have difficulty in deciding whether an offence is one of strict liability or not. The first rule is that where an Act of Parliament includes words indicating *mens rea* (eg 'knowingly', 'intentionally', 'maliciously' or 'permitting'), the offence requires *mens rea* and is not one of strict liability. However, if an Act of Parliament makes it clear that *mens rea* is not required, the offence will be one of strict liability.

However, in many instances a section in an Act of Parliament is silent about the need for *mens rea*. Parliament is criticised for this. If it made clear in all sections which create a criminal offence whether *mens rea* was required or not, then there would be no problem. As it is, where there are no express words indicating *mens rea* or strict liability, the courts have to decide which offences are ones of strict liability.

4.6.2 Principle in *Sweet v Parsley*

Where an Act of Parliament does not include any words indicating *mens rea*, the judges will start by presuming that all criminal offences require *mens rea*. This was made clear in the case of *Sweet v Parsley* (1969).

Sweet v Parsley (1969)

D rented a farmhouse and let it out to students. The police found cannabis at the farmhouse and D was charged with 'being concerned in the management of premises used for the purpose of smoking cannabis resin'. D did not know that cannabis was being smoked there. It was decided that she was not guilty as the court presumed that the offence required *mens rea*.

In giving judgment, Lord Reid said:

'There has for centuries been a presumption that Parliament did not intend to make criminals of persons who were in no way blameworthy in what they did. That means that whenever a section is silent as to *mens rea* there is a presumption that ... we must read in words appropriate to require *mens rea*.'

Although the courts start with the presumption that *mens rea* is required, they look at a variety of points to decide whether the presumption should stand or should be displaced and the offence made one of strict liability.

4.6.3 The *Gammon* tests

In *Gammon (Hong Kong) Ltd v Attorney-General of Hong Kong* (1984) the appellants had been charged with deviating from building work in a material way from the approved plan, contrary to the Hong Kong Building Ordinances. It was necessary to decide whether it had to be proved that they knew that their deviation was material or whether the offence was one of strict liability on this point.

The Privy Council started with the presumption that *mens rea* is required before a person can be held guilty of a criminal offence and that this presumption of *mens rea* applies to statutory offences.

They went on to give four other factors to be considered. These were that:

- the presumption can only be displaced if this is clearly or by necessary implication the effect of the words of the statute
- the presumption is particularly strong where the offence is 'truly criminal' in character
- the presumption can only be displaced if the statute is concerned with an issue of social concern such as public safety
- strict liability should only apply if it will help enforce the law by encouraging greater vigilance to prevent the commission of the prohibited act.

4.6.4 Looking at the wording of an Act

As already stated, where words indicating *mens rea* are used, the offence is not one of strict liability. If the particular section is silent on the point then the courts will look at other sections in the Act. Where the particular offence has no words of intention, but other sections in the Act do, then it is likely that this offence is a strict liability offence.

In *Storkwain* (1986) (see the beginning of this chapter) the relevant section, s 58(2) of the Medicines Act 1968, was silent on *mens rea*. The court looked at other sections in the Act and decided that, as there were express provisions for *mens rea* in other sections, Parliament had intended s 58(2) to be one of strict liability.

Where other sections allow for a defence of 'due diligence' but another section does not, then this is another possible indicator from within the statute that the offence is meant to be one of strict liability.

In *Harrow LBC v Shah and Shah* (1999) the defendants were charged under s 13(1)(c) of the National Lottery Act 1993. This subsection does not include any words indicating either that *mens rea* is required or that it is not, nor does it contain any provision for a defence of 'due diligence'. However, another subsection, s 13(1)(a), clearly allows a defence of 'due diligence'. The inclusion

of a 'due diligence' defence in part of s 13 but not in the section under which the defendants were charged, was an important point in the Divisional Court coming to the decision that s 13(1)(c) was an offence of strict liability.

4.6.5 Quasi-criminal offences

In *Gammon* (1984) the Privy Council stated that the presumption that *mens rea* is required is particularly strong where the offence is 'truly criminal' in character. Offences which are regulatory in nature are not thought of as being truly criminal matters and are, therefore, more likely to be interpreted as being of strict liability.

Regulatory offences are also referred to as 'quasi-crimes'. They affect large areas of everyday life. They include offences such as breaches of regulations in a variety of fields such as:

- selling food, as in *Callow v Tillstone* (1900)
- the selling of alcohol, as in *Cundy v le Cocq* (1884)
- building regulations, as occurred in *Gammon* (1984)
- sales of lottery tickets to an under-age child, as in *Harrow LBC v Shah and Shah* (1999) and
- regulations preventing pollution from being caused, as in *Alphacell Ltd v Woodward* (1972).

Alphacell (1972)

The company was charged with causing polluted matter to enter a river, contrary to s 2(1)(a) of the Rivers (Prevention of Pollution) Act 1951, when pumps which they had installed failed, causing polluted effluent to overflow into a river. There was no evidence either that the company knew of the pollution or that it had been negligent. The offence was held by the House of Lords to be one of strict liability and the company was found guilty because it was of the 'utmost public importance' that rivers should not be polluted.

4.6.6 Penalty of imprisonment

Where an offence carries a penalty of imprisonment, it is more likely to be considered 'truly criminal' and so less likely to be interpreted as an offence of strict liability. This was an important factor in *B v DPP* (2000).

B v DPP (2000)

D, a 15-year-old boy, asked a 13-year-old girl on a bus to give him a 'shiner' (ie have oral sex with him). He believed she was over the age of 14. He was charged with inciting a child under the age of 14 to commit an act of gross indecency, under s 1(1) of the Indecency with Children Act 1960. The House of Lords quashed his conviction, as *mens rea* was required for the offence.

The offence, inciting a child under the age of 14 to commit an act of gross indecency, carried a maximum penalty of two years' imprisonment. Lord Nicholls pointed out that this was a serious offence and that:

'the more serious the offence, the greater was the weight to be attached to the presumption [of *mens rea*], because the more severe was the punishment and the graver the stigma that accompanied a conviction.'

However, some offences carrying imprisonment have been made strict liability offences. For example in *Storkwain* (1986) (see the beginning of this chapter) the offence carried a maximum sentence of two years' imprisonment. Despite this, the House of Lords still held that the offence was one of strict liability.

It appears unjust that an individual should be liable to imprisonment even though the offence does not require proof of any fault by the defendant.

4.6.7 Issues of social concern

The type of crime and whether it is 'truly criminal' are linked to another condition laid down by the case of *Gammon* (1984): that is the question of whether the crime involves an issue of social concern. The Privy Council ruled that the only situation in which the presumption of *mens rea* can be displaced is where the statute is concerned with an issue of social concern.

This allows strict liability to be justified in a wide range of offences, as issues of social concern can be seen to cover any activity which is a 'potential danger to public health, safety or morals'.

Regulations covering health and safety matters in relation to food, drink, pollution, building and road use are obviously issues of social concern, but other issues such as possession of guns are also regarded as matters of public safety.

Even transmitting an unlicensed broadcast has been held to be a matter of social concern. This was decided in *Blake* (1997).

Blake (1997)

D was a disc jockey who was convicted of using a station for wireless telegraphy without a licence, contrary to s 1(1) of the Wireless Telegraphy Act 1949. His defence was that he believed he was making a demonstration tape and did not know he was transmitting. He was convicted on the basis that the offence was one of strict liability. He appealed to the Court of Appeal but his appeal was dismissed.

4.6.8 Promoting enforcement of the law

In *Gammon* (1984) the final point in considering whether strict liability should be imposed, even where the statute is concerned with an issue of social concern, was whether it would be effective to promote the objects of the statute by encouraging greater vigilance to prevent the commission of the prohibited act. If the imposition of strict liability will not make the law more effective then there is no reason to make the offence one of strict liability.

In *Lim Chin Aik v The Queen* (1963) the appellant had been convicted under s 6(2) of the Immigration Ordinance of Singapore of remaining (having entered) in Singapore when he had been prohibited from entering by an order made by the Minister under s 9 of the same Ordinance.

The Ordinance was aimed at preventing illegal immigration. However, the appellant had no knowledge of the prohibition and there was no evidence that the authorities had even tried to bring it to his attention. The Privy Council thought that it was not enough to be sure that the statute dealt with a grave social evil in order to infer strict liability. It was also important to consider whether the imposition of strict liability would assist in the enforcement of the regulations.

If it did not, then the offence should not be one of strict liability.

4.7 Justification for strict liability

4.7.1 Policy issues

Many statutory offences created by Parliament are aimed at preventing danger or other problems to the public. The risks of such danger are thought to outweigh the defendant's individual rights. It is more important to protect the public, even though this may in some cases mean that defendants who have taken every possible care will be convicted of an offence.

For example, many statutory offences are connected with cars and other transport. It is important that all vehicles are in a safe condition and operated safely. If they are not, then there are obvious risks of causing death or injury. It is thought that by having offences of strict liability, people who operate vehicles will take greater care to carry out regular safety checks.

Roscoe Pound explained it in this way:

Key facts

	Law	Cases
Presumption of *mens rea*	Unless the words make it clear that *mens rea* is not required, the courts will always start with the presumption that *mens rea* is required.	*Sweet v Parsley* (1969)
Looking at the rest of the Act	If other subsections state that *mens rea* is required but the section being considered does not state this, it is likely that the offence will be held to be one of strict liability.	*Storkwain* (1986)
Quasi-criminal offences	Regulatory crimes (not truly criminal) are *more* likely to be held to be strict liability offences.	*Harrow LBC v Shah and Shah* (1999)
Penalty of imprisonment	Where an offence is punishable by imprisonment, it is *less* likely that it will be held to be one of strict liability.	*B v DPP* (2000)
Issue of social concern	Where the offence involves potential danger to public health, safety or morals then it is *more* likely to be held to be a strict liability offence.	*Blake* (1997)
Would strict liability promote enforcement of the law?	If making the offence one of strict liability would *not* help law enforcement then there is no reason to make the offence a strict liability one.	*Lim Chin Aik v The Queen* (1963)

Figure 4.2 Key facts chart on how the courts decide whether strict liability applies

> 'Such statutes are not meant to punish the vicious but to put pressure upon the thoughtless and inefficient to do their whole duty in the interests of public health or safety.'

4.7.2 Social utility

The main justification for strict liability offences is their usefulness to the public as a whole. Strict liability offences help protect society by regulating activities 'involving potential danger to public health, safety or morals'. Making an offence one of strict liability promotes greater care over these matters by encouraging higher standards in such matters as hygiene in processing and selling food, or in obeying building or transport regulations. It makes sure that businesses are run properly.

As failure to comply with high standards may cause risk to the life and health of large numbers of the general public, there is good reason to support this point of view. However, some opponents of strict liability argue that there is no evidence that strict liability leads to businesses taking a higher standard of care. Some even argue that strict liability may be counter-productive. If people realise that they could be prosecuted even though they have taken every possible care, they may be tempted not to take any precautions.

4.7.3 Other justifications

Other justifications for the imposition of strict liability include the following:

- It is easier to enforce as there is no need to prove *mens rea*.
- It saves court time as people are more likely to plead guilty.
- Parliament can provide a 'due diligence' defence where this is thought to be appropriate.
- Lack of blameworthiness can be taken into account when sentencing.

As there is no need to prove *mens rea*, it is clear that enforcement of the law is more straightforward. In addition, rather than prosecute for minor regulatory breaches, the Health and Safety Executive and local Trading Standards officers are more likely to serve improvement notices or prohibition notices in the first instance. This can help to ensure that the law is complied with, without the need for a court hearing. When a case is taken to court, the fact that only the act has to be proved saves time and also leads to many 'guilty' pleas.

The use of a 'due diligence' defence (or a 'no negligence' defence) can soften the law on strict liability. In many instances Parliament provides such a defence in the statute creating the offence. If the inclusion of such defences was done in a consistent way, then many of the objectors to the imposition of strict liability would be satisfied.

However, the use of 'due diligence' clauses in Acts often seems haphazard. For example, in *Harrow LBC v Shah and Shah* (1999) the relevant section allowed a 'due diligence' defence for promoters of the lottery but not for those managing a business in which lottery tickets were sold (see section 4.3.2).

The final justification for strict liability is that allowances for levels of blameworthiness can be made in sentencing. A judge can pass a very lenient sentence where he feels that the defendant's level of blameworthiness was low.

4.7.4 Arguments against strict liability

Although there are sound justifications for imposing strict liability, there are equally persuasive arguments against its use. The arguments against strict liability include:

- it imposes liability on people who are not blameworthy
- those who are unaware of risks may be guilty
- there is no evidence that it improves standards
- the imposition of strict liability is contrary to human rights
- some strict liability offences carry a social stigma.

Liable even though not blameworthy

The main argument against strict liability is that it imposes guilt on people who are not blameworthy in any way. Even those who have taken all possible care will be found guilty and can be punished.

This happened in the case of *Harrow LBC v Shah and Shah* (1999) where the defendants had done their best to prevent sales of lottery tickets to anyone under the age of 16. Another case where all possible care had been taken was *Callow v Tillstone* (1900). In this case even the use of an expert (a vet) was insufficient to avoid liability.

Guilty even though unaware of risk

Strict liability may be imposed even though the defendant was unaware of any risks.

In *Environment Agency v Empress Car Co (Abertillery) Ltd* (1998) the House of Lords considered the word 'cause' in an Act where there was strict liability. They held that a defendant could only escape liability if he could show that the occurrence arising from the operations of his business was 'abnormal and extraordinary' rather than a normal fact of life.

At first sight this seems to allow a defence for defendants who had no knowledge of the possibility that the event might happen. However, the Law Lords went on to say that even though it was not foreseeable that it would happen to the particular defendant or take the particular form, a defendant would be liable if the matter was one of ordinary occurrence.

So defendants can be guilty of a happening caused by a risk of which they were unaware. An example of this was seen in *Environment Agency v Brook plc* (1998).

Environment Agency v Brook plc (1998)

A leakage was caused by a hidden defect in a seal. The leak caused pollution. It was pointed out that defects in valves are a rare but ordinary fact of life. The company were liable for the leak.

Does not improve standards

Although an important reason for imposition of strict liability is the maintenance of high standards so that health and safety are not put in jeopardy, there is, as mentioned earlier, no evidence that it improves standards. In fact, if the precautions against a very small risk are too expensive, then company managers may decide not to pay for the precautions, but to take the risk. This is the idea of 'profit from risk'. The company's profits are more important than spending large sums of money on protecting against a small risk. The cost of the precautions may even be far greater than any fine that will be imposed on the company for breaking the law.

Contrary to human rights

Another argument against the imposition of strict liability where an offence is punishable by imprisonment is contrary to the principles of human rights. This point was raised in *R v G* (2008).

R v G (2008)

G was a 15-year-old boy who had consensual sex with a girl he thought was aged 15. In fact she was only aged 12, but agreed that she had told him she was 15. G was prosecuted under s 5 of the Sexual Offences Act 2003 for the offence of rape of a child under 13. He was advised that this was a strict liability offence and his belief that she was 15 was irrelevant. He, therefore, pleaded guilty. The case was referred to the House of Lords on two points. The first was whether the fact that the offence was one of strict liability violated article 6(1) (entitlement to a fair hearing) and/or 6(2) (presumption of innocence) of the European Convention on Human Rights.

The Law Lords unanimously decided that there was no breach of either part of article 6. Article 6(1) only guaranteed fair procedure: it was not concerned with the content of the law. Article 6(2) required a defendant to be presumed innocent of the offence, but did not say anything about what the mental or other elements of the offence should be.

So, in the case of G, the defendant was guilty of a very serious offence, even though he genuinely (and on reasonable grounds) believed that the girl was the same age as himself.

Social stigma

The case of *R v G* also shows that strict liability can be imposed even where it creates serious social stigma. As a result of his conviction, G was put on the register of sex offenders. This was a particularly serious consequence for G. This is a strong argument against the imposition of strict liability in crimes which do lead to serious social stigma.

This is not an issue in regulatory quasi-criminal offences as these carry little or no social stigma.

4.8 Proposals for reform of strict liability

The main problem is that there is no way of knowing whether Parliament has deliberately decided to make an offence one of strict liability, or whether they did not realise that that was the effect of the wording of the Act.

It has, therefore, been suggested that Parliament should always state expressly whether an offence is meant to be one of strict liability or not. This would mean that there would be no need for the courts to use complicated rules of interpretation in order to decide if an offence is one of strict liability or not. It would be clear to everybody.

The Draft Criminal Code suggested this could be done by including the presumption of *mens rea* in the Code. Clause 20 of the draft Code states:

> 'Every offence requires a fault element of recklessness with respect to each of its elements other than fault elements, unless otherwise provided.'

Another way of reforming strict liability could be by requiring each offence to have a defence of due diligence. This would avoid the injustice of those who have taken all possible care being guilty of an offence. This would be in line with the law in Australia and Canada where judges have developed a general 'no-negligence' defence.

Yet another way of reforming the law on strict liability could be to have a rule that no offence carrying the penalty of imprisonment could be an offence of strict liability. This reform is not so wide-ranging as the two ideas above, but it still promotes justice as it would ensure that no one could be imprisoned for a breach of strict liability.

Finally, an alternative way of reforming strict liability law might be by removing regulatory offences from the criminal system. These could instead be treated as administrative issues.

However, this type of reform could not be applied to mainstream criminal offences of strict liability, such as those in the Sexual Offences Act 2003. These would have to remain in the criminal law with the risk of injustice to those convicted of such offences as in the case of *R v G*.

Examination question

'Strict liability offences are an exception to the general rule that the prosecution has the burden of proving that a person accused of a crime possesses the relevant guilty mind.'

Discuss, in the light of the above statement, whether you agree that the creation of strict liability offences can ever be justified.

(OCR, Specimen Paper)

Chapter 5

Attempts

An attempt is where a person tries to commit an offence but, for some reason, fails to complete it. For example, D fires a gun at V, intending to kill V. Just as D pulls the trigger, V stoops to tie his shoelace. The bullet misses V and goes over his head. D intended to kill V but has not succeeded, so D cannot be charged with murder as V is still alive. However, it is obvious that D ought to be criminally liable for some offence. It would be ridiculous if he were just allowed to go free. D is clearly a dangerous person and should be liable under the criminal law. In this type of situation D can be charged with attempted murder.

A case example of an attempt to murder is *White* (1910).

White (1910)

D put cyanide in his mother's drink, intending to kill her. She died of a heart attack before she could drink it. He tried to commit murder but did not actually kill his mother. He was convicted of attempted murder.

5.1 Definition of 'attempt'

'Attempt' is now defined by s 1(1) of the Criminal Attempts Act 1981.

Definition

'If, with intent to commit an offence to which this section applies, a person does an act which is more than merely preparatory to the commission of the offence, he is guilty of attempting to commit the offence.'

As with all offences the prosecution must prove the *actus reus* and the *mens rea*. The definition above sets these out. They are:

- *Actus reus* – a person does an act which is more than merely preparatory to the commission of the offence
- *Mens rea* – with intent to commit that offence.

5.2 *Actus reus* of attempt

Before 'attempt' was defined in the 1981 Act, the courts used several different tests to decide whether the defendant had actually done enough towards the commission of the main offence for him to have committed the *actus reus*. The main tests were:

- the 'last act' test: had D done the last act he could do before committing the main crime?
- the 'proximity' test: were the defendant's acts so 'immediately connected' to the *actus reus* of the offence as to justify liability for attempt?

The courts have held that these common-law tests are irrelevant, the important point being whether the defendant has done an act which is 'more than merely preparatory' to the commission of the main offence.

5.2.1 'More than merely preparatory'

The act that the defendant commits has to be more than merely preparation for the main crime. Some acts are obviously mere preparation, but other acts are more difficult to categorise.

Let's take the example where D decides to rob a bank. First, he buys himself a shotgun and converts it into a sawn-off shotgun. Both the buying and the converting are 'merely preparatory'. Next, he drives around the area, checking escape routes. Again, this is 'merely preparatory'.

On the day of the robbery, D steals a car ('merely preparatory') and drives to the bank (still 'merely preparatory'). He stands on the pavement outside the bank, carrying the sawn-off shotgun in a bag. This is getting nearer, but, according to the case of *Campbell* (1990) (see below), is still only 'merely preparatory'. Then he walks into the bank. Now he has gone beyond mere preparation and can be charged with attempted robbery.

There have been many cases on the meaning of 'merely preparatory'. It is difficult to draw any general principle from them. In *Attorney-General's Reference (No 1 of 1992)* (1993) it was decided that D need not have performed the last act before the crime proper, nor need he have reached the 'point of no return'.

Attorney-General's Reference (No 1 of 1992) (1993)

D dragged a girl up some steps to a shed. He lowered his trousers and interfered with her private parts. His penis remained flaccid. He argued that he could not therefore attempt to commit rape. His conviction for attempted rape was upheld.

Looking at the whole of D's acts, this seems a sensible decision. However, if he had been stopped immediately after he had dragged the girl to the shed, and before he lowered his trousers or interfered with her, then it is unlikely that he could have been convicted. His act of dragging her was probably 'merely preparatory'.

In *Gullefer* (1987) the Court of Appeal held that 'more than merely preparatory' means that the defendant must have gone beyond purely preparatory acts and be 'embarked on the crime proper'.

Gullefer (1987)

D jumped onto a race track in order to have the race declared void and so enable him to reclaim money he had bet on the race. His conviction for attempting to steal was quashed because his action was merely preparatory to committing the offence.

5.2.2 Cases showing mere preparation

The case of *Gullefer* (above) illustrates a situation in which D's acts were mere preparation. Although D had tried to interfere with the race, he had several other acts to do before the theft (the point at which he would get his betting money back). He had to go to one of the betting points and ask for his money back. Even just going towards the point would not be sufficient. However, asking for the money would change his actions into 'more than merely preparatory'. He would be guilty of attempted theft. It is worth noting that when the money was handed to him, he would then be guilty of the main offence of theft.

The Court of Appeal stated that an attempt begins when 'the merely preparatory acts have come to an end and the defendant embarks upon the crime proper'. It also pointed out that when this moment occurs will depend on the facts in any particular case.

The case of *Geddes* (1996) also illustrates acts which were only preparatory.

Geddes (1996)

D was found in the boys' toilet block of a school, in possession of a large kitchen knife, some rope and masking tape. He had no right to be in the school. He had not contacted any of the pupils. His conviction for attempted false imprisonment was quashed.

This case is difficult to justify. D had no right to be on the premises. He had entered the school with all the equipment for falsely imprisoning a student. The next step would be for him to approach one of the students. If the law of attempt is to be effective in protecting people from the main offence, then surely he should have been guilty of an attempt at that point. Is it sensible to wait until he approaches one of the students?

However, the Court of Appeal thought that attempts should be considered by asking two questions:

1. Had the accused moved from planning or preparation to execution or implementation?
2. Had the accused done an act showing that he was actually trying to commit the full offence, or had he got only as far as getting ready, or putting himself in a position, or equipping himself, to do so?

Using these two questions, it can be seen that Geddes had not quite moved from planning or preparation to execution. Also, it can be argued that he had got only as far as getting ready, or putting himself in a position, to commit the full offence.

Another case which is perhaps even more difficult to justify is *Campbell* (1990).

Campbell (1990)

D, who had an imitation gun, sunglasses and a threatening note in his pocket, was in the street outside a post office. His conviction for attempted robbery was quashed.

The next step in this case would have been for D to enter the post office. Again, if the law of attempt is to be effective in protecting people from the main offence, surely he should have been guilty of an attempt at that point? Is it sensible to wait until he enters the post office? If the gun had been real then customers and staff in the post office would have been put at risk.

5.2.3 Cases in which there was an attempt

The following two cases show situations where the defendant had gone beyond mere preparation. In each case the defendants were held to be guilty of an attempt to commit the full offence.

Boyle and Boyle (1987)

The defendants were found standing by a door of which the lock and one hinge were broken. Their conviction for attempted burglary was upheld.

The Court of Appeal held that the test to use was whether the defendant was embarking on the crime proper. In this case, once the defendants had entered they would be committing burglary, so trying to gain entry was an attempt.

The difference from *Campbell* is that burglary is committed at the moment D enters as a trespasser with intent to steal (or do certain other offences). Robbery is not committed until D uses force in order to steal. Walking into a building still leaves another step before the crime proper is committed.

In the next case, *Jones* (1990), the defendant had done almost everything he could before committing the full offence.

Key cases

Case	Facts	Offence attempted	Point of law
Cases where there was sufficient for an attempt			
A-G's reference (No 1 of 1992) (1993)	D tried to rape a girl but could not get an erection.	Rape	Need not have performed the last act.
Boyle and Boyle (1987)	Standing by door with broken lock.	Burglary	Had done part of a series of acts.
Jones (1990)	Gun safety catch was left on.	Murder	Sufficient evidence to leave the question of whether there was an attempt to the jury.
Cases which were merely preparatory			
Gullefer (1987)	Disrupted race intending to reclaim bet.	Theft	Has D 'embarked upon the crime proper'?
Geddes (1996)	In school with knife, rope and tape.	False imprisonment	Has D 'actually tried to commit the offence in question'?
Campbell (1990)	Outside post office with imitation gun and threatening note.	Robbery	Merely preparatory.

Figure 5.1 Key cases chart on 'merely preparatory' in attempts

Jones (1990)

D's partner told him that she wanted their relationship to end and that she was seeing another man, V. D bought a shotgun and shortened the barrel. D then found V, who was in his car. D, who was wearing a crash helmet with the visor down, got into V's car and pointed the gun at V. V grabbed the gun and managed to throw it out of the car window. D's conviction for attempted murder was upheld.

D tried to argue that, as the safety catch was still on, he had not done the last act before the crime proper. The Court of Appeal said that buying the gun, shortening it, loading it and disguising himself with the visor were all preparatory acts. But once D got into V's car and pointed the gun at V, then there was sufficient evidence to leave to the jury the question of whether there was an attempt.

5.3 *Mens rea* of attempt

For an attempt, the defendant must normally have the same intention as would be required for the full offence. If the prosecution cannot prove that D had that intention then D is not guilty of the attempt. This was shown by the case of *Easom* (1971).

Easom (1971)

D picked up a woman's handbag in a cinema, rummaged through it, then put it back on the floor without removing anything from it. His conviction for theft of the bag and its contents was quashed. The Court of Appeal also refused to substitute a conviction for attempted theft of the bag and specific contents (including a purse and a pen), as there was no evidence that D intended to steal the items.

In this case there was no evidence that the defendant had intended to permanently deprive the owner of the bag or items in it (part of the required *mens rea* for theft). As a result, he could not be guilty of attempted theft.

A similar decision was made in the case of *Husseyn* (1977).

Husseyn (1977)

D and another man were seen loitering near the back of a van. When the police approached, they ran off. D was convicted of attempting to steal some sub-aqua equipment that was in the van. The Court of Appeal quashed his conviction.

The decisions by the Court of Appeal in both these cases can be criticised. Surely the defendant did intend to steal something? The fact that Easom did not do so (presumably because there was nothing really worth stealing) should not make him not guilty of attempting to steal. Equally, in the case of Husseyn, the fact that he ran off because the police arrived does not mean that he was not trying to steal.

These problems were resolved in *Attorney-General's Reference (Nos 1 and 2 of 1979)* (1979) where the Court of Appeal decided that if D had a conditional intent (ie D intended stealing if there was anything worth stealing), D could be charged with an attempt to steal some or all of the contents.

So, Eason would now be charged with attempting to steal all or some of the contents of the bag, rather than the bag itself and specific items in it. Husseyn would be charged with attempting to steal some or all of the contents of the van.

5.3.1 Is recklessness enough for the *mens rea*?

What if it can be proved that the defendant was reckless? Is this sufficient for him to be guilty of an attempt? In *Millard and Vernon* (1987) it was decided that it was not sufficient.

Millard and Vernon (1987)

Ds repeatedly pushed against a wooden fence on a stand at a football ground. The prosecution alleged that they were trying to break it and they were convicted of attempted criminal damage. The Court of Appeal quashed their convictions.

Recklessness is not normally sufficient *mens rea* for an attempt. This is so even where recklessness would suffice for the completed offence. However, there is an exception in that recklessness as to one part of the offence can be sufficient. This is illustrated by *Attorney-General's Reference (No 3 of 1992) (1994)*.

Attorney-General's Reference (No 3 of 1992) (1994)

D threw a petrol bomb towards a car containing four men. The bomb missed the car and smashed harmlessly against a wall. D was charged with attempting to commit arson with intent to endanger life. The trial judge ruled that it had to be proved that D intended to damage property *and* to endanger life. D was acquitted.

The Court of Appeal held that the trial judge was wrong. It was necessary to prove that D intended to damage property, but it was only necessary to prove that he was reckless as to whether life would be endangered.

5.4 Attempting the impossible

In some situations a person may intend to commit an offence and may do everything they possibly can to commit it, but in fact the offence is impossible to commit.

An example of this would be where D goes to V's room and stabs V as he lies in bed. In fact, V died of a heart attack two hours before D stabbed him. D has merely stabbed a dead body.

Murdering V is physically impossible so D cannot be guilty of his murder, but can D be guilty of attempting to murder V?

Another example is where D thinks that the goods he is buying very cheaply are stolen goods. He is willing to go ahead, thinking he is 'handling stolen property'. In fact, the goods are not stolen, so the offence of handling stolen property is legally impossible in this situation. Should D be guilty of attempting to handle stolen property?

Under the common law, before 1981, the House of Lords had held that where a crime was legally or physically impossible to commit, then the defendant could not be guilty of attempting to commit it. When the Criminal Attempts Act 1981 was passed it contained a subsection (s 1(2)) which was intended to close this loophole and make defendants guilty of an attempt even though the full offence was impossible.

Section 1(2) of the Criminal Attempts Act 1981 states:

> 'A person may be guilty of attempting to commit an offence … even though the facts are such that the commission of the offence is impossible.'

After the Act was passed, the House of Lords had to consider this section and the problem of attempting the impossible in the case of *Anderton v Ryan* (1985).

Anderton v Ryan (1985)

Mrs Ryan bought a video recorder very cheaply. She thought it was stolen. Later she admitted this to police who were investigating a burglary at her home. Her conviction was quashed because the video recorder was not in fact stolen.

The House of Lords held that even though Mrs Ryan had gone beyond merely preparatory acts, in fact all her acts were innocent. The video recorder was not stolen. On this basis, they thought that s 1(2) did not make her guilty.

However, less than a year later, the House of Lords overruled this decision in *Shivpuri* (1986).

Shivpuri (1986)

D agreed to receive a suitcase which he thought contained prohibited drugs. The suitcase was delivered to him, but it contained only snuff and harmless vegetable matter. D was convicted of attempting to be knowingly concerned in dealing with prohibited drugs.

This time the House of Lords said that both ss 1(2) and 1(3) were relevant. Subsection 1(3) states:

'In any case where–

(a) apart from this subsection a person's intention would not be regarded as having amounted to an intent to commit an offence; but

(b) if the facts of the case had been as he believed them to be, his intention would be so regarded,

then, for the purpose of subsection (1) he shall be regarded as having an intent to commit that offence.'

The combined effect of ss 1(2) and 1(3) of the Criminal Attempts Act 1981 meant that a person could be guilty of an attempt even if the commission of the full offence was impossible. In *Shivpuri* the facts as he believed them to be were that the suitcase contained prohibited drugs. He intended dealing in drugs so his intention, under s 1(3), is regarded as being an intention to commit that offence.

The House of Lords accepted that its decision in *Anderton v Ryan* (1985) had been wrong and they used the Practice Statement to overrule that decision.

Key facts

	Attempt	Case or statute
Definition of 'attempt'	With intent to commit an offence, a person does an act which is more than merely preparatory to the commission of the offence.	s 1(1) Criminal Attempts Act 1981
'More than merely preparatory'	D must have embarked on the crime proper *or* D must be trying to commit the full offence.	*Gullefer* (1987) *Geddes* (1996)
Mens rea of attempt	D must have intention for the full offence. A conditional intention is sufficient.	*Easom* (1971) *Attorney-General's Reference (Nos 1 and 2 of 1979)* (1979)
	Recklessness is not normally sufficient *but* recklessness as to part of the offence may be sufficient.	*Millard and Vernon* (1987) *Attorney-General's Reference (No 3 of 1992)* (1994)
Attempting the impossible	Sections 1(2) and 1(3) of the Criminal Attempts Act 1981 mean that D is guilty even if the full offence is legally or physically impossible.	*Shivpuri* (1986)

Figure 5.2 Key facts chart on attempts

Activity

Explain whether in each of the following scenarios there is an attempt to commit an offence.

1. Amir knows his girlfriend has been going out with Blake. Amir plans to disfigure Blake. He buys some acid which he intends to throw in Blake's face and then drives to Blake's house. As he is about to get out of the car, he sees a police car nearby. Amir immediately drives off.
2. Connor puts some poison in Donna's drink, intending to kill her. The amount he puts in the drink is insufficient to kill and Donna survives.
3. Faye sees a handbag in the ladies' cloakroom. She hopes there will be some money in it, so she opens it. In fact, the bag contains only make-up and tissues. Faye closes the bag and replaces it.
4. Greg and Hans are found in the garden of a house with masks, a torch and screwdrivers in their pockets. They admit they intended to burgle the house.
5. Ian fires a shot at Jani but misses her. He admits he intended to kill her.

5.5 Is the law on attempts satisfactory?

There are several points which can be argued to be unsatisfactory.

- The courts have not been very clear in deciding the dividing line between what is 'merely preparatory' and what is an attempt.
- Some of the decisions in this area are not effective for protecting the public.
- The early decisions on *mens rea* left a loophole where D intended to steal if he could find anything worth stealing, but the concept of conditional intent has now clarified this (see section 5.3).
- Should D be guilty just because of intention?

5.5.1 What is 'more than merely preparatory'?

The cases *Gullefer*, *Geddes* and *Campbell* that we looked at in section 5.2.1 show that the courts are not always prepared to take a broad approach when deciding what is 'more than merely preparatory'.

However, it can be argued that the 'more than merely preparatory' test is an improvement on the law as it stood prior to the passing of the Criminal Attempts Act 1981. The old law used a variety of different tests, so that it was not easy to predict which test would be used in any given case.

The 'more than merely preparatory' test has helped to clarify and simplify the law. It also makes it easier for juries to apply the law, as they can use their common sense in deciding if the things the defendant did were 'more than merely preparatory'.

5.5.2 Protection of the public

In considering this it is also necessary to ask why attempting an offence should make someone criminally liable. The main justification is that it can prevent the full offence from being committed. It would be ridiculous if the police had to wait until D fired the shot and killed V, instead of being able to arrest D for attempted murder. So, given that prevention of crime and protection of potential victims are important, the decisions in *Geddes* and *Campbell* in particular are hard to reconcile with this.

5.5.3 Should intention alone make a defendant guilty?

The opposite point of view is that a defendant should not be criminally liable for his intentions. He must do something toward the commission of the full offence. This raises the question of whether Parliament should have made defendants liable where the facts are such that the commission of the full offence is impossible. Should Shivpuri have been guilty? He did not actually deal in drugs or do any wrong act. Is it enough that he intended to?

Again, it can be argued that it is in the public interest to be able to convict someone like Shivpuri. Drug dealing causes society many problems.

Level of *mens rea*

Another issue in relation to attempt is that a higher level of *mens rea* is required for an attempt of some offences than is required for the full offence.

For example, in the offence of murder, *mens rea* can be proved by showing either that the defendant intended to kill or that he intended to cause really serious harm. However, for attempted murder it is necessary to prove that the defendant intended to kill. Intention to cause really serious harm is not sufficient for the *mens rea* of attempted murder.

This makes it appear that the law is more favourable to those charged with attempt than to those charged with the full offence. However, a defendant who intended to cause really serious harm but did not commit the full offence can be charged with the offence of attempting to commit grievous bodily harm contrary to s 18 of the Offences Against the Person Act 1861, so the defendant does not escape liability completely.

Recklessness

There is also a discrepancy in the law in that recklessness is not usually sufficient for the *mens rea* of an attempt even though it is sufficient for the full offence.

Was the acquittal in *Millard and Vernon* justified (see section 5.3)? Should the fact that they were reckless in repeatedly pushing against the fence have made them liable for attempted criminal damage?

Or it is more justified that the prosecution had to prove that they intended to damage the fence? If they had been liable for attempt through recklessness, this would have meant that they were being found guilty even though they had not formed any *mens rea*. After all, it is a key principle of criminal law that a person should not be guilty unless they have a guilty mind.

Examination questions

1. Discuss whether the current law relating to attempted crimes strikes the right balance between protecting society and convicting those who deserve to be punished.

   (OCR, Specimen Paper)

2. 'A person who genuinely attempts to commit a crime and fails, still deserves to be punished just as much as a person who succeeds in committing an offence'.

   Consider whether you agree with this view of attempts.

   (OCR, Unit 2571, June 2007)

Chapter 6

Murder

Homicide is the unlawful killing of a human being. There are different offences, depending on the *mens rea* of the defendant and whether there is a special defence available to the defendant. The most serious homicide offence is murder.

6.1 Definition of 'murder'

Murder is a common-law offence. This means that it is not defined by any Act of Parliament. It has been defined by the decisions of judges in different cases, and the accepted definition is based on one given by a seventeenth-century judge, Lord Coke.

Definition

'Murder is the unlawful killing of a reasonable person in being and under the King's (or Queen's) Peace with malice aforethought, express or implied'.

The different elements of this definition are considered in detail under the *actus reus* and *mens rea* of murder below at sections 6.2 and 6.3.

Jurisdiction

Obviously, a person can be charged with a murder committed anywhere in England and Wales. But murder is unusual in that jurisdiction over it also includes any murder in any country by a British citizen. This means that if the defendant is a British citizen, he may be tried in an English court for a murder he is alleged to have committed in another country.

6.2 *Actus reus* of murder

The *actus reus* of murder is the unlawful killing of a reasonable creature in being and under the Queen's Peace. Breaking this down, it has to be proved that:

- D killed
- a reasonable creature in being
- under the Queen's Peace and
- the killing was unlawful.

6.2.1 'Killed'

Act or omission

The *actus reus* of killing can be by an act or omission, but it must cause the death of the victim. Usually in murder cases, the *actus reus* is an act. But remember that we saw in Chapter 2 at section 2.2 that an omission (a failure to act) can make a person liable for an offence.

This applies to murder, as seen by the case of

Gibbins and Proctor (1918) where the father of a seven-year-old girl and his mistress kept the girl separate from the father's other children and deliberately starved her to death. The father had a duty to feed her because he was her parent and the mistress was held to have undertaken to look after the children, including the girl, so she was also under a duty to feed the child. The omission or failure to feed her was deliberate with the intention of killing or causing serious harm to her. In these circumstances they were guilty of murder. The failure to feed the girl was enough for the *actus reus* of murder.

Causation

Murder is a *result crime*. The defendant cannot be guilty unless his act or omission caused the death. In most cases there is no problem with this. For example, D shoots V in the head and V is killed instantly. However, in some cases there may be other causes contributing to the death, such as poor medical treatment. This type of situation raises questions of causation.

The law on causation is considered fully in Chapter 2 in section 2.3 and you need to know the law stated there.

6.2.2 'Reasonable creature in being'

This phrase means 'a human being'. So, for murder, a person must be killed. Normally, this part of the definition does not cause any difficulties. The only two problem areas are:

- Is a foetus in the womb a 'reasonable creature in being'?
- Is a victim still considered to be alive (and so a 'reasonable creature in being') if they are 'brain-dead' but being kept alive by a life-support machine?

Foetus

A homicide offence cannot be charged in respect of the killing of a foetus. The child has to have an 'existence independent of the mother' for it to be considered a 'creature in being'. This means that it must have been expelled from her body and have an independent circulation. However, the umbilical cord connecting the child and the mother need not have been cut. Also, it is probable that the child need not have taken its first breath for it to be considered a 'reasonable creature in being'.

In addition, in *Attorney-General's Reference (No 3 of 1994)* (1997) it was stated by the House of Lords that where the foetus is injured and the child is born alive but dies afterwards as a result of the injuries, this can be the *actus reus* for murder or manslaughter.

Attorney-General's Reference (No 3 of 1994) (1997)

The defendant stabbed his girlfriend who was about 23 weeks' pregnant. She recovered from the stab wound but it caused her to give birth prematurely some seven weeks after the stabbing. The baby was born alive but died at the age of four months as a result of the premature birth. The defendant was charged with the murder of the child. At the trial the judge directed that a foetus was not a 'reasonable creature in being' and so the defendant could not in law be guilty of either the murder or manslaughter of the child. The defendant was acquitted.

The House of Lords agreed that this was correct where the foetus died before being born but stated *obiter* that:

'violence towards a foetus which results in harm suffered after the baby has been born alive can give rise to criminal responsibility'.

However, they held that in the circumstances the offence was manslaughter as there was no *mens rea* for murder.

Brain-dead

It is not certain whether a person who is 'brain-dead' would be considered as a 'reasonable creature in being' or not. Doctors are allowed to switch off life-support machines without being liable for homicide. This suggests that 'brain-death' is the recognised test for death, but there has been no case on this point. It is possible that the courts might decide that a defendant who switches off a life-support machine, not as a medical decision but intending to kill the victim, could be guilty of murder.

'Year and a day' rule

There used to be a rule that death must have occurred within a year and a day of the attack. This rule was sensible in past centuries when medical knowledge was not sufficient to prove that an attack had caused the death after such a long time. However, with improvements in medical skill, the rule became out of date. In particular, it meant that, where a victim was in a coma and did not die until more than a year after the attack, the attacker could not be charged with his murder. So the 'year and a day' rule was abolished by the Law Reform (Year and a Day Rule) Act 1996. There is now no time limit on when the death may occur after the unlawful act but, where it is more than three years after the attack, the consent of the Attorney-General is needed for the prosecution.

6.2.3 'Queen's Peace'

'Under the Queen's Peace' means that the killing of an enemy in the course of war is not murder. However, the killing of a prisoner of war would be sufficient for the *actus reus* of murder.

6.2.4 'Unlawful'

The killing must be unlawful. If the killing is in self-defence or defence of another or in the prevention of crime and the defendant used reasonable force in the circumstances, then the killing is not unlawful.

The defences of self-defence and defence of another are common-law defences which justify the defendant's actions. They can be a defence to any crime, including murder, as the defendant is justifying the use of force. In addition there is a statutory defence of prevention of crime under s 3(1) of the Criminal Law Act 1967 which states that:

> 'a person may use such force as is reasonable in the circumstances in the prevention of crime'.

This also can be a defence to any offence, including murder.

An interesting case in which the killing of one person was thought to be justified is *Re A (Children) (Conjoined Twins)* (2000).

Re A (Children) (Conjoined Twins) (2000)

Twin girls were born joined at the lower abdomen. The one twin (J) was capable of a separate existence, but the other twin (M) was not. M was being kept alive by a common artery through which J's stronger heart circulated enough oxygenated blood for both of them. If the twins were not separated, then both girls would die within six months as J's heart would eventually not be strong enough to pump the blood around. If the twins were separated, M would inevitably die.

The twins' parents refused permission to separate them, so the hospital authorities applied for a declaration that it would be lawful to separate them. The Court of Appeal held that it would be lawful. The main reason for this finding was that the defence of necessity justified the separation (see section 12.5 for necessity). However, one of the judges (Ward LJ) thought that M's dependence on blood from J's heart was the equivalent of a potentially fatal attack on J. This entitled doctors to intervene and use force to save J.

For all these three defences the key point is whether the use of force and level of the force was reasonable in the circumstances.

Reasonable force

In deciding whether the force used was reasonable, the fact that the defendant had only done what he honestly and instinctively thought was necessary in a moment of unexpected anguish is very strong evidence that the defensive action taken was reasonable.

In looking at the circumstances, the defendant must be judged on the facts as he genuinely believed them to be. This is so, even if the defendant was mistaken about the true facts. This rule is illustrated by *Beckford* (1988).

Beckford (1988)

D was a police officer in Jamaica. He and other police officers had gone to a house to investigate a report that a man armed with a gun was terrorising his family. As D approached the house, he saw a man running out of it. D shot and killed the man. D claimed that he believed his own life was in danger as he thought the man still had a gun. In fact, when the man was shot he did not have a gun. D was convicted and appealed to the Privy Council, which quashed his conviction as the jury should have been allowed to consider whether D genuinely believed his own life was in danger.

Lord Griffiths when giving judgment in the case pointed out that:

'a genuine belief in a fact which if true would justify self-defence [must] be a defence to a crime of personal violence because the belief negates the intent to act unlawfully.'

So what the defendant genuinely believed is the important fact, even if that belief was mistaken and even if it was unreasonable.

Excessive force

The amount of force used to defend oneself or another must be reasonable in the circumstances. If excessive force is used the defence will fail as shown by the case of *Clegg* (1995).

Clegg (1995)

D was a soldier on duty at a checkpoint in Northern Ireland. A car came towards the checkpoint at speed and with its headlights full on. One of the soldiers shouted for it to stop but it did not. Clegg fired three shots at the windscreen of the car and one as it passed him. This final shot hit a passenger in the back and killed her. The evidence showed that the car had gone past Clegg by the time this last shot was fired. So it was held that he could not use self-defence as a defence because there was no danger when he fired that shot. The force was excessive in the circumstances and his conviction for murder was upheld.

Note that in 1999 the case of *Clegg* was referred back to the Court of Appeal by the Criminal Case Review Commission. On this occasion his conviction was quashed because new forensic evidence cast doubt on whether the fatal shot had actually been fired by Clegg.

Another case in which it was decided that the level of the force used was not reasonable was *Martin (Anthony)* (2002).

Martin (Anthony) (2002)

D shot two burglars who had broken into his farmhouse, one of whom died. The evidence was that the burglars were leaving when D shot them, and the burglar who died had been shot in the back. D was found guilty of murder. He appealed on the basis that the defence of self-defence should have been allowed as he was suffering from a paranoid personality disorder which meant that he may have genuinely (but mistakenly) thought he was in an extremely dangerous situation.

The Court of Appeal rejected the appeal on this basis as they held that personality disorders could not be taken into account when considering the defence of self-defence. However, the conviction was reduced to manslaughter on the grounds that D was suffering from diminished responsibility (see section 7.1 for an explanation of diminished responsibility).

So the rules on when use of force can justify the defendant's actions are as follows:

- The defences of self-defence/defence of another/prevention of crime are defences which justify D's actions so that he is held not to have acted unlawfully.

- The force used must be reasonable in the circumstances.
- The circumstances include what D genuinely believed to be the situation. This is so even if that belief was mistaken or unreasonable, provided the jury accepts that D genuinely believed it.
- However, a personality disorder which affects D's perceptions of the situation cannot be taken into account.
- The amount of force must not be excessive in the circumstances as D believed them to be.

6.3 *Mens rea* of murder

The *mens rea* for murder is stated as being 'malice aforethought, express or implied'. This means that there are two different intentions, either of which can be used to prove the defendant guilty of murder:

Activity

Read the following situations and explain whether the *actus reus* for murder is present.

1. Jane is angry because Karina is pregnant by Jane's boyfriend. When Karina is eight months' pregnant, Jane stabs her in the stomach, intending to kill the foetus. Karina is rushed to hospital, where a Caesarian section is carried out. The baby is alive when it is removed from Karina's womb, but dies two hours later.
2. Anya is offered a lift home by Barnaby. After a few minutes, she realises he is driving away from her home. He then puts his hand on her thigh as he is driving and says that they can enjoy themselves. Anya is so afraid that she jumps out of the car while it is going at about 40 mph. She is hit by another car and killed.
3. Boris has been threatened by Clint in the past. He also knows that Clint often carries

a knife. One day Clint runs towards Boris shouting, 'You're for it now'. Boris picks up a heavy piece of concrete and throws it at Clint's head. Clint suffers head injuries and dies as a result.
4. Lily decides to kill Kevin. She takes his shotgun and loads it. She waits until he has gone to sleep, then she goes into his bedroom and shoots him in the head. Unbeknown to her, Kevin died from a drug overdose 20 minutes before she shot him.
5. Martha has an argument with her husband, Desmond. Desmond then goes into the kitchen and a few minutes later comes out shouting abuse at her. Martha sees what she thinks is a knife in his hand, although it is actually a child's toy. Believing that he is about to stab her, Martha throws an ash-tray at Desmond's head. This hits him on the temple and kills him.

- *express* malice aforethought, which is the intention to kill, or
- *implied* malice aforethought, which is the intention to cause grievous bodily harm.

A defendant has the *mens rea* for murder if he has either of these intentions. This means that a person can be guilty of murder even though they did not intend to kill. This was decided in *Vickers* (1957).

Vickers (1957)

Vickers broke into the cellar of a local sweet shop. He knew that the old lady who ran the shop was deaf. However, the old lady came into the cellar and saw Vickers. He then hit her several times with his fists and kicked her once in the head. She died as a result of her injuries. The Court of Appeal upheld Vickers' conviction for murder. It pointed out that where a defendant intends to inflict grievous bodily harm and the victim dies, that has always been sufficient in English law to imply malice aforethought.

The same point was considered by the House of Lords in *Cunningham* (1981) when it confirmed that an intention to cause grievous bodily harm was sufficient for the *mens rea* of murder.

Cunningham (1981)

D attacked V in a pub, attacking him repeatedly with a chair. V died from his injuries and D was convicted of murder. The House of Lords dismissed his appeal. It held that the law was firmly established. An intention to cause grievous bodily harm was sufficient for the *mens rea* of murder.

The other issue is what is meant by 'grievous bodily harm'? In *DPP v Smith* (1961) the House of Lords decided that 'grievous bodily harm' has the natural meaning of 'really serious harm'.

However, even if the judge directed the jury leaving out the word 'really' and just saying 'serious harm', this was not a misdirection.

Intention to injure a foetus

In *Attorney-General's Reference (No 3 of 1994)* (1997) it was held that it was not possible for a defendant to have the *mens rea* to kill or seriously injure a foetus. This was because a foetus does not have a separate existence from its mother.

6.3.1 Intention

The general rules on intention apply to murder. These were discussed in Chapter 3 at section 3.1 and should be referred back to. The main problem with proving intention is in cases where the defendant's main aim was not to cause the death or serious injury of the victim, but something quite different, but in achieving the aim a death is caused. This is referred to as *oblique intent*. The defendant does not have the *mens rea* for murder unless he foresaw that he would also cause death or serious injury. This is known as *foresight of consequences* and was considered in detail at section 3.1.2. However, as the law in this area is complex and important, the three main cases are set out here again.

Foresight of consequences

The main rule is that foresight of consequences is not intention. In *Moloney* (1985), where the defendant shot and killed his step-father in a drunken challenge to see who was quicker on the draw, it was held that foresight of consequences is only evidence from which intention may be inferred.

In *Nedrick* (1986) the defendant poured paraffin through the letter box of a house in order to frighten the woman who lived there. A child died in the fire. The Court of Appeal suggested that juries ask themselves two questions:

- How probable was the consequence which resulted from the defendant's voluntary act? and
- Did the defendant foresee that consequence?

I don't intend to hurt you.

The Court of Appeal also said that the jury should be directed that they are not entitled to infer the necessary intention unless they feel sure that death or serious injury was a virtual certainty as a result of the defendant's actions, and that the defendant appreciated that such was the case.

In *Woollin* (1998) the House of Lords approved this direction but disapproved of the use of the two questions. The Law Lords said that 'substantial risk' was not the correct test. Using this phrase blurred the line between intention and recklessness. They approved the direction given in *Nedrick*, provided that the word 'find' was used instead of 'infer'. So, the jury should be directed that they are not entitled to *find* the necessary intention unless they feel sure that death or serious injury was a virtual certainty as a result of the defendant's actions, and that the defendant appreciated that such was the case.

In each of the following situations, explain whether the defendant has the required intention for murder.

1. Jamie is annoyed because Harry has being trying to date Jamie's girlfriend. Jamie sees Harry in a local pub and goes over and punches him hard in the face saying 'Perhaps that will make you leave my girlfriend alone'. Harry has a thin skull and the punch causes a brain haemorrhage from which he dies.
2. Diana intends to kill Edward. She fixes an explosive booby trap to the front door of his house, so that when he opens it the explosive will go off. Unbeknown to Diana, Edward has given Felix the keys to his house and told him to collect some papers from there. Felix opens the door and is killed by the explosion.
3. Ravinder's business has been losing a lot of money. He decides to set fire to one of the smaller buildings in the unit so that he can claim insurance on it. Ravinder knows that there is no one in his building, so he sets it alight. Unfortunately, the fire spreads to another building on the site. Nancy, who is working in that building, is trapped by the fire and dies.

6.4 The need for reform of the law

In 2006 the Law Commission published a report, *Murder, Manslaughter and Infanticide* (Report Law Com 304). In this report the Law Commission pointed out that there were many problems with the law on murder.

In its general comments on the law of murder, the report said (at paragraph 1.8):

Key facts

	Law	Source/case
Definition	'The unlawful killing of a reasonable person in being and under the King's (or Queen's) Peace, with malice aforethought, express or implied'	Lord Coke (17th century)
Actus reus	Must unlawfully kill a person under the Queen's Peace.	
	Can be an act or an omission.	*Gibbins and Proctor* (1918)
	A foetus is not considered a person for the purposes of murder.	*Attorney-General's Reference (No 3 of 1994)* (1997)
	A killing is not unlawful if it is in self-defence, defence of another or prevention of crime and the use of force is reasonable in the circumstances.	*Beckford* (1988)
Mens rea	Intention to kill *or* intention to cause grievous bodily harm.	*Vickers* (1957) *Cunningham* (1981)
	Foresight of consequences is evidence of intention.	*Moloney* (1985)
	Jury can *find* intention if death or serious injury was a virtual certainty as a result of D's actions and D appreciated this.	*Woollin* (1998)

Figure 6.1 Key facts chart for murder

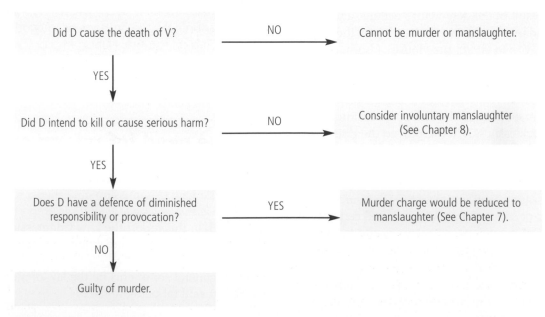

Figure 6.2 Flow chart on homicide

> 'The law governing homicide in England and Wales is a rickety structure set upon shaky foundations. Some of its rules have remained unaltered since the seventeenth century, even though it has long been acknowledged that they are in dire need of reform. Other rules are of uncertain content, often because they have been constantly changed to the point that they can no longer be stated with any certainty or clarity.'

In the report the Law Commission set out the existing problems with the law on murder. They listed the following:

- The law on murder has developed bit-by-bit in individual cases and is not a coherent whole.
- A defendant can be convicted of murder even though he only intended to cause serious harm (the serious harm rule).
- There is no defence available if excessive force is used in self defence.
- The defence of duress is not available as a defence to murder.
- The mandatory life sentence and the Government's sentencing guidelines do not allow sufficient differentiation in sentencing to cover the wide variety of levels of blameworthiness in the current law of murder.

Each of these is discussed in the section below.

The Law Commission also pointed out that there are problems with the special defences to murder of diminished responsibility and provocation. These problems are considered in Chapter 7, sections 7.1.5 and 7.2.5.

6.4.1 Bit-by-bit development of the law

One of the main areas where the bit-by-bit development by the courts has caused problems is the meaning of 'intention'. Intention is a concept which affects all specific intent offences but most of the cases which have been heard by the House of Lords have involved murder.

Section 8 of the Criminal Justice Act 1967 tried to make the law clear on this point. It states:

> 'A court or jury in determining whether a person has committed an offence—
>
> (a) shall not be bound in law to infer that he intended or foresaw a result of his actions by reason only of its being a natural and probable consequence of those actions; but
>
> (b) shall decide whether he did intend or foresee that result by reference to all the evidence, drawing such inferences from the evidence as appear proper in the circumstances.'

The main problems in the law are on foresight of consequences. The House of Lords has tried on many occasions to explain the effect of foresight of consequences. In *Moloney* (1985) it ruled that foresight of consequences was not intention; it was only evidence from which intention could be inferred in accordance with s 8(b) above.

However, the later decision in *Woollin* (1998), where the House of Lords speaks about intention being *found* from foresight of consequences, has made the law uncertain. It is not clear whether there is a substantive rule of criminal law that foresight of consequences is intention, or if there is only a rule of evidence that intention can be found from foresight of consequences. In *Matthews and Alleyne* (2003) the Court of Appeal even said that there was little to choose between a rule of evidence and one of substantive law, leaving it even more unclear (see section 3.1.2).

6.4.2 The serious harm rule

The Law Commission in its report, *Murder, Manslaughter and Infanticide*, pointed out that Parliament, when it passed the Homicide Act 1957, never intended a killing to amount to murder unless the defendant realised that his or her conduct might cause death. It stated that in its view the present offence of murder is too wide.

Under the present law on murder, a defendant is guilty of murder if he had the intention to cause grievous bodily harm and actually causes the victim's death. In some of these cases the defendant may not even realise that death could occur. Yet he is just as guilty of murder as the man who deliberately sets out to kill his victim.

The Law Commission gives the following example in its report (paragraph 1.17):

> 'D intentionally punches V in the face. The punch breaks V's nose and causes V to fall to the ground. In falling, V hits his or her head on the kerb causing a massive and fatal brain haemorrhage.'

It points out that, if the jury decides that the harm D intended the punch to cause can be described as 'serious', then this would be murder. Yet, most people would agree that this should not be the most serious offence of homicide and D should not receive a mandatory life sentence for it.

Not only is the Law Commission very critical of this rule, but the problem had already been pointed out by judges as far back as 1981 in the case of *Cunningham* (1981). When the law was considered by the House of Lords, Lord Edmund Davies stated that he thought the *mens rea* for murder should be limited to an intention to kill. He said:

> '[It is] strange that a person can be convicted of murder if death results from, say, his intentional breaking of another's arm, an action which, while undoubtedly involving the infliction of "really serious harm" and as such, calling for severe punishment, would in most cases be unlikely to kill.'

Although he was very critical of the law, Lord Edmund Davies felt that any change to the law had to be made by Parliament. This was because the law has been the same for over 200 years and it would therefore be wrong for judges to change such a well-established law.

As yet no reform to the law has been made, but the Law Commission has made very specific proposals for how the law could be reformed.

6.4.3 No defence where excessive force is used

If a defendant can show that he used reasonable force in self-defence or prevention of crime in doing the killing, he is not guilty of murder. However, where force is necessary in self-defence or prevention of crime, but the defendant uses excessive force in the circumstances, he is guilty of murder. This 'all or nothing' effect of the defence is very harsh in murder cases, as the defendant is either acquitted or given a life sentence. He was justified in using some force and his only 'fault' is that he used more force than was reasonable. This surely does not justify a life sentence.

Two recent cases have highlighted this problem. The first was *Clegg* (1995) where a soldier was initially convicted of murder when he shot a passenger in a car that had gone through a checkpoint. The second case was *Martin (Anthony)* (2002) who shot a burglar in the back when the burglar was leaving Martin's farmhouse.

Both these decisions have been criticised. Many people believe that a person who kills where he has an honest, but unreasonable, belief as to the degree of force needed is not as blameworthy as a 'true' murderer. It is unjust that such a person is found guilty of the same crime of murder and sentenced to the same punishment.

The Law Commission proposed that use of excessive force in a situation where some force is justified should be a partial defence to murder. If the defence was successful, the offence would be reduced to manslaughter. The judge would then have more discretion over sentencing in such a case. A life sentence could be given but it would not be mandatory.

6.4.4 No defence of duress

Duress is where the defendant is threatened with death or serious injury so that he takes part in an offence. Duress is allowed as a defence to almost all offences, but it is not allowed as a defence to murder (or attempted murder). See section 12.4 for full discussion of the defence of duress.

The Law Commission gave the following example:

> 'A taxi driver has his vehicle commandeered by a gunman, who holds a gun to the driver's head and tells him to drive to a place where the gunman says he may shoot someone. The taxi driver does as the gunman demands and the gunman goes on to shoot and kill someone.'

The report points out that, under the existing law, the taxi driver is an accomplice in the killing and could be convicted of murder. He would then receive a mandatory life sentence just as the gunman would. This is clearly not fair.

The Law Commission proposed that duress should be a complete defence to murder. However, a defendant claiming this defence would have to prove that he or she was threatened with death or life-threatening harm and had had no realistic opportunity to seek police protection. The jury would also have to find that a person of ordinary courage might have responded in the same way as D did by taking part in the commission of the crime.

6.4.5 Mandatory life sentence

If a defendant aged 18 or over is convicted of murder, the judge has to pass a sentence of life imprisonment. For offenders aged 10–17 who are found guilty of murder, the judge has to order that they be detained at Her Majesty's Pleasure. Because the judge has no discretion in what sentence to impose, this is known as a *mandatory* sentence. The judge cannot give a different sentence even if he feels that the defendant is not as blameworthy as a deliberate killer.

For other offences, including attempted murder, the judge can decide what the most appropriate sentence is for the offence and the offender. This makes it possible for a judge to give even a community sentence where the circumstances justify it. This happened in the case of *Gotts* (1992), where the father of a 16-year-old boy threatened to kill the boy unless he stabbed his mother. The boy did stab her and seriously injured her, but the injury did not kill her. He was convicted of attempted murder and because of the circumstances the judge put him on probation for three years. If the stabbing had caused the death of the mother, the judge would have had to order the boy (because of his age) to be detained at Her Majesty's Pleasure.

It is because of the mandatory life sentence for murder that the 1957 Homicide Act sets out special defences: of diminished responsibility and provocation (see Chapter 7), which reduce the charge to manslaughter. This allows the judge flexibility in passing sentence which he does not have when the defendant is convicted of murder.

Minimum sentences

In each case the judge will impose a life sentence but will then state the minimum number of years the offender must serve before any application can be made for release on licence.

The sentencing problems have been aggravated by the Government's guidelines on these minimum sentences as laid down in the Criminal Justice Act 2003. This gives three starting points for adult offenders:

- A whole life term for exceptionally serious cases, such as premeditated killings of two or more people, sexual or sadistic child murders or politically motivated murders.
- Thirty years' minimum for serious cases such as murders of police or prison officers, murders involving firearms, sexual or sadistic killings or killings aggravated by racial or sexual orientation.
- Fifteen years' minimum for murders not falling within the two higher categories.

Under these rules the defendant in *Martin (Anthony)* (2002) who shot and killed a burglar would have had to have been given a minimum sentence of 30 years. This is the same length of sentence as a contract killer would receive who deliberately kills a victim. The guidelines do not allow sufficient differentiation between levels of blameworthiness.

The Law Commission was not asked to consider sentencing. However, in their proposals for making murder into a two-tier offence, they state that the mandatory life sentence and the guidelines on minimum sentences should only apply to first degree murder. This would create a fairer sentence structure.

6.4.6 Law Commission's proposals for reform

The Law Commission proposed that murder should be reformed by dividing into two separate offences:

- first degree murder, and
- second degree murder.

First degree murder would cover cases in which the defendant intended to kill. It would also cover situations where the defendant intended to cause serious harm and was aware that his or her conduct posed a serious risk of death.

Cases in which the defendant intended to do serious injury, but was not aware that there was a serious risk of death, would be second degree murder. By dividing murder into two separate categories the mandatory life sentence would apply only to first degree murder. Second degree murder would carry a maximum of a life sentence but would allow the judge discretion in sentencing.

NB The Law Commission's summary of its proposals is set out in full in Appendix 4.

6.4.7 Government's response to the Law Commission's proposals

In July 2008 the Government issued a consultation paper, *Murder, manslaughter and infanticide: proposals for reform of the law*, CP

19/08. This paper rejected the Law Commission's proposal of completely reforming murder by making it a two-tier offence. The Government's proposals do not, therefore, address the problems of no intent to kill, the difficulty of the meaning of intention, the lack of a defence of duress and the use of the mandatory life sentence. These would continue to be problems in the law of murder.

The only area where the Government accepted that reform is needed is the lack of a defence for those who use excessive force in self-defence. For this the Government proposes that there should be a partial defence of 'killing in response to a fear of serious violence'.

This would form part of a new defence which it is proposed would replace the partial defence of provocation. See section 7.2.8 for a discussion of how this would affect provocation.

The Government's consultation paper points out that there are two likely scenarios where the partial defence of 'killing in response to a fear of serious violence' would be available. These are where:

- a victim of sustained abuse kills his or her abuser in order to thwart an attack which is anticipated but not immediately imminent; or
- someone overreacts to what they perceive as an imminent threat.

If this proposal is accepted then defendants in cases such as *Clegg* (1995) and *Martin (Anthony)* (2002) would have a partial defence to a charge of murder which could reduce the charge to manslaughter.

6.4.8 Euthanasia

There is also the problem of euthanasia. This is also known as 'mercy killing' and is where D kills V because V is suffering through an incurable illness. Quite often, D is the spouse or partner of V and has seen V suffering for a long period of time.

Under the present law, if D kills V because he or she can no longer bear to see V in such pain, then D is guilty of murder. This is so, even if V has begged D to do the killing. This means that D will be sentenced to life imprisonment with a minimum term of 15 years before D can be considered for release on licence.

As such a defendant is unlikely to be a dangerous person, surely there should be more discretion in the sentence that the courts impose.

In some countries, in particular the Netherlands, doctors are allowed to end the life of terminally ill patients. There are, of course, strict controls on when this can be done.

In the UK, although euthanasia is not allowed, doctors can withdraw treatment from patients in certain circumstances under the decision in *Airedale NHS Trust v Bland* (1993).

Airedale NHS Trust v Bland (1993)

Bland had been suffocated in the Hillsborough Stadium tragedy of 1989. This had so starved his brain of oxygen that he had been in persistent vegetative state in hospital for over three years. He was being fed through tubes. The hospital applied for permission to stop feeding him.

The House of Lords stated that there was no rule that a patient's life be prolonged regardless of the quality of life. Sanctity of life was an important principle, but quality of life could also be considered. If it was in the best interests of the patient to discontinue life support, then that was allowed to happen.

So although doctors can withdraw treatment where a patient is in a persistent vegetative state, the doctors are not allowed to do anything positive to kill the patient. It can be argued that it is better to administer a drug which kills such a patient painlessly, rather than deprive them of food and drink, so that they effectively starve to death.

Examination questions

1. Discuss whether the common law governing the offence of murder is satisfactory or is in need of reform by Parliament. (Do not consider causation issues in answering this question.)

(OCR, Unit G143, June 2008)

2. Sarev owes Dipak £40,000 as the result of a gambling debt. When Sarev refuses to pay, Dipak is very angry and decides to frighten Sarev. One night, he cuts the brake fluid pipe beneath Sarev's car hoping that Sarev will be involved in a crash that will scare him into repaying the debt. Outside Sarev's house there is a steep hill with a bend at the bottom. Next morning Sarev drives down the hill but is unable to slow down as he approaches the sharp bend. The car collides at speed with a stone wall and Sarev is critically injured and knocked unconscious.

An ambulance arrives within ten minutes to take Sarev to hospital. The paramedics, John and Carol, who are the crew on the ambulance, fail to close the rear door of the ambulance correctly and, as it accelerates away, the stretcher on which Sarev is lying is thrown out on to the road. Sarev is run over and killed by a van driven by Ron that is travelling closely behind the ambulance.

Discuss Dipak's liability for the murder of Sarev.

(OCR, Unit 2571, January 2006)

Chapter 7

Voluntary manslaughter

There are three special defences to a charge of murder. These are where the killing occurs when the defendant is under:

- diminished responsibility
- provocation or
- a suicide pact.

All of these defences are set out in the Homicide Act 1957. These defences are available only to murder. They are also only *partial* defences, which means that the defendant is not completely acquitted. Instead, when one of these defences is successful, the charge of murder is reduced to manslaughter.

This is important because it means that the judge has discretion in what sentence he imposes. When a person is found guilty of murder, the judge has to pass a sentence of life imprisonment. However, for manslaughter the judge can choose *any* sentence which is suitable. This means that where the defendant is dangerous and his mental problems cannot be treated, the judge may pass a sentence of life imprisonment, as happened in *Byrne* (1960) (see section 7.1.2). However, if the defendant is not dangerous then he may be given a short term of imprisonment or even a community sentence.

The defences of diminished responsibility and provocation are now explained in detail.

7.1 Diminished responsibility

This defence was introduced by the Homicide Act 1957; it did not exist in English law until then. Before 1957, if a person with mental problems killed, then their only defence was insanity. The test for insanity is a very narrow one and defendants who clearly suffer from a mental illness do not always come within it. (See Chapter 12 for further information on the defence of insanity.)

7.1.1 Definition

The definition of diminished responsibility is given in s 2(1) of the Homicide Act.

Definition

Diminished responsibility

Where a person kills or is party to a killing of another, he shall not be convicted of murder if he was suffering from such abnormality of mind (whether arising from a condition of arrested or retarded development of mind or any inherent causes or induced by disease or injury) as substantially impaired his mental responsibility for his acts and omission in doing or being a party to the killing.

The burden of proving the defence is on the defendant, but the defendant need only prove it on the balance of probabilities.

This means that a defendant who pleads diminished responsibility must prove that:

- he was suffering from an abnormality of mind
- which was caused by arrested or retarded development of mind or an inherent cause or disease or injury, and
- the abnormality of mind substantially impaired his mental responsibility for the killing.

The meanings of each of these points are considered in the next sections. The defence of diminished responsibility is currently used in less than 20 cases a year.

7.1.2 'Abnormality of mind'

'Abnormality of mind' covers a wide range of situations. In *Byrne* (1960) the Court of Appeal described it as 'a state of mind so different from that of ordinary human beings that the reasonable man would term it abnormal'.

Byrne (1960)

The defendant was a sexual psychopath who strangled a young woman and then mutilated her body. The medical evidence was that, because of his condition, he was unable to control his perverted desires. He was convicted of murder, but the Court of Appeal quashed the conviction and substituted a conviction for manslaughter as it held that his condition came within the definition of diminished responsibility.

The Court of Appeal held that 'abnormality of mind' is wide enough to cover:

- the perception of physical acts and matters
- the ability to form a rational judgement as to whether an act is right or wrong, and
- the ability to exercise will power to control physical acts in accordance with that rational judgment.

This final point covers 'irresistible impulse', as with the defendant, where he could not resist his perverted desires. This meant that the defence of diminished responsibility was available to Byrne. However, although the Court of Appeal substituted a conviction for manslaughter, Byrne was still sentenced to life imprisonment.

In *Byrne* the medical experts had described his condition as amounting to 'partial insanity' and the Court of Criminal Appeal had approved of this. However, in *Seers* (1984) it was held that comparisons with insanity are not helpful and should be avoided.

Seers (1984)

D, who was suffering from chronic reactive depression, killed his wife. The trial judge had directed the jury that the defence was only available to those who were 'partially insane' or 'on the borderline of insanity'. Seers was convicted of murder but the Court of Appeal quashed this conviction and substituted a conviction for manslaughter.

Diminished responsibility covers a wide range of mental conditions, including depressive illnesses, paranoia, epilepsy, pre-menstrual tension and 'battered wife syndrome'.

Some of the conditions have been well known for years, but some of the conditions have been recognised more recently. In particular, 'battered wife syndrome' was only recently recognised. This is demonstrated by the case of *Hobson* (1998).

Hobson (1998)

D was tried in October 1992 for the murder of her abusive, alcoholic partner. At the trial she described the abuse she had endured. The trial judge left the question of whether there was self-defence and/or provocation to the jury. Diminished responsibility was not specifically raised as a defence and the judge did not mention it to the jury. D was convicted. In May 1997 she appealed on the ground that the evidence at her trial raised the defence of diminished responsibility based on 'battered woman syndrome'. The Court of Appeal allowed the appeal and ordered a retrial. The court noted that 'battered woman syndrome' had not been regarded as an abnormality of mind until 1994, two years after D's trial.

7.1.3 Causes of the abnormality of mind

The abnormality of mind must be caused by one of the matters set out in the brackets within s 2(1) of the Homicide Act 1957. These are:

- a condition of arrested or retarded development of mind or
- any inherent cause or
- induced by any disease or
- induced by injury.

'Inherent cause' means one which comes from within the defendant, as opposed to an outside factor. It does not have to be permanent. A totally external factor, such as alcohol or drugs or a traumatic event or environmental influences, is not an inherent cause. However, if a traumatic event causes the defendant to suffer from post-traumatic stress disorder then this is recognised as a disease.

The important point is that there must be medical evidence given at the trial, of an abnormality of mind arising from one of the specified causes.

7.1.4 'Substantially impairs'

The abnormality of mind must substantially impair the defendant's mental responsibility for his acts and omissions in doing or being a party to the killing.

In *Byrne* (1960) the appeal court said that the question of whether the impairment was substantial was one of degree and that it was for the jury to decide. In *Lloyd* (1967) it was held that 'substantial' does not mean 'total', nor does it

mean 'trivial' or 'minimal'. It is something in between, and it is for the jury to decide if the defendant's mental responsibility is impaired and, if so, whether it is substantially impaired. However, as it is a question of fact, the judge can withdraw the point from the jury if there is no evidence on which a reasonable jury could conclude that the defendant's mental responsibility was substantially impaired.

In *Seers* (1984) the court also considered the phrase 'substantially impaired' and held that 'substantially' means more than 'trivial' but not 'total' or 'absolute' impairment.

7.1.5 Diminished responsibility and intoxication

The defence of diminished responsibility becomes more complicated when the defendant was also intoxicated at the time of the killing. There are various combinations of intoxication and diminished responsibility that have to be considered. These are:

- intoxication only
- intoxication and a pre-existing abnormality of mind not connected to the intoxication
- intoxication which has caused brain damage
- intoxication due to addiction/dependency.

Intoxication only

There is a clear rule that intoxication alone is not diminished responsibility. In *Di Duca* (1959) the Court of Appeal held that the immediate effects of taking alcohol or drugs was not an injury, even if it did have an effect on the brain. So a 'transient' state of intoxication was not an abnormality of mind.

So, if the jury decide that the defendant was not suffering from an abnormality of mind, the defence of diminished responsibility is not available. The defendant will be guilty of murder.

Intoxication and a pre-existing abnormality of mind

There are also difficulties in cases where the defendant has some abnormality of mind but, in addition, is intoxicated at the time he does the killing. This problem was considered in *Gittens* (1984).

Gittens (1984)

D suffered from depression and had medication for this. One night he drank a lot and also took several anti-depressant pills. He then clubbed his wife to death and strangled his step-daughter. He was convicted of murder. The conviction was quashed because the trial judge had misdirected the jury on the effect of intoxication in the case. The Court of Appeal held that where there was a combination of factors, one of which was intoxication, the jury had to decide whether the combination of the factors excluding the intoxication amounted to a substantial impairment of the defendant's responsibility for his acts.

This decision was later interpreted as meaning that the defendant could only prove diminished responsibility if he could satisfy the jury that he would have killed because of the abnormality of mind even if he had not been intoxicated. However, in *Dietschmann* (2003) the House of Lords said that this was the wrong approach and was not what had been decided in *Gittens*.

Dietschmann (2003)

The defendant was upset by the fact that, in his view, the victim was behaving in a way which was disrespectful to the memory of the defendant's aunt who had just died, and he killed the victim by repeatedly kicking him and stamping on him. The defendant was suffering from an adjustment disorder in the form of a depressed grief reaction to the death of his aunt.

This was agreed on by the psychiatrists called by both the prosecution and the defence. However, they disagreed on whether this had substantially impaired his mental responsibility for the killing. The defendant had also drunk about a third of a bottle of whisky and two and a half pints of cider before the killing. He was convicted and appealed. The Court of Appeal dismissed the appeal, but the House of Lords allowed it.

Although the Court of Appeal dismissed the appeal, they certified the following questions for the House of Lords:

> '(1) Does a defendant seeking to prove a defence of diminished responsibility under section 2(1) of the Homicide Act 1957 in a case where he had taken drink prior to the killing of the victim, have to show (a) he would have killed as in fact he did; and (b) he would have been under diminished responsibility when he did so?
>
> (2) If not, what direction ought to be given to a jury as to the approach to be taken to self-induced intoxication which was present at the material time in conjunction with an abnormality of mind which falls within section 2(1) of the 1957 Act?'

In the House of Lords, Lord Hutton said that the meaning of s 2(1) was reasonably clear. It meant that if the defendant satisfied the jury that, notwithstanding the alcohol he had consumed and its effect on him, his abnormality of mind substantially impaired his mental responsibility for his acts in doing the killing, the jury should not find him guilty of murder but, instead guilty of manslaughter under s 2(1).

Lord Hutton also pointed out that s 2(1) does not require the abnormality of mind to be the sole cause of the defendant's acts in doing the killing.

Even if the defendant would not have killed if he had not taken the drink, the causative effect of the drink does not necessarily prevent an abnormality of mind from substantially impairing his mental responsibility. Lord Hutton highlighted three points from the decision in *Gittens*:

1. The abnormality of mind and the drink might each play a part in impairing the defendant's mental responsibility for the killing.
2. The jury's task was to decide whether, despite the disinhibiting effect of the drink on the defendant's mind, the abnormality of mind nevertheless substantially impaired his mental responsibility for his fatal acts.
3. It was not correct for the judge to direct the jury that unless they were satisfied that if the defendant had not taken drink he would have killed, the defence must fail. The direction was incorrect because it failed to recognise that drink and the abnormality of mind might each play a part in impairing the defendant's mental responsibility for the killing.

The House of Lords allowed the appeal and sent the case back to the Court of Appeal to decide whether to substitute a verdict of manslaughter or to order a new trial.

Intoxication which has caused brain damage

If the brain has been injured through alcoholism, then that injury or disease can support a finding of diminished responsibility. This was stated in *Tandy* (1989) (see below).

Intoxication due to addiction/dependency

In *Tandy* (1989) the Court of Appeal held that where the defendant is unable to resist drinking, so that it is involuntary, this may amount to diminished responsibility.

Tandy (1989)

Mrs Tandy had been an alcoholic for a number of years, usually drinking barley wine or Cinzano. One day, she drank nearly a whole bottle of vodka. That evening she told her mother that her (Tandy's) second husband had sexually interfered with her 11-year-old daughter. She then strangled her daughter. The trial judge told the jury to decide whether Tandy was suffering from an abnormality of mind as a direct result of her alcoholism or whether she was just drunk. She was convicted. The Court of Appeal dismissed her appeal because Tandy had not shown that her brain had been injured or that her drinking was involuntary.

The decision in this case has been criticised as it only looks at whether the defendant was unable to prevent themselves from drinking. It does not consider whether alcoholism is a disease.

The point was considered again in *Wood* (2008) when the Court of Appeal pointed out that the 'sharp effect of the distinction drawn in *Tandy* between cases where brain damage has occurred as a result of alcohol dependency syndrome and those where it has not, is no longer appropriate'.

Wood (2008)

The defendant, after drinking heavily, had gone to the victim's flat. The defendant claimed he had fallen asleep there and been woken by the victim trying to perform oral sex on him. The defendant repeatedly hit the victim with a meat cleaver, killing him. At the trial medical experts agreed that the defendant was suffering from alcohol dependency syndrome but disagreed as to whether this had damaged his brain.

The judge directed the jury that if they found that the defendant had suffered brain damage from his long-term abuse of alcohol then the defence of diminished responsibility was available to him. But if they found that he had not suffered brain damage, they then had to decide whether the drinking had been voluntary or not. If it was voluntary then the defendant could not use the defence of diminished responsibility.

The defendant was convicted. He appealed and the Court of Appeal quashed the conviction holding that the judge was wrong to direct the jury that all of the defendant's drinking had to be involuntary.

When hearing the appeal in this case of *Wood* the Court of Appeal considered the effect of the judgment in *Dietschmann* on the decision in *Tandy*. They held that alcohol dependency syndrome could be considered as a possible source of abnormality of mind. This was for the jury to decide. If the jury found that it was an abnormality of mind, then they had to consider the effect of any alcohol consumed by the defendant as a result of his dependency.

This involved questions such as whether the defendant's craving for alcohol was or was not irresistible and whether his consumption of alcohol in the period leading up to the killing was voluntary – and, if so, to what extent.

The view in *Tandy* that all the drinking had to be involuntary for the defence of diminished responsibility to be available was incompatible with the House of Lords' approach in *Dietschmann*.

The jury could take into consideration the effect of any drinking which they decided was involuntary when determining whether the defendant's mental responsibility for his actions at the time of the killing was substantially impaired.

Although the approach recognises that that a person suffering from alcohol dependency syndrome cannot always control their drinking, it does make the task for the jury a difficult one. They have to decide which drinks were involuntary and then consider the effect of those while ignoring any consumption of alcohol which they decide was voluntary.

7.1.6 Problems with the law on diminished responsibility

Although diminished responsibility has provided a more satisfactory defence than insanity for defendants who kill but are suffering from a mental abnormality, there are still problems with the defence.

Burden of proof

One problem is that the burden of proof should not be on the defendant; in most other defences the defendant only has to raise the issue and the prosecution has to disprove it. This should also apply to diminished responsibility. At the moment, defendants pleading diminished responsibility are at a disadvantage which is not faced by those raising provocation.

There is also the possibility that putting the burden of proof on the defendant may be a breach of Art 6(2) of the European Convention on Human Rights which states that 'everyone charged with a criminal offence shall be presumed to be innocent until proven guilty according to law'. Making the defendant prove diminished responsibility could be considered a breach of this right to be presumed innocent.

Medical evidence

In order to prove that the defendant is suffering from diminished responsibility, the defence have to supply evidence from two doctors that the defendants' condition does come within the mental condition required by s 2.

Quite often the whole case turns on conflicting evidence about the defendant's mental condition. There will be evidence from doctors for the defence stating that it does, while the prosecution will produce other doctors who are of the opinion that the defendant is not suffering from diminished responsibility.

This means that the jury have to decide which medical evidence to accept. This is surely not a proper task for a panel of ordinary people with no medical knowledge. It would be better for such issues to be decided by medical experts.

Policy issues

In some cases the prosecution are prepared to accept the defendant's plea of not guilty to murder but guilty of manslaughter on the ground of diminished responsibility. In other cases the prosecution will not accept such a plea. This leaves a major decision being largely made by the lawyers in the Crown Prosecution Service.

However, the judge at the trial does not have to agree with the prosecution and can insist that the trial goes ahead. This happened in the case of Peter Sutcliffe in 1981 (the Yorkshire Ripper case) where the defendant was charged with the murder of several women.

The prosecution was prepared to agree to a plea of guilty to manslaughter on the basis of diminished responsibility, because of a desire to avoid a long and expensive murder trial together with a wish to shield the relatives of victims from unpleasant details of their murders. However, the judge refused to accept such a plea, so Sutcliffe was tried for murder and convicted.

This raises another problem with juries making the decision as to whether a defendant is suffering from diminished responsibility or not. Where the defendant has committed several murders or particularly unpleasant murders, the jury may decide to convict him of murder even though there is evidence that he is suffering from diminished responsibility.

Wording of s 2 Homicide Act 1957

There are also problems with the wording in s 2 of the Homicide Act 1957. The definition in this section has been constantly criticised. Lord Justice Buxton described the wording as a 'disgrace'.

The Law Commission in its report, *Murder, Manslaughter and Infanticide* (2006), pointed out two principal problems with the current law. These were:

1. The section does not explain what is involved in a 'substantial impairment of mental responsibility'. Section 2 implies that the effects of an abnormality of mind must significantly reduce the offender's culpability. But the Act does not make this clear. It also fails to say in what way the effects of an abnormality of mind can reduce the culpability for an intentional killing so as to make a manslaughter verdict the right one instead of murder.

2. The definition in s 2 was not drafted with the needs and practices of medical experts in mind. In particular the term 'abnormality of mind' is not a psychiatric term. The meaning of the phrase has had to be developed through case law. It would be better to have a clearer medical definition.

In addition, medical knowledge of mental illness has developed beyond the simple list given in the words in brackets in the section (whether arising from a condition of arrested or retarded development of mind or any inherent causes or induced by disease or injury).

The Law Commission quotes one psychiatrist as pointing out that:

> '[A]ttempting to specify the cause of mental disorders … is irrelevant [and] misleading, and in fact there are almost always multiple causes stemming from the interaction between genetic vulnerability and life events.'

An example of improved medical knowledge is the recognition of what is commonly called 'battered wife syndrome'. This is where a woman has been physically and mentally abused over many years to the point where she has lost touch with reality and is no longer fully responsible for her actions.

7.1.7 Proposals for reform

The Law Commission in 2006 in its report, *Murder, Manslaughter and Infanticide*, recommended that the definition of diminished responsibility should be modernised so as to take into account changing medical knowledge. The Law Commission also thought that the definition

Key facts

	Law	Act/Case
Definition	• Suffering from an abnormality of mind. • Caused by arrested or retarded development of mind, an inherent cause, disease or injury. • The abnormality of mind substantially impaired his mental responsibility for the killing.	s 2(1) Homicide Act 1957
Abnormality of mind	A state of mind so different from that of ordinary human beings that the reasonable man would term it abnormal.	*Byrne* (1960)
Substantially impaired	A question of degree for the jury to decide. 'Substantial' neither means 'total', 'trivial' nor 'minimal' but something in between.	*Byrne* (1960) *Lloyd* (1967)
Effect of intoxication	• Brain damage caused by alcohol/drug abuse can be diminished responsibility. • Alcohol dependency syndrome can be an abnormality of mind – jury must consider effects of involuntary drinking.	*Tandy* (1989) *Wood* (2008)
Burden of proof	It is for the defence to prove on the balance of probabilities.	s 2(2) Homicide Act 1957
Effect of defence	The charge of murder is reduced to manslaughter.	s 2(3) Homicide Act 1957
Proposal for reform	Partial defence where P was suffering from a relevant mental impairment; and this substantially impairs P's ability to: • understand the nature of P's conduct; or • form a rational judgment; or • to exercise self-control.	2008 Government's consultation paper

Figure 7.1 Key facts chart on diminished responsibility

should be flexible enough to allow for future developments in medical knowledge.

The Government in their consultation paper, *Murder, manslaughter and infanticide: proposals for reform of the law*, CP 19/08 accepted the Law Commission's recommendations and proposed that there should be a new partial defence of diminished responsibility. The definition they suggest in the consultation paper is as follows:

> '(1) A person (P) who kills or is a party to the killing of another is not to be convicted of murder if P was suffering from a relevant mental impairment which provides an explanation for P's acts and omissions in doing or being a party to the killing.'

The paper gives the following explanation of 'relevant mental impairment':

> '"Relevant mental impairment" means an abnormality of mental functioning which:
>
> (a) arises from a recognised medical condition, and

(b) substantially impairs P's ability to do one or more of the following:

   (i) to understand the nature of P's conduct; or

   (ii) form a rational judgment; or

   (iii) to exercise self-control.'

This would base the defence on a 'recognised medical condition'. This wording allows for the law to develop with changing medical knowledge of mental health conditions. It is not restrictive, unlike the present wording of the defence.

It also sets out clearly the aspects of the defendant's functioning which must be

---

Activity

Read the following extract from a newspaper report by Stewart Payne in the *Daily Telegraph* of 3rd November 2005 and answer the question below.

Mercy for mother who was driven to kill her Down's Syndrome son

'The desperate plight of a loving mother who killed her Down's Syndrome son after caring for him for 36 years led a judge to spare her a jail sentence yesterday.

Wendolyn Markcrow, 67, described as having lived a "saintly" life, finally reached her wits' end, a court heard.

During another sleepless night she "snapped" and gave her son Patrick 14 tranquillisers and suffocated him with a plastic bag.

She then slashed her neck and arm with a kitchen knife and sat down in the garden shed where she hoped to die.

She was "overwhelmed with despair" and wanted to end her life. Yet she feared for what would happen to Patrick if she were not there.

Oxford Crown Court heard that she had never thought to put her own needs before those of her son and, in the end, "spiralled into depression". Markcrow, a mother of four, who admitted manslaughter on the grounds of diminished responsibility at an earlier hearing, survived her suicide attempt. She told police: "I feel sad, desperate, defeated and ashamed."

Mr Justice Gross sentenced her to two years' prison, suspended for 18 months, and told her: "The pressures you faced were extreme."'

Questions

1. Which section of which Act allows a defence of diminished responsibility?

2. What would Mrs Markcrow's lawyers have had to prove in order to establish the defence of diminished responsibility?

3. What points in the extract support the defence?

4. The original charge against the defendant would have been murder. What effect does the defence of diminished responsibility have on that charge?

5. What sentence did the judge pass on the defendant?

6. The mandatory sentence for murder is life imprisonment. Why was the judge able to pass such a lenient sentence?

substantially impaired in order for the partial defence of diminished responsibility to succeed.

The Law Commission had also recommended that developmental immaturity in those aged under 18 should be included. There is evidence to show that frontal lobes of the brain which play an important role in the development of self-control and in controlling impulsive behaviour do not mature until the age of 14.

If there is no such defence, children as young as 10 may be convicted of murder when they are developmentally immature. They cannot use the defence of diminished responsibility under the existing law as they are not suffering from an abnormality of mind.

However, the Law Commission recognised that this proposal was controversial; the Government rejected it and it was not included in their consultation paper published in July 2008.

7.2 Provocation

Provocation had been a common-law defence prior to the Homicide Act 1957, and the Act recognised and built on that old common-law defence.

7.2.1 Definition

The defence of provocation is now set out in s 3 of the Homicide Act 1957.

Definition

Provocation

Where, on a charge of murder, there is evidence on which the jury can find that the person charged was provoked (whether by things done or by things said or by both together) to lose his self-control, the question whether the provocation was enough to make a reasonable man do as he did shall be left to be determined by the jury.

This section does not explain what can amount to provocation, except to state that it can be 'by things done or by things said or by both together'. The section also imposes a two-stage test for the jury to apply:

1. A *subjective* test – did the defendant lose his self-control?
2. An *objective* test – would a reasonable man have lost his self-control?

7.2.2 What amounts to provocation?

The Act states that provocation can be things done or said or both. This has been held to include a wide range of behaviour, such as:

- physical assaults, both on the defendant or on his relatives: *Pearson* (1992)
- homosexual advances
- the continual crying of a 19-day-old baby: *Doughty* (1986)
- a denial of stealing the defendant's tools: *Smith (Morgan James)* (2000)
- the actions of the wife's lover in going to meet her, where the husband was provoked into killing his wife: *Davies* (1975)
- supplying drugs to the defendant's son: *Baillie* (1995).

From these examples it can be seen that the victim does not have to aim the provocation deliberately at the defendant. In *Doughty* (1986) the defendant killed his baby son aged 19 days because the child would not stop crying. He was convicted but the Court of Appeal quashed the conviction because it should have been left to the jury to decide if the baby's crying was provocation by 'things done'. Clearly, a 19-day-old child is not deliberately trying to provoke anyone.

The acts which provoke the defendant can also be aimed at another person. This happened in *Pearson* (1992) where a father abused the defendant's younger brother. Although this behaviour was not aimed at the defendant, it was still 'things done' which caused the defendant to lose his self-control.

This has to be provocation.

7.2.3 Loss of self-control

The first test is that the jury must be satisfied that the defendant lost his self-control as a result of the provocation. The accepted test comes from *Duffy* (1949) (a case which was decided under the common law before the Homicide Act was passed).

Duffy (1949)

D, who was an abused wife, had a quarrel with her husband. She then left the room and changed her clothes. When her husband was in bed she attacked him with a hammer and a hatchet. D's conviction for murder was upheld because the court stated that there must be 'a sudden and temporary loss of self-control, rendering the accused so subject to passion as to make him or her for the moment not master of his mind'.

This concept in *Duffy* of a sudden and temporary loss of self-control has been approved by the Court of Appeal in later cases since the 1957 Act. This means that provocation is only available as a defence where D suffers a sudden loss of self-control.

Time lapse

One of the points that may be looked at to decide whether there was a 'sudden and temporary' loss of self-control is the time lapse between the provocation and the killing. The longer the time lapse between the provocation and the killing, the less likely that the defence will succeed. This was shown in the case of *Ibrams and Gregory* (1981).

Ibrams and Gregory (1981)

The ex-boyfriend of Ibrams' current girlfriend had been visiting the flat which Ibrams and the girlfriend shared, and had been terrorising them. On 7th October Ibrams called the police but the police did nothing. On 10th October the two defendants made a plan to attack the ex-boyfriend and they carried out this plan and killed him on 12th October. They were convicted of murder. The Court of Appeal upheld their convictions because there was no evidence of any provocation after 7th October and the gap of five days between this and the attack negatived their claims that they had lost their self-control.

This does not mean that there can never be any time lapse. Other cases have pointed out that there can still be a 'sudden and temporary loss of self-control' even after a time gap. This was seen in *Baillie* (1995).

Baillie (1995)

D discovered that a drug dealer had supplied his teenage sons with drugs and was now threatening the sons with violence. D armed himself with a sawn-off shotgun and a cut-throat razor and drove to the drug dealer's home and shot him. The Court of Appeal quashed his conviction for murder and ordered a re-trial. It held that even though there are factors, such as a lapse of time, which tend to equate with a desire for revenge, it is still possible for there to be a sudden and temporary loss of self-control.

It is argued that this need for a sudden loss of self-control makes the defence more available to men than women. This is because men are more likely than women to respond quickly with violence. In many cases women will take longer before they lose their self-control. This is known as 'slow burn' and was considered in *Thornton (No 2)* (1996).

Thornton (No 2) (1996)

Sara Thornton's husband was jealous and possessive and physically abused her. He also drank heavily. One night, when Sara returned home, her husband was lying on the sofa in the living room. He called her names and told her that he would kill her when she was asleep. Sara went into the kitchen and sharpened a bread-knife. She returned to the living room and stabbed her husband in the stomach. She was convicted of murder and her first appeal failed but on the second appeal the Court of Appeal held that there could be a sudden loss of self-control triggered by a minor incident. In other words, it is the last straw which sparks the killing. The Court of Appeal also said that medical evidence that the defendant was suffering from 'battered woman syndrome' could be relevant in explaining the 'slow-burn' reaction. It quashed the conviction and ordered a re-trial at which the jury acquitted the defendant.

This 'slow burn' was also seen in *Ahluwalia* (1992), where the defendant had been physically abused over many years by her husband. One night, her husband, before he went to bed, threatened her with violence the next day unless she paid a bill. Later, after the husband was asleep, the defendant poured petrol over him and set him alight. He died six days later. She was convicted of murder and appealed. The Court of Appeal did not allow her appeal on the basis of provocation. It pointed out that the defendant's reaction to the provocation had to be 'sudden' rather than 'immediate' and the longer the delay, the more likely that the act had been deliberate, so that the prosecution could negative the defence of provocation. However, the Court of Appeal did allow her appeal on the basis of diminished responsibility.

Course of conduct

In *Humphreys* (1995) the Court of Appeal held that a course of conduct by the victim towards the defendant before the final act of provocation was important. This course of conduct must be taken into account when the jury were deciding whether or not the defendant suffered a temporary loss of self-control as a result of the final event.

7.2.4 The 'reasonable man' test

Under s 3 of the Homicide Act 1957, the jury must take into account the effect the provocation would have on a reasonable man. This phrase 'reasonable man' has caused many problems. Before the 1957 Act, under the common law, the courts ruled that the reasonable man was an adult who was normal both mentally and physically. This ruling often appeared unfair, as in *Bedder v DPP* (1954) where the defendant was impotent. A prostitute taunted him about this and he stabbed her to death. His conviction for murder was upheld because under the 'reasonable man' test the jury had to ignore the fact of impotence and the effect it would have on the provocation.

This was the leading case until 1978 when in *Camplin* the House of Lords held that the 1957

Act had effectively overruled *Bedder* (1954). In *Camplin* it was held that age, sex and other relevant characteristics should be taken into account when considering how the reasonable man would have responded to the provocation.

Camplin (1978)

The defendant, who was a 15-year-old boy, had been sexually abused by an older man who had then laughed at him. Camplin had reacted to this by hitting the man over the head with a chapatti pan. At the trial the judge directed the jury to ignore the boy's age and to consider what effect the provocation would have had on the reasonable adult, and he was convicted of murder. On appeal, the House of Lords overruled *Bedder* and allowed the appeal, substituting a conviction for manslaughter.

In the judgment of the House of Lords in *Camplin*, Lord Diplock said:

> '… the reasonable man is a person having the power of self-control to be expected of an ordinary person of the sex and age of the accused, but in other respects sharing such of the accused's characteristics as they think would affect the gravity of the provocation to him; and that the question is not merely whether such a person would in like circumstances be provoked to lose his self-control but whether he would react to the provocation as the accused did.'

This made it clear that there were two parts to the 'reasonable man' test in s 3 of the Homicide Act 1957. These were:

1. for the purposes of self-control, the level is the power of self-control to be expected from a person of the age and sex of the defendant, but
2. for the gravity of the provocation, the

reasonable man shares such of the defendant's characteristics as the jury thinks would affect the gravity to the defendant.

Gravity of the provocation

In *Camplin* the House of Lords gave examples of a number of characteristics which could affect the gravity of the provocation where the provocation was aimed at one of those characteristics.

These included age, sex, race, colour, ethnic origin, physical deformity or infirmity, impotence (as in *Bedder*), a shameful incident in the past or even a painful abscess on the cheek where the provocation relied on a blow to the face. Also, for female defendants they accepted that pregnancy or menstruation might be a relevant characteristic if the provocation was aimed at this.

Subsequent cases tried to set down which 'other characteristics' might be relevant. For example, in *Morhall* (1995) the fact that the defendant was a glue-sniffer was a relevant characteristic to be taken into account. Morhall had been persistently criticised by the victim about this immediately before the killing.

The important point is that such characteristics can only be taken into account when considering the way in which the defendant would be likely to respond to the provocation. They are known as 'response' characteristics.

These characteristics are not relevant to the defendant's power of self-control.

Power of self-control

Camplin (1978) clearly stated that age and sex could be taken into account when considering the power of self-control to be expected from the reasonable man. However, the courts were uncertain as to whether any other characteristics could be taken into account on this point. In *Thornton (No 2)* (1996) the Court of Appeal stated that 'battered woman syndrome' might be relevant to the level of self-control.

However, in *Luc Thiet Thuan* (1997), where the defendant had suffered a previous head injury which caused him to have outbursts of temper which he could not control, the Privy Council held that mental abnormality could not be taken into account when considering the level of self-control to be expected from the defendant. The same point on level of self-control was considered by the House of Lords in *Smith (Morgan James)* (2000).

Smith (Morgan James) (2000)

During an argument with a friend about whether the friend had stolen some tools belonging to D, D picked up a kitchen knife and stabbed the victim. There was evidence that D was suffering from a depressive illness which might have reduced his threshold for reacting to provocation. The trial judge ruled that this characteristic was not relevant to the reasonable man's loss of self-control. The Court of Appeal allowed D's appeal against his conviction for murder. The prosecution appealed to the House of Lords and the Court of Appeal certified the following question as a point of law of general public importance:

'Are characteristics other than age and sex, attributable to a reasonable man for the purpose of s 3 of the Homicide Act 1957 relevant not only to the gravity of the provocation to him but also to the standard of self-control to be expected?'

The Lords, by a majority of three to two, rejected the prosecution's appeal.

In *Smith (Morgan James)* (2000) Lord Hoffmann pointed out that Lord Diplock's judgment in *Camplin* (1978) allows juries to take into account two characteristics (age and sex) and that age may be relevant to the power of self-control. There was no suggestion in *Camplin* that age and sex were the only factors which could be taken into account when considering self-control, or that all other factors should be excluded.

The question was whether in all the circumstances the jury considered that the defendant's loss of self-control was excusable, and this is judged by reference to how a person in his position, exercising ordinary powers of self-control, would have behaved. The objective element of the test for provocation was whether the jury thought that the circumstances were such as to make the loss of self-control sufficiently excusable to reduce the gravity of the offence from murder to manslaughter.

The House of Lords did, however, point out that the law expects people to exercise control over their emotions. A tendency to violent rages or childish tantrums is a defect in character rather than an excuse.

This decision in *Smith (Morgan James)* (2000) laid down general principles and left the matter to the jury, as the Homicide Act 1957 clearly set out. The general principle in the case was that the same standards of behaviour should be expected of everyone, and whether the accused's loss of self-control was excusable should be judged by reference to how a person in his position, exercising ordinary powers of self-control, would have behaved.

However, the House of Lords accepted that this general principle may 'sometimes have to yield to a more important principle, which is to do justice in the particular case'. If the jury thinks 'that there was some characteristic of the accused, whether temporary or permanent, which affected the degree of control which society could reasonably have expected of him', they may take that into account if they think it is just to do so. This was thought to be the law but a Privy Council decision has had a major impact on this area of law.

Privy Council decision in *Holley* (2005)

Following the decision in *Smith* (2000), the same point had to be considered by the Privy Council in *Attorney-General for Jersey v Holley* (2005). Unusually, a panel of nine judges was used to decide this case.

Attorney-General for Jersey v Holley (2005)

D was an alcoholic who had been drinking heavily. He claimed that his long-standing girlfriend told him she had had sex with another man and taunted him. He struck and killed her with an axe he was using to chop wood. He was convicted of murder and his conviction was upheld by the Privy Council by a majority of six judges to three.

The conclusion of the majority of judges in the Privy Council was that only age and sex should be considered when identifying and applying the objective standard of self-control. Other characteristics of D are not relevant. So D is, for the purposes of the defence of provocation, to be judged by the standard of a person having ordinary powers of self-control. This has the merits of being a constant, objective standard in all cases.

This obviously differed from the House of Lords' decision in *Smith (Morgan James)* and the Privy Council recognised this, with Lord Nicholls stating that that decision was 'erroneous'.

However, the Privy Council did accept that other characteristics can be taken into account in assessing the gravity of the provocation to D. There is still a subjective test for the gravity of the provocation to the defendant. For this purpose the jury must 'take the defendant as they find him, "warts and all"'.

The decision in *Holley* (2005) was by the Privy Council. Normally, in the system of judicial precedent which operates in the courts in England and Wales, decisions by the Privy Council are only persuasive. But decisions by the House of Lords are binding on all lower courts. So it was not immediately certain what influence the decision in *Holley* would have.

However, in *Mohammed* (2005) a three-judge

panel in the Court of Appeal followed *Holley* (2005) rather than the decision in *Smith (Morgan James)* (2000). Then in *James: Karimi* (2006) a five-judge panel was used to decide two cases, and this panel again followed the decision in *Holley* from the Privy Council. The Court of Appeal stated that, although it would normally follow decisions of the House of Lords, in exceptional circumstances it would follow the Privy Council.

It therefore appears that the law is as decided in *Holley* (2005). There is a subjective test for the gravity of the provocation in which characteristics of the defendant can be taken into account. The test for the standard of self-control is objective: that of the reasonable person of the same age and sex as the defendant.

7.2.5 Proof of provocation

The judge decides if there is evidence of provocation for the defence to be left to the jury. If there is evidence which raises the possibility of provocation, the prosecution must then prove beyond reasonable doubt that the accused was not provoked.

In some cases the defendant may put forward both the defence of provocation and the defence of diminished responsibility. This causes a problem over the burden of proof, as for provocation the defence only has to raise the issue, but for diminished responsibility the defence has to *prove* it on the balance of probabilities. This may cause confusion to juries in such cases.

7.2.6 Problems in the law on provocation

In 2003, when the Law Commission was reviewing the law on special defences to murder, it issued a consultation paper on the special defences to murder. In this it pointed out a number of problems with the defence of provocation:

- The defence as stated in s 3 of the Homicide Act 1957 contradicts itself; it raises the

Key facts

	Law	Section/case
Definition	Evidence on which the jury can find that the person charged was provoked (whether by things done or by things said or by both together) to lose his self-control.	s 3 Homicide Act 1957
Examples of provocation	• Physical assaults, both on the defendant or on his relatives. • The continual crying of a 19-day-old baby. • A denial of stealing the defendant's tools. • Supplying drugs to the defendant's son.	*Pearson* (1992) *Doughty* (1986) *Smith (Morgan James)* (2000) *Baillie* (1995)
Loss of self-control	• There must be a sudden and temporary loss of self-control, so that D is not master of his mind. • A time lapse may negative this. • It must be sudden but need not be immediate.	*Duffy* (1949) *Ibrams and Gregory* (1981) *Thornton (No 2)* (1996)
'Reasonable man' test	Was the provocation enough to make a reasonable man do as D did? For the gravity of the provocation, the characteristics of D are taken into account. For the standard of self-control expected of D, the test is objective. D is judged by the standard expected of a reasonable person of the age and sex of D.	s 3 Homicide Act 1957 *Morhall* (1995) *Camplin* (1978) *Holley* (2005)
Effect of defence	The charge of murder is reduced to manslaughter.	s 3 Homicide Act 1957

Figure 7.2 Key facts chart on provocation

question of whether a reasonable man would ever respond to provocation.

• The term 'reasonable man' has proved difficult for the judge to explain. The phrase has been considered by the House of Lords four times in 20 years and on the last occasion in *Smith (Morgan James)* (2000) the judges were split 3:2. (The matter has also now been considered by the Privy Council in *Holley* (2005) when the panel of nine judges were split 6:3.)

• There is no limit to the conduct which is capable of 'provoking', so that completely innocent conduct may be regarded as provocation. This was seen in *Doughty* (1986) when the crying of a very young baby was held to be provocation.

• It allows a defence for anger, when there is no defence if the defendant kills in fear, despair or compassion.

• The effect of the decision in *Smith (Morgan James)* (2000) was to reduce the threshold of self-control that people are entitled to demand of all members of society. (Note that if the case of *Holley* (2005) continues to be followed by the courts in England and Wales, then this criticism disappears.)

As already pointed out in section 7.2.3, the defence is also seen as a 'male' defence, because men are more likely to suffer a sudden loss of self-control.

7.2.7 Proposals for reform

The Law Commission's report in 2004, *Partial Defences and Murder*, suggested reforming the defence of provocation in the following way.

" 1. An unlawful homicide that would otherwise be murder should instead be manslaughter if:

   (a) the defendant acted in response to:

      (i) gross provocation (meaning words or conduct or a combination of words and conduct which caused the defendant to have a justifiable sense of being seriously wronged); or

      (ii) fear of serious violence towards the defendant or another; or

      (iii) a combination of (i) and (ii).

   (b) a person of the defendant's age and of ordinary temperament, ie ordinary tolerance and self-restraint, in the circumstances of the defendant might have acted in the same or a similar way.

2. In deciding whether a person of ordinary temperament in the circumstances of the defendant might have acted in the same or a similar way, the court should take into account the defendant's age and all the circumstances of the defendant other than matters whose only relevance to the defendant's conduct is that they bear simply on his or her general capacity for self-control.

3. The partial defence should not apply where:

   (a) the provocation was incited by the defendant for the purpose of providing an excuse to use violence, or

   (b) the defendant acted in considered desire for revenge.' "

These proposals would make several changes to the current law on provocation.

In their report, *Murder, Manslaughter and Infanticide* (2006), the Law Commission confirmed the proposals made in the 2004 report as the ones that it recommended.

The first main difference between the proposals and the current law is that only 'gross provocation' would suffice under the proposals. This would presumably prevent such matters as the crying of a 19-day-old baby being provocation, as in *Doughty* (1986).

A second difference is that a test of whether the words and/or conduct caused the defendant to have a justifiable sense of being seriously wronged would be introduced. Two words appear to be especially important in the phrase 'justifiable sense of being seriously wronged'. These are 'justifiable' and 'seriously'. The combination of the two would be likely to restrict the operation of the defence of provocation, compared with its present operation. Again, it would prevent the crying of a 19-day-old baby from being provocation. This could scarcely give rise to a phrase 'justifiable sense of being seriously wronged'.

Abolition of the defence

If the mandatory sentence of life imprisonment for murder were to be abolished, this would then allow the defence of provocation to be abolished, as the judge would have discretion in sentencing.

However, this would leave two problems. Firstly, if the prosecution did not accept the defendant's version of what had happened, then there would still need to be an investigation of the facts before the judge could decide on a suitable sentence. Secondly, surely a jury is better placed than a judge to decide on the level of self-control to be expected by society from a defendant? If the defence of provocation is abolished then the matter will be entirely in the hands of a judge.

7.2.8 The Government's response

In its consultation paper, *Murder, manslaughter and infanticide: proposals for reform of the law*, CP 19/08, the Government proposed a different approach to reform of provocation. They wish to abolish the current defence of provocation.

Instead they would like to replace it with a defence of:

> 'Killing in response to words and conduct which caused the defendant to have a justifiable sense of being seriously wronged.'

The draft clause for this new partial defence to murder states:

> '1. Where a person ("D") kills or is a party to the killing of another ("V"), D is not to be convicted of murder if –
>
> (a) D's acts and omissions in doing or being a party to the killing resulted from D's loss of self-control,
>
> (b) the loss of self-control had a qualifying trigger, and
>
> (c) a person of D's sex and age, with a normal degree of tolerance and self-restraint and in the circumstances of D, might have reacted in the same or in a similar way to D.'

The first point to note is that under this defence there would still be a requirement that the defendant had lost self-control but this loss would not have to be 'sudden'. This would allow for situations where the defendant's reaction has been delayed or builds gradually. This would solve the problem of cases such as *Thornton (No 2)* (1996).

Reasonable person

The Government proposes that this new partial defence should apply only if a person of the defendant's sex and age, with a normal degree of tolerance and self-restraint and in the circumstances of the defendant, might have reacted in the same or a similar way.

Other limitations

The Government also proposes limiting when the defence is available. They propose that words and conduct should be a partial defence to murder only in exceptional circumstances.

Also, under their proposals, they make it clear that a partner having an affair does not of itself constitute such conduct for the purposes of the partial defence.

Activity

Applying the law

Explain whether any of the special defences to murder could apply in the following situations.

1. Roscoe, aged 25, has a mental age of 8. In a fit of temper, he attacks Arun and kicks him to death.
2. Cameron and Jacob are working together on a building site. Cameron knows that Jacob's wife is having an affair with another man. He taunts Jacob about this. Jacob loses his temper and hits Cameron on the head with a brick, killing him.
3. Ellie's husband, Gwyn, is an alcoholic and when drunk is often violent to her. Ellie has recently been suffering from depression for which she takes medication. One evening, Gwyn comes home drunk and hits Ellie several times. He then goes to bed. Ellie stays up and, after about four hours, in a sudden burst of rage, she gets a knife and stabs Gwyn, killing him.
4. Brigid, an immature, attention-seeking, 16-year-old, tries to commit suicide by slashing her wrists with a knife, but the cuts she makes are only superficial. Carol teases her about her inability to do anything properly. Brigid rushes at Carol and stabs her with the knife, killing her.

Examination questions

1. 'Judicial decisions during the last 15 years about provocation as a special and partial defence to murder suggest that provocation has become too wide in its application and is in need of reform.'

Critically consider whether there is any justification for this statement.

(OCR, Unit 2571, June 2006)

2. Zandra, who is aged 16, has had an unhappy childhood. She has left home and has turned to drugs and prostitution. She is living with Shaun, aged 33, who is a weightlifter. Shaun regularly forces Zandra to give him her earnings. He is jealous and possessive and has beaten her on a number of occasions. She is immature and has often harmed herself to seek attention. One night, fearing that Shaun will beat her up and force her to have sex with him, Zandra cuts her wrists. When Shaun comes into the lounge and sees what she has done he taunts her saying she has made a pathetic job of slashing her wrists. Zandra goes to her bedroom to get her knife, returns to the lounge and stabs Shaun in the chest killing him instantly.

Discuss Zandra's potential liability for the murder of Shaun.

(OCR, G143, January 2008)

3. Holly lives with Ian, who frequently hits her. He threatens that if she tries to leave him she will 'pay'. One evening Holly and Ian argue and Ian calls her 'a worthless slave'. Ian goes to bed. Holly watches television for two hours and drinks a bottle of vodka. On her way to the bedroom Holly takes a knife from the kitchen and, seeing Ian asleep, stabs him in the chest killing him instantly.

Evaluate the accuracy of each of the four statements A, B, C, and D individually, as they apply to the facts in the above scenario.

Statement A: Holly cannot plead provocation as a defence to a charge of murder because there is no evidence that she has been provoked.

Statement B: Holly still cannot successfully plead provocation as a defence because her loss of self-control was not 'immediate'.

Statement C: Holly will be successful in reducing her potential conviction for murder to voluntary manslaughter because she lost her self-control.

Statement D: Holly will be successful in reducing her potential conviction from murder to manslaughter by pleading intoxication as a defence.

(OCR, Unit G143, June 2008)

Chapter 8

Involuntary manslaughter

I nvoluntary manslaughter is an unlawful killing where the defendant does not
have the intention, either direct or oblique, to kill or to cause grievous bodily
harm. The lack of this intention is what distinguishes involuntary
manslaughter from murder.

It is also important not to confuse involuntary manslaughter with voluntary
manslaughter. For voluntary manslaughter, the defendant has the intention to
kill or cause grievous bodily harm but the charge is reduced from murder
because the defendant can use one of the special defences to murder. Those
special defences were explained in Chapter 7.

Range of involuntary manslaughter

Involuntary manslaughter covers a wide range of
circumstances. At the top end of the range, the
behaviour of the defendant which caused the
death can be highly blameworthy, as there was a
high risk of causing death or serious injury. At the
bottom end of the range, the defendant's
behaviour may verge on carelessness and only
just enough to be considered blameworthy. There
have been criticisms that the same offence covers
such a wide range of behaviour, and proposals for
reform are considered at section 8.4.

The maximum sentence for involuntary
manslaughter is life imprisonment, so this gives
the judge discretion to impose any sentence
which is suitable for the particular circumstances
of the offence. In some cases the judge may even
pass a non-custodial sentence.

Ways of committing involuntary manslaughter

There are three ways of committing involuntary
manslaughter. These are:

1. *unlawful act* manslaughter
2. *gross negligence* manslaughter
3. *reckless* manslaughter.

Each of these must be considered separately.

8.1 Unlawful act manslaughter

This is also known as *constructive* manslaughter because the liability for the death is built up or constructed from the facts that the defendant has done a dangerous unlawful act which caused the death. This makes the defendant liable even though he did not realise that death or injury might occur.

Definition

Unlawful act manslaughter
The elements of unlawful act manslaughter are:

- The defendant must do an unlawful act.
- That act must be dangerous on an objective test.
- The act must cause the death.
- The defendant must have the required *mens rea* for the unlawful act.

8.1.1 Unlawful act

The death must be caused by an unlawful act. The unlawful act must be a criminal offence. A civil wrong (tort) is not enough. In *Franklin* (1883) the defendant threw a large box into the sea from the West Pier at Brighton. The box hit and killed a swimmer. It was held that a civil wrong was not enough to create liability for unlawful act manslaughter. Another case illustrating that there must be a criminal unlawful act is *Lamb* (1967).

Lamb (1967)

Lamb and his friend were fooling around with a revolver. They both knew that it was loaded with two bullets in a five-chamber cylinder but thought that it would not fire unless one of the bullets was opposite the barrel. They knew that there was no bullet in this position, but did not realise that the cylinder turned so that a bullet from the next chamber along would be fired. Lamb pointed the gun at his friend and pulled the trigger, killing him. It was held that the defendant had not done an unlawful act. The pointing of the gun at the friend was not an assault as the friend did not fear any violence from Lamb.

There must be an act. An omission cannot create liability for unlawful act manslaughter. This was shown by the case of *Lowe* (1973).

Lowe (1973)

The defendant was convicted of wilfully neglecting his baby son and of his manslaughter. The trial judge had directed the jury that if they found the defendant guilty of wilful neglect he was also guilty of manslaughter. The Court of Appeal quashed the conviction for manslaughter because a finding of wilful neglect involved a failure to act, and this could not support a conviction for unlawful act manslaughter.

In many cases the unlawful act will be some kind of assault, but any criminal offence can form the unlawful act, provided that it involves an act which is dangerous in the sense that it is likely to cause some injury. Examples of the offences which have led to a finding of unlawful act manslaughter include:

- arson – *Goodfellow* (1986) (see 8.1.2)
- criminal damage – *Newbury and Jones* (1976) (see 8.1.4)
- burglary – *Watson* (1989) (see 8.1.2).

8.1.2 Dangerous act

The unlawful act must be dangerous on an objective test. In *Church* (1966) it was held that it must be:

'such as all sober and reasonable people would inevitably recognise must subject the other person to, at least, the risk of some harm resulting therefrom, albeit not serious harm'.

From this, it can be seen that the risk need only be of 'some harm'. The harm need not be serious. If a sober and reasonable person realises that the unlawful act might cause some injury, then this part of the test for unlawful act manslaughter is satisfied. It does not matter that the defendant did not realise there was any risk of harm to another person. The case of *Larkin* (1943) illustrates both the need for an unlawful act and for there to be, on an objective viewpoint, the risk of some harm.

Larkin (1943)

D threatened another man with an open cut-throat razor, in order to frighten him. The mistress of the other man tried to intervene and, because she was drunk, accidentally fell onto the open blade which cut her throat and killed her. On appeal, D's conviction for manslaughter was upheld. The act of threatening the other man with the razor was a technical assault. (See Chapter 9 for explanation of assaults.) It was also an act which was dangerous because it was likely to injure someone.

Humphries J explained this in the judgment when he said:

'Where the act which a person is engaged in performing is unlawful, then, if at the same time it is a dangerous act, that is, an act which is likely to injure another person, and quite inadvertently he causes the death of that other person by that act, then he is guilty of manslaughter.'

It is clear that the act need not be aimed at the victim. This was the situation in *Larkin* where the assault was against the man but the woman dies. It is also shown by the case of *Mitchell* (1983).

Mitchell (1983)

D tried to push his way into a queue at the post office. A 72-year-old man told him off for this. D then punched the man, causing him to stagger backwards into an 89-year-old woman. The woman was knocked over and injured, and a few days later died of her injuries. D was convicted of unlawful act manslaughter. He had done an unlawful act by punching the man. This act was dangerous as it was an act which was likely to injure another person. Finally, the act inadvertently caused the death of the woman.

I'm only playing dominoes.

It can be seen that all the elements set by Humphries J in the statement in *Larkin* (1943) are present. The defendants in both *Larkin* and *Mitchell* were guilty of unlawful act manslaughter, despite the fact that in each case the person threatened (or punched) was not the one who died.

Act against property

The act need not even be aimed at a person; it can be aimed at property, provided it is 'such that all sober and reasonable people would inevitably recognise must subject another person to, at least, the risk of some harm'. This was illustrated by *Goodfellow* (1986).

Goodfellow (1986)

D decided to set fire to his council flat so that the council would have to re-house him. The fire got out of control and his wife, son and another woman died in the fire. He was convicted of manslaughter and appealed. The Court of Appeal upheld the conviction because all the elements of unlawful act manslaughter were present.

If you look at the facts of *Goodfellow* you can see the elements of unlawful act manslaughter. These were:

- The act was committed intentionally: Goodfellow intended to set the flat on fire.
- It was unlawful: it was arson, an offence under the Criminal Damage Act 1971.
- Reasonable people would recognise that it might cause some harm to another person: there was an obvious risk that someone in the flat might be hurt.
- The act caused the death.

Physical harm

The 'risk of harm' refers to physical harm. Something which causes fear and apprehension is not sufficient. This is so even if it causes the victim to have a heart attack. This meant that in the case of *Dawson* (1985) convictions for manslaughter were quashed.

Dawson (1985)

Three defendants attempted to rob a petrol station. They were masked and armed with pick-axe handles. The petrol station attendant managed to sound the alarm but then dropped dead from a heart attack. Causing him fear through the attempted robbery was not a 'dangerous' act and did not make this manslaughter.

However, where a reasonable person would be aware of the victim's frailty and the risk of physical harm to him, then the defendant will be liable. This was stated in *Watson* (1989).

Watson (1989)

Two defendants threw a brick through the window of a house and entered it, intending to steal property. The occupier was a frail 87-year-old man who heard the noise and came to investigate what had happened. The two defendants physically abused him and then left. The man died of a heart attack 90 minutes later. Although the Court of Appeal quashed the convictions for manslaughter, the court stated that the act of burglary could be 'dangerous' in that it became dangerous as soon as the old man's condition would have been apparent to the reasonable man.

8.1.3 Causing the death

The unlawful act must cause the death. The rules on causation are the same as for murder and are set out in Chapter 2 at section 2.3. An important point is that if there is an intervening act which breaks the chain of causation then the defendant cannot be liable for manslaughter.

This point has caused problems in cases where the defendant has supplied V with an illegal drug. If the defendant also injects the drug into V, then there is no break in the chain of causation. This was shown in the case of *Cato* (1976).

Key cases

Case	Facts	Law
Lamb (1967)	D fired gun at a friend; both thought it was safe because there was no bullet in the firing chamber.	There must be an unlawful act. In this case there was no assault as the friend did not fear violence.
Lowe (1973)	Failed to care properly for baby.	There has to be an act – unlawful act manslaughter cannot be committed by an omission.
Larkin (1943)	Threatened a man with a razor – a woman fell on blade and died.	The unlawful act need not be aimed at V but it must be objectively dangerous in the sense that it is likely to cause harm.
Goodfellow (1986)	Set fire to flat, causing three deaths.	The unlawful act can be aimed at property. The test is whether it is objectively dangerous in the sense that it is likely to cause harm.
Dawson (1985)	Petrol station attendant died of a heart attack when his petrol station was robbed.	Causing fear is not enough. The unlawful act must put V at risk of physical harm.
Newbury and Jones (1976)	Pushed a paving stone onto a passing train, killing the guard.	D need only have the intention to do the unlawful act; there is no need for D to foresee that it might cause some harm.

Figure 8.1 Key cases chart on unlawful act manslaughter

Cato (1976)

D and V each prepared an injection of a mix of heroin and water. They then injected each other. V died. By injecting V with the heroin, D had committed the unlawful act of administering a noxious substance to V, contrary to s 23 of the Offences against the Person Act 1861. As V died from the effects of the injection, D was convicted of unlawful act manslaughter.

The problem has been with situations where the defendant has prepared the injection, handed the syringe to V, and V has then injected himself. There have been several cases on this. There are two points at issue:

- whether the defendant has done an unlawful act; and
- whether the defendant caused the victim's death, or the self-injection is an intervening act.

The first case on this issue was *Dalby* (1982).

Dalby (1982)

D supplied a drug called Diconal which the victim then self-injected and subsequently died. The defendant's conviction for manslaughter was quashed because the Court of Appeal held that although supplying the drug was an unlawful act, it was not the act of supplying which had caused the death. The injection was the cause of the death and, as this was a voluntary act by the victim, the chain of causation had been broken.

However, in later cases it was suggested that the defendant could be guilty in similar circumstances as he was considered to have administered a noxious substance to V, contrary to s 23 of the Offences Against the Person Act 1861. This was an unlawful act, and if V died the defendant could be guilty of unlawful act manslaughter. This idea was criticised and was not followed in all cases, thus causing confusion in the law.

The debate was finally settled in *Kennedy* (2007) when the House of Lords ruled that there was no unlawful act by the defendant under s 23. The defendant did not administer the noxious substance by filling a syringe and handing it to V. The act of self-injection was a voluntary intervening act by V which broke the chain of causation.

Kennedy (2007)

D had prepared an injection of heroin and water for V to inject himself. He handed the syringe to V who injected himself and then handed the syringe back to D. V died. Initially Kennedy was convicted and the Court of Appeal upheld his conviction. The case was then referred back to the Court of Appeal by the Criminal Case Review Commission. Again the Court of Appeal upheld the conviction on the basis that filling the syringe and handing it to V was administering a noxious substance and an unlawful act.

The case was then appealed to the House of Lords. They quashed the conviction on the basis that D had not done an unlawful act which caused the death. D had not administered a noxious substance for an offence under s 23 of the Offences against the Person Act 1861. V's act in injecting the heroin himself was an intervening act which broke any chain of causation.

In *Kennedy* the Law Lords pointed out that the criminal law generally assumes the existence of free will. The victim had freely and voluntarily administered the injection to himself. The defendant could only be guilty if he was involved in administering the injection. In this case he had not been.

Joint involvement

The Law Lords did accept that there could be situations in which it could be regarded that both defendant and victim were involved in administering the injection. However, they did not give any examples of when this could be considered to have happened. In fact they specifically stated that the case of *Rogers* (2003) had been wrongly decided.

In *Rogers* the defendant had participated in the injection of heroin by holding his belt round the victim's arm as a tourniquet to make it easier for the victim to find the vein to inject. The Court of Appeal had held that the act causing death was the injection of the heroin and it was 'artificial and unreal' to separate the tourniquet from the injection. By applying and holding the tourniquet, the defendant was playing a part in the mechanics of the injection. This made him guilty of an offence under s 23 of the Offences Against the Person Act 1861 and, if death occurred as a result, he was also guilty of manslaughter.

The case of *Rogers* was not appealed to the House of Lords. However, the Law Lords stated in *Kennedy* (2007) that *Rogers* was wrongly decided. There was no unlawful act of administering a noxious substance by helping V inject by providing a tourniquet. If this is not administering a noxious substance then it is difficult to think of situations in which D and V could be regarded as being jointly involved in the act of injecting.

Alternative of gross negligence manslaughter

It is possible that in situations where the defendant has supplied the drugs the defendant could be liable for gross negligence manslaughter. This view was put forward in *Dias* (2002).

Dias (2002)

D was a heroin addict used to injecting heroin. The victim was also a drug user but was not known to inject heroin. They were living rough and went into the stairway of a block of flats where D prepared a syringe of heroin and gave it to the victim who injected himself. D then injected himself. When D had recovered from the effects of the heroin he realised that the victim was very ill. He asked a passer-by to call an ambulance and then left the scene. The victim was taken to hospital but died. D's conviction for manslaughter on the basis of an unlawful act was quashed.

Although the conviction for unlawful act manslaughter was quashed, the Court of Appeal suggested that a conviction for gross negligence manslaughter might be possible where a duty of care could be established. This might possibly be through a duty not to supply and prepare drugs.

There have been convictions on this basis where there has been a close relationship between D and V. In these cases it is possible to show that D owed V a duty of care. (For the law on gross negligence manslaughter, see section 8.2.) It may also be possible to rely on gross negligence manslaughter if the drug user is either particularly vulnerable, eg a young first-time user, or the defendant is aware of problems following V's self-injection. But it is clear following the House of

Key facts

Elements	Comment	Cases
Unlawful act	Must be unlawful.	*Lamb* (1967)
	A civil wrong is not enough.	*Franklin* (1883)
	It must be an act; an omission is not sufficient.	*Lowe* (1973)
Dangerous act	The test for this is objective – would a sober and reasonable person realise the risk of some harm?	*Church* (1966)
	The risk need only be of some harm – not serious harm.	*Larkin* (1943)
	The act need not be aimed at the final victim.	*Mitchell* (1983)
	An act aimed at property can still be such that a sober and reasonable person would realise the risk of some harm.	*Goodfellow* (1986)
	There must be a risk of physical harm; mere fear is not enough.	*Dawson* (1985)
Causes death	Normal rules of causation apply; the act must be the physical and legal cause of death.	*Dalby* (1982)
	An intervening act such as the victim self-injecting a drug breaks the chain of causation.	*Kennedy* (2007)
	But merely preparing the injection is not a cause of death. V's self-injection breaks the chain of causation.	
Mens rea	D must have *mens rea* for the unlawful act but it is not necessary to prove that D foresaw any harm from his act.	*Newbury and Jones* (1976)

Figure 8.2 Key facts chart on unlawful act manslaughter

Lords' decision in *Kennedy* (2007) that unlawful act manslaughter cannot be proved if the victim dies after self-injecting a drug.

8.1.4 *Mens rea*

It must be proved that the defendant had the *mens rea* for the unlawful act, but it is not necessary for the defendant to realise that the act is unlawful or dangerous. This was made clear in the case of *Newbury and Jones* (1976).

Newbury and Jones (1976)

The defendants were two teenage boys who pushed a piece of paving stone from a bridge onto a railway line as a train was approaching. The stone hit the train and killed the guard. They were convicted of manslaughter and the House of Lords was asked to decide the question of whether a defendant could be convicted of unlawful act manslaughter if he did not foresee that his act might cause harm to another. The House of Lords confirmed it was not necessary to prove that the defendant foresaw any harm from his act.

So, a defendant can be convicted provided that the unlawful act was dangerous and the defendant had the necessary *mens rea* for that act.

8.2 Gross negligence manslaughter

Gross negligence manslaughter is another way of committing manslaughter. It is completely different from unlawful act manslaughter. It is committed where the defendant owes the victim a duty of care but breaches that duty in a very negligent way, causing the death of the victim. It can be committed by an act or an omission, neither of which has to be unlawful. The leading case on gross negligence manslaughter is *Adomako* (1994).

Adomako (1994)

D was the anaesthetist for a man who was having an operation on a detached retina. During the operation, one of the tubes supplying oxygen to the patient became disconnected. D failed to notice this until some minutes later when the patient suffered a heart attack caused by the lack of oxygen. The patient suffered brain damage and died six months later as a result. Doctors giving evidence in the trial said that a competent anaesthetist would have noticed the disconnection of the tube within 15 seconds and that D's failure to react was 'abysmal'. The trial judge directed the jury on gross negligence and they convicted. The conviction was upheld by the House of Lords.

Definition

Gross negligence manslaughter

From *Adomako* (1994) it appears that the elements of gross negligence manslaughter are:

- the existence of a duty of care towards the victim
- a breach of that duty of care which causes death
- gross negligence over the risk of death which the jury considers to be criminal.

Each of these elements needs to be considered.

8.2.1 Duty of care

A duty of care has been held to exist for the purposes of the criminal law in various situations. These include the duty of a doctor to his patient, as in *Adomako* (1994). In that case Lord Mackay said that the ordinary principles of negligence in the civil law applied to ascertain whether there was a duty of care and whether that duty had been breached.

The civil principles come from the case of *Donoghue v Stevenson* (1932) where it was stated that:

> 'You must take reasonable care to avoid acts and omissions which you can reasonably foresee would be likely to injure your neighbour. Who then is my neighbour? The answer seems to be – persons who are so closely and directly affected by my act that I ought reasonably to have them in contemplation as being so affected when I am directing my mind to the acts or omissions which are called into question.'

Note that an act or an omission can form the basis of negligence.

Case examples of duty of care

Since the case of *Adomako* (1994), the criminal courts have decided that a duty of care exists in very different situations. Some of these are set out below.

Singh (1999)

D was the landlord of property in which a faulty gas fire caused the deaths of tenants. It was recognised that there was a duty on D to manage and maintain property properly.

Litchfield (1998)

D was the owner and master of a sailing ship. He sailed, knowing that the engines might fail because of contamination to the fuel. The ship was blown onto rocks and three crew members died. It was held that D owed a duty to the crew.

In both the above cases there was a contractual duty of care. However, there does not need to be a contractual duty. Other situations can lead to a duty of care, as shown by the cases of *Khan and Khan* (1998) and *Dias* (2002) (see section 8.1.3).

Khan and Khan (1998)

The defendants had supplied heroin to a new user who took it in their presence and then collapsed. They left her alone and by the time they returned to the flat she had died. Their conviction for unlawful act manslaughter was quashed but the Court of Appeal thought there could be a duty to summon medical assistance in certain circumstances.

In *Khan and Khan* (1998) the Court of Appeal stated *obiter* that duty situations could be extended to other areas, and a further extension of the type of duty recognised by the courts occurred in *Wacker* (2002).

Wacker (2002)

D agreed to bring 60 illegal immigrants into England. They were put in the back of his lorry for a cross-channel ferry crossing. The only air into the lorry was through a small vent and it was agreed that this vent should be closed at certain times to prevent the immigrants from being discovered. D closed the vent before boarding the ferry. The crossing took an hour longer than usual and at Dover the Customs officers found that 58 of the immigrants were dead. D's conviction for manslaughter was upheld by the Court of Appeal.

The defendant argued that it was impossible to determine the extent of his duty, but the Court of Appeal held it was a simple matter on the facts. The defendant knew that the safety of the immigrants depended on his own actions in relation to the vent and he clearly assumed the duty of care.

An interesting point in *Wacker* was that the victims were parties to an illegal act. In the civil law of negligence this would have meant that the victims (or their dependants) could not have made a claim against the defendant. However, the Court of Appeal held that for the criminal law, it was irrelevant that the victims were parties to an illegal act. It pointed out that the purposes of civil and criminal law were different and public policy demanded that defendants in this type of situation were liable under the criminal law.

The case of *Wacker* indicates that this area of the law may be extended in the future, and it is difficult to predict what duties may be recognised.

8.2.2 Breach of duty causing death

Once a duty of care has been shown to exist, it must be proved that the defendant was in breach of that duty of care *and* that this breach caused the death of the victim.

Whether there is a breach of duty is a factual matter. Did the defendant negligently do or fail to do something? Causation is important, as it must be proved that the breach caused the death. The general rules on causation apply; see Chapter 2 at section 2.3.

8.2.3 Gross negligence

The fact that a defendant has been negligent is not enough to convict him of gross negligence manslaughter. The negligence has to be 'gross'. This was first explained in *Bateman* (1925) which involved negligent treatment of a patient by a doctor.

Bateman (1925)

D was a doctor who attended a woman for the birth of her child at her home. During the childbirth, part of the woman's uterus came

away. D did not send V to hospital for five days, and she later died. D's conviction was quashed on the basis that he had carried out the normal procedures that any competent doctor would have done. He had not been grossly negligent.

In his judgment Lord Hewart said:

'The facts must be such that, in the opinion of the jury, the negligence of the accused went beyond a mere matter of compensation between subjects and showed such disregard for the life and safety of others as to amount to a crime against the State and conduct deserving of punishment.'

In *Adomako* (1994) the House of Lords approved this test and stressed that it was a matter for the jury. The jury had to decide whether, having regard to the risk of death involved, the conduct of the defendant was so bad in all the circumstances as to amount, in their judgment, to a criminal act or omission.

The jury has to consider the seriousness of the breach of duty in all the circumstances in which the defendant was placed when it occurred. In *Adomako* Lord Mackay said:

> 'The jury will have to consider whether the extent to which the defendant's conduct departed from the proper standard of care incumbent upon him, involving as it must have done a risk of death to the patient, was such that it should be judged as criminal.'

There have been criticisms of these tests because it is left to individual jury panels to decide the appropriate standard for 'gross' negligence. This may lead to inconsistent decisions in similar cases. There is also little guidance on what should be considered as 'gross' negligence.

Key facts

Elements	Comment	Cases
Duty of care	D must owe V a duty of care.	*Adomako* (1994)
	The civil concept of negligence applies.	*Adomako* (1994)
	Covers wide range of situations, eg maintaining a gas fire.	*Singh* (1999)
	May even cover a duty not to supply drugs.	*Rogers* (2003)
	The fact that V was party to an illegal act is not relevant.	*Wacker* (2003)
Breach of duty	This can be by an act or an omission.	
Gross negligence	Beyond a matter of mere compensation and showed such disregard for the life and safety of others as to amount to a crime.	*Bateman* (1925)
	Conduct so bad in all the circumstances as to amount to a criminal act or omission.	*Adomako* (1994)
Risk of death	There must be a risk of death from D's conduct.	*Adomako* (1994) *Misra and another* (2004).

Figure 8.3 Key facts chart on gross negligence manslaughter

Risk of death

In *Adomako* (1994) it was not totally clear whether there has to be a risk of death through the defendant's conduct or whether the risk need only be to 'health and welfare' of the victim. In *Stone and Dobinson* (1977), where the defendants had undertaken the care of Stone's sister, the test was expressed as the risk being to the 'health and welfare' of the sister who died. When Lord Mackay gave judgment in *Adomako*, he approved this way of explaining the matter. However, Lord Mackay also approved the test in *Bateman* (1925) where the test is 'disregard for the life and safety of others'. In addition, Lord Mackay specifically mentioned 'a risk of death' on two occasions in his judgment.

The matter has now been resolved in *Misra and another* (2004).

Misra and another (2004)

V had an operation on his knee. The two defendants were senior house doctors who were responsible for the post-operative care of V. They failed to identify and treat V for an infection which occurred after the operation. V died from the infection. The defendants were convicted and appealed on the basis that the elements of gross negligence manslaughter were uncertain and so breached Art 7 of the European Convention on Human Rights.

The Court of Appeal held that *Adomako* (1994) had clearly laid down the elements, so there was no breach of Art 7. The test in gross negligence manslaughter involves consideration of the risk of death. It is not sufficient to show a risk of bodily injury or injury to health. The defendants' conviction for manslaughter was upheld.

8.3 Reckless manslaughter

After the decision in *Adomako* (1994), it was thought that reckless manslaughter no longer existed. However, in *Lidar* (2000) the Court of Appeal upheld the defendant's conviction for manslaughter even though the judge referred to subjective recklessness (rather than gross negligence) in his directions to the jury.

Lidar (2000)

D and others had been asked to leave a public house in Leicester. They went into the pub car park and got into a Range Rover, with D as driver. One of the passengers shouted something at V, who was the doorman of the pub. V approached the vehicle and put his arms through the open front passenger window. D then drove off, with V half in and half out of the window. After about 225 metres, V was dragged under the rear wheel of the Range Rover and suffered injuries from which he died. D was convicted of manslaughter.

Although the trial judge directed the jury in the basis of recklessness, it is obvious from the facts that the defendant could have been convicted on the basis of gross negligence manslaughter. The defendant clearly owed V a duty of care. In fact, all road users owe a duty of care to others on the road (whether as drivers, passengers or pedestrians). By driving off with V half in and half out of the window, the defendant was in breach of that duty of care. It was open to the jury to decide that the breach was gross negligence.

In view of this, it is difficult to see why it is necessary to have a separate category of subjectively reckless manslaughter.

8.4 Reform of the law of manslaughter

There have been many criticisms of manslaughter as an offence. The first general one is that the same offence covers such a wide range of behaviour. The levels of blameworthiness of individual defendants vary enormously, yet all are convicted of the same offence. There are also specific criticisms of both unlawful act manslaughter and gross negligence manslaughter.

8.4.1 Problems with unlawful act manslaughter

For unlawful act manslaughter the main criticisms are:

- It covers a very wide range of conduct.
- Death may be an unexpected result; if the same act resulted in minor injury, the defendant would only be liable for the offence of assault occasioning actual bodily harm.
- A defendant who did not realise there was risk of any injury is still guilty because of the objective nature of the test.

In 1996 the Law Commission recommended the abolition of unlawful act manslaughter. It criticised the concept of unlawful act manslaughter, pointing out:

> 'It ... is inappropriate to convict a defendant for an offence of homicide where the most that can be said is that he or she ought to have realised that there was the risk of some, albeit not serious, harm to another resulting from his or her commission of an unlawful act.'

8.4.2 Reform of unlawful act manslaughter

Although in 1996 the Law Commission had recommended abolishing unlawful act manslaughter, it did not recommend abolition in its 2006 report, *Murder, Manslaughter and Infanticide*. Instead, it recommended a three-tier structure of homicide offences. These were:

- first degree murder;
- second degree murder; and
- manslaughter.

Under these proposals manslaughter would cover:

1. killing another person through gross negligence (this proposal is discussed at 8.4.4); or

2. killing another person:

    (a) through the commission of a criminal act intended by the defendant to cause injury, or

    (b) through the commission of a criminal act that the defendant was aware involved a serious risk of causing some injury.

This second category would be known as 'criminal act manslaughter'. It would be different to the present unlawful act manslaughter as a defendant could only be convicted on a subjective test; ie he or she must either intend to cause injury or be aware that the act involved a serious risk of causing some injury. This would prevent defendants being convicted of the serious offence of manslaughter where they did not intend any injury and were unaware of the risk of injury.

In addition, more serious situations which at the moment are classed as manslaughter could become second degree murder under the Law Commission's proposals. These are killings where the defendant intended to cause injury or a fear or risk of injury and was aware that his or her conduct involved a serious risk of causing death.

This allows greater differentiation between the blameworthiness of defendants.

NB The Law Commission's summary of its proposals for murder and manslaughter is set out in Appendix 4.

8.4.3 Problems with gross negligence manslaughter

The main criticisms of gross negligence manslaughter are:

- The test is circular, as the jury is directed to convict of a crime if they think that the conduct was criminal.
- The test may lead to inconsistent verdicts, as it depends on what different juries think.
- The civil test for negligence should not be used in criminal cases: the purpose of the two branches of law is quite different.

Circular test

The fact that the jury have to decide whether to convict the defendant of manslaughter (a criminal offence) by deciding whether his conduct was criminal is regarded as a circular test.

In other words, the starting point of 'is the defendant's conduct criminal?' is almost the same as saying 'has he committed a crime?'. There is no sequence of reasoning, instead the argument goes round in a circle. It's a crime because it's criminal!

The other problem with this test is that it leaves the jury to decide a question of law. Normally, in other offences, the judge decides if the conduct is capable of being a crime and the jury then decide on the facts whether the defendant has committed the alleged crime. In gross negligence manslaughter the jury decide whether the conduct is capable of being criminal.

There also used to be a criticism that it was unclear whether the risk had to be of death or whether risk of serious injury was sufficient to prove gross negligence manslaughter. This point was clarified in *Misra* (2004) where the Court of Appeal held that the test in gross negligence manslaughter involves consideration of the risk of death. It is not sufficient to show a risk of bodily injury or injury to health.

8.4.4 Reform of gross negligence manslaughter

In 1996, the Law Commission proposed that instead of gross negligence manslaughter there should be two categories of killing involving negligence. These were reckless killing and killing by gross carelessness. Reckless killing would be the more serious offence as the prosecution would have to prove that:

- the defendant is aware that his conduct will cause death or serious injury and
- it is unreasonable in the circumstances for him to take that risk, having regard to the circumstances as he believes them to be.

This would answer the criticism that a defendant can at present be liable for the very serious offence of manslaughter, without any awareness of the consequences of his act.

Killing by gross carelessness would be a lower-level offence, covering situations where the risk of death or serious injury would be obvious to a reasonable person in the position of the defendant, the defendant is capable of appreciating that risk and either:

- his conduct falls far below what can reasonably be expected of him in the circumstances, or
- he intends by his conduct to cause some injury, or unreasonably takes the risk that it may do so, and the conduct causing (or intended to cause) the injury constitutes an offence.

Although the Government issued a paper on reform in 2000, no other action was taken on the 1996 proposals. However, the Government did ask the Law Commission to review the whole of the homicide law. The Law Commission's report, *Murder, Manslaughter and Infanticide,* was published in 2006.

Law Commission Report of 2006

In their 2006 report, *Murder, Manslaughter and Infanticide,* the Law Commission did not recommend having two categories of killing in cases where there had been negligence. Instead they recommended that there should only be gross negligence manslaughter which would be committed where:

- a person by his or her conduct causes the death of another;
- a risk that his or her conduct will cause death … would be obvious to a reasonable person in his or her position;
- he or she is capable of appreciating that risk at the material time; and
- … his or her conduct falls far below what can reasonably be expected of him or her in the circumstances.

This largely restates the existing law. It makes it absolutely clear that the risk must be to cause death. A risk of serious injury is not sufficient.

However, the Law Commission recommended keeping the rule that gross negligence manslaughter can be committed even when D was unaware that his or her conduct might cause death. They justified this by pointing out:

> 'This is because negligence, however gross, does not necessarily involve any actual realisation that one is posing a risk of harm. It is a question of how glaringly obvious the risk would have been to a reasonable person.'

But, under the proposal, this rule is softened by the fact that the prosecution would have to prove that the defendant is capable of appreciating that risk at the material time. This would prevent those with mental disabilities or younger defendants being convicted if they were not capable of appreciating the risk.

8.4.5 Reform of reckless manslaughter

If the Law Commission's recommendations of 2006 were carried out, 'reckless manslaughter' would become a very narrow category. In many cases it would be almost indistinguishable from gross negligence manslaughter. The Law Commission, therefore, thought that to have a separate category would make the law too complex. Instead they recommended the abolition of reckless manslaughter as a separate category.

However, the Law Commission pointed out that the worst cases of recklessness (those in which there was also an intention to cause injury or a fear or risk of injury) would be accounted for within second degree murder.

For the less serious cases, the Law Commission thought that most cases would be covered by gross negligence manslaughter. This was because D would be hard-pressed to deny that he or she was perfectly well aware of the risk of his or her conduct killing someone. For example, the situation in *Lidar* (2000), where D drove off knowing that the victim was hanging from the car window with his body half in the car, would be covered under the Law Commission's proposal for gross negligence manslaughter.

Activity

Applying the law

Explain whether the following situations could be unlawful act manslaughter and/or gross negligence manslaughter.

1. Asif is throwing stones at passing cars. One of the stones goes through the open side window in Dawn's car and hits her on the side of the head. She loses control of the car and hits a pedestrian, Keith, who is killed.

2. Justine and Oliver have spent the evening at Justine's flat, drinking heavily. Oliver also knows that Justine has taken an Ecstasy tablet, although he has not taken any drugs. Justine passes out and Oliver, who is afraid he may get into trouble, decides to leave. The next morning, Justine is discovered to be dead.

3. Liam is very angry with Sam and kicks out at him. This causes Sam to trip and fall down some steps, breaking his neck and killing him.

4. Patsy has been caring for her elderly aunt who is very frail and unable to walk without assistance. Patsy goes away on a fortnight's holiday, leaving her aunt on her own. The aunt dies through lack of food and cold.

5. Brett decides to rob a local post office. He puts a mask over his face and takes an imitation gun with him. He enters the post office and tells the two members of the staff who are there, Karina and Sven, to put their hands up. Karina is so shocked that she suffers a heart attack. When her colleague, Sven, tries to go to her assistance, Brett pushes him away. Sven falls, hitting his head, and dies. Karina dies two hours later.

Examination questions

1. Emma hires Fred, a qualified electrician, to re-wire her house. She is unhappy when she notices sparks coming from some of the switches as she turns some lights on and off. Emma complains to Fred who returns to do some checks. He assures her that everything is in order and perfectly safe. The next morning, Emma goes to take a shower in the bathroom. When she turns on the shower control, she receives an electric shock that causes her to fall and bang her head, knocking her unconscious. Fortunately her friend, Gita, arrives almost immediately and discovers Emma. Gita calls an ambulance and Emma is rushed to hospital. While Emma is still critically ill she develops an infection.

   Hugh, a junior doctor employed by the hospital, fails to read Emma's medical notes properly. The notes clearly show that Emma is allergic to penicillin. Hugh gives penicillin to Emma to treat the infection. As a result of her allergy, Emma dies.

   Discuss the liability of Fred and Hugh for Emma's death.

   (OCR Specimen Paper)

2. Raul and Christiano are standing in a queue at a bus stop when they begin arguing with one another. Raul pushes Christiano, who staggers backwards and collides with Margaret, an 83-year-old lady. Margaret falls backwards onto the pavement. She is injured and in pain. Margaret is taken to hospital where x-rays reveal that she has broken her hip. Doctors agree that the injuries are made worse partly because she suffers from osteoporosis (a disease which makes her bones unusually brittle).

   Although Margaret is elderly, Dr Smith decides to operate in order to give Margaret a chance of being able to walk again in the future. A few days later, Margaret is recovering slowly from the operation when she develops a secondary infection. Dr Smith prescribes penicillin for Margaret but she is allergic to the drug and dies.

   Discuss the potential liability of both Raul and Dr Smith for the death of Margaret.

   (OCR, Unit 2571, January 2008)

Chapter 9

Non-fatal offences against the person

The main offences are set out in the Offences Against the Person Act 1861 (OAPA). They are based on whether or not the victim was injured; if there were injuries, their level of seriousness; and the intention of the defendant. The main offences are in ascending order of seriousness:

- assault – common law but charged under s 39 Criminal Justice Act 1988
- battery – common law but charged under s 39 Criminal Justice Act 1988
- assault occasioning actual bodily harm – s 47 OAPA 1861
- malicious wounding or inflicting grievous bodily harm – s 20 OAPA 1861
- wounding or causing grievous bodily harm with intent – s 18 OAPA 1861.

9.1 Common assault

There are two ways of committing this:

- assault
- battery.

Assault and battery are common-law offences. There is no statutory definition for either assault or for battery. However, statute law recognises their existence as both of these offences are charged under s 39 Criminal Justice Act 1988 which sets out that the maximum punishment for them is six months' imprisonment or a fine of £5,000, or both.

The act involved is different for assault and battery. For assault, there is no touching, only the fear of immediate, unlawful force. For battery, there must be actual force. There are often situations in which both occur. For example, where the defendant approaches the victim shouting that he is going to 'get him', then punches the victim in the face. The approaching, shouting and raising his arm prior to the punch constitute an assault, while the punch is the battery. As the act is different for each it is easier to consider assault and battery separately. The next section gives the definition of each and the following sections explain the individual elements.

9.1.1 Definition of assault and battery

Definition

Assault

An act which causes the victim to apprehend the infliction of immediate, unlawful force with either an intention to cause another to fear immediate unlawful personal violence or recklessness as to whether such fear is caused.

Definition

Battery

The application of unlawful force to another person intending either to apply unlawful physical force to another or recklessness as to whether unlawful force is applied.

9.1.2 *Actus reus* of assault

An assault is also known as a technical assault or a psychic assault. There must be:

- an act
- which causes the victim to apprehend the infliction of immediate, unlawful force.

An 'act'

An assault requires some act or words. An omission is not sufficient to constitute an assault. However, words are sufficient for an assault. These can be verbal or written. In *Constanza* (1997) the Court of Appeal held that letters could be an assault. The defendant had written 800 letters and made a number of phone calls to the victim. The victim interpreted the last two letters as clear threats. The Court of Appeal said there was an assault as there was a 'fear of violence at some time, not excluding the immediate future'.

In *Ireland* (1997) it was held that even silent telephone calls can be an assault. It depends on the facts of the case.

'Apprehend immediate unlawful force'

The important point is that the act or words must cause the victim to apprehend that immediate force is going to be used against them. There is no assault if the situation is such that it is obvious that the defendant cannot actually use force. For example, where the defendant shouts threats from a passing train there is no possibility that he can carry out the threats in the immediate future.

It was decided in *Lamb* (1967) that pointing an unloaded gun at someone who knows that it is unloaded cannot be an assault. This is because the other person does not fear immediate force. However, if the other person thought the gun was loaded then this could be an assault.

Fear of immediate force is necessary; immediate does not mean instantaneous, but 'imminent', so an assault can be through a closed window, as in *Smith v Chief Superintendent of Woking Police Station* (1983).

Smith v Chief Superintendent of Woking Police Station (1983)

D broke into a garden and looked through V's bedroom window on the ground floor at about 11 pm one evening. V was terrified and thought that D was about to enter the room. Although D was outside the house and no attack could be made at that immediate moment, the court held that V was frightened by his conduct. The basis of the fear was that she did not know what he was going to do next, but that it was likely to be of a violent nature. Fear of what he might do next was sufficiently immediate for the purposes of the offence.

Words indicating that there will be no violence may prevent an act from being an assault. This is a principle which comes from the old case of *Tuberville v Savage* (1669) where the defendant placed one hand on his sword and said, 'If it were not assize time, I would not take such language from you'. This was held not to be an assault, because what he said showed he was not going to do anything.

However, it will depend on all the circumstances. For example, in *Light* (1857) the defendant raised a sword above the head of his wife and said, 'Were it not for the bloody policeman outside, I would split your head open.' It was held that this was an assault. The wife feared that force was going to be used on her and the words in the circumstances were not enough to negate that fear.

Fear of any unwanted touching is sufficient: the force or unlawful personal violence which is feared need not be serious.

There are many examples of assault:

- raising a fist as though about to hit the victim
- throwing a stone at the victim which just misses
- pointing a loaded gun at someone within range
- making a threat by saying 'I am going to hit you'.

Unlawfulness of the force

The force which is threatened must be unlawful. If it is lawful, there is no offence of common assault. Whether force is lawful or unlawful is discussed in detail under the *actus reus* of battery in the next section.

9.1.3 *Actus reus* of battery

The *actus reus* of battery is the application of unlawful force to another person. Force is a slightly misleading word as it can include the slightest touching, as shown by the case of *Collins v Wilcock* (1984).

Collins v Wilcock (1984)

Two police officers saw two women apparently soliciting for the purposes of prostitution. They asked the appellant to get into the police car for questioning but she refused and walked away. As she was not known to the police, one of the officers walked after her to try to find out her identity. She refused to speak to the officer and again walked away. The officer then took hold of her by the arm to prevent her leaving. She became abusive and scratched the officer's arm. She was convicted of assaulting a police officer in the execution of his duty. She appealed against that conviction on the basis that the officer was not acting in the execution of his duty, but was acting unlawfully by holding her arm as the officer was not arresting her. The court held that the officer had committed a battery and the defendant was entitled to free herself.

In this case, the court pointed out that touching a person to get his attention was acceptable, provided that no greater degree of physical contact was used than was necessary. However, physical restraint was not acceptable.

A similar point arose in *Wood v DPP* (2008) where a police officer took hold of Wood's arm to check his identity.

Wood (Fraser) v DPP (2008)

The police had received a report that a man named Fraser had thrown an ashtray at another person in a public house. The ashtray had missed the person but had been smashed. Three police officers went to the scene. They saw a man (the appellant, W) who fitted the description of 'Fraser' leave the public house. One of the police officers took hold of W by the arm and asked if he was Fraser. W denied this and struggled, trying to pull away. At that point another officer took hold of W's other arm. W was charged with assaulting two of the police officers while they were acting in the execution of their duty.

The police officer who had first caught hold of W's arm said that he had done this in order to detain W, but was not at that point arresting him. It was held that as the officer had not arrested W, then there was a technical assault (battery) by the police officers. This meant that W was entitled to struggle and was not guilty of any offence of assault against the police.

Even touching the victim's clothing can be sufficient to form a battery. In *Thomas* (1985) the defendant touched the bottom of a woman's skirt and rubbed it. The Court of Appeal said, *obiter*, 'There could be no dispute that if you touch a person's clothes while he is wearing them that is equivalent to touching him'.

Continuing act

A battery may be committed through a continuing act, as in *Fagan v Metropolitan Police Commander* (1968) where the defendant parked his car with one of the tyres on a police officer's foot. When he parked he was unaware that he had done this, but when the police officer asked

him to remove it, he refused to do so for several minutes. The court said that at the start there was an act which could be a battery but the full offence of battery was not committed at that point because there was no element of intention. However, it became an offence of battery the moment the intention was formed to leave the wheel on the officer's foot.

Indirect act

A battery can also be through an indirect act such as a booby trap. In this situation the defendant causes force to be applied, even though he does not personally touch the victim. This occurred in *Martin* (1881) where the defendant placed an iron bar across the doorway of a theatre. He then switched off the lights. In the panic which followed several of the audience were injured when they were trapped and unable to open the door. Martin was convicted of an offence under s 20 OAPA 1861.

A more modern example is *DPP v K* (1990).

DPP v K (1990)

D was a 15-year-old schoolboy who took sulphuric acid without permission from his science lesson, to try its reaction on some toilet paper. While he was in the toilet he heard footsteps in the corridor, panicked and put the acid into a hot-air hand drier to hide it. He returned to his class intending to remove the acid later. Before he could do so another pupil used the drier and was sprayed by the acid. D was charged with assault occasioning actual bodily harm (s 47). The magistrates acquitted him because he said he had not intended to hurt anyone (see section 9.2.3 for the *mens rea* of s 47). The prosecution appealed, by way of case stated, to the Queen's Bench Divisional Court which held that a common assault (which includes both an assault and a battery) could be committed by an indirect act.

Another example of indirect force occurred in *Haystead v Chief Constable of Derbyshire* (2000) where the defendant caused a small child to fall to the floor by punching the woman holding the child. The defendant was found guilty because he was reckless as to whether or not his acts would injure the child. It is worth noting that, in this case, the conviction could also be justified by the principle of transferred malice.

Omissions

Criminal liability can arise by way of an omission, but only if the defendant is under a duty to act. Such a duty can arise out of a contract, a relationship, from the assumption of care for another or from the creation of a dangerous situation. As the *actus reus* of battery is the application of unlawful force it is difficult to think how examples could arise under these duty situations, but there has been one reported case, *DPP v Santana-Bermudez* (2003).

DPP v Santana-Bermudez (2003)

In this case a policewoman, before searching D's pockets, asked him if he had any needles or other sharp objects on him. D said 'no', but when the police officer put her hand in his pocket she was injured by a needle which caused bleeding. The Divisional Court held that the defendant's failure to tell her of the needle could amount to the *actus reus* for the purposes of an assault causing actual bodily harm.

Other scenarios which could make a defendant liable by way of omission are where the defendant has created a dangerous situation which may lead to force being applied to the victim. This can be seen by analogy with *Miller* (1983) where D accidentally set fire to his mattress but failed to do anything to prevent damage to the building in which he was sleeping. He was convicted of arson.

No other person was involved, but if there had been someone else asleep in the room and Miller had failed to wake them and warn them of the danger, then he could have been liable for a battery if there had been any problem. For example, if the person was hit by plaster falling from the ceiling as a result of the fire, then there appears to be no reason why Miller could not have been charged with battery of that person.

Unlawful force

For a battery to be committed, the force must be unlawful. If the victim gives genuine consent to it then the force may be lawful. (See section 9.8 for further information on consent as a defence.) Force may also be lawful where it is used in self-defence or prevention of crime. This can only be so if the force used is reasonable in the situation as the defendant believed it to be (see section 9.7 for information on self-defence). If the force is lawful, then the person using the force is not guilty of a battery.

Another situation where force may be lawful is in the correction of a child by a parent. English law recognises that moderate and reasonable physical chastisement of a child is lawful. However, in *A v UK* (1998) where a jury had acquitted a father who had beaten his son with a garden cane, the European Court of Human Rights ruled that a law allowing force to be used on children offends Art 3 of the European Convention on Human Rights. This article prohibits torture and inhuman or degrading treatment of punishment.

Despite this ruling, force used to correct a child can be lawful in the United Kingdom, provided the judge in such a case directs the jury to take account of the nature, context and duration of the force used by the parent, the physical and mental effect on the child and the reasons for the punishment. If the force is excessive then it is a criminal offence.

Battery without an assault

It is possible for there to be a battery even though there is no assault. This can occur where the victim is unaware that unlawful force is about to be used on him, such as where the attacker comes up unseen behind the victim's back. The first thing the victim knows is when he is struck; there has been a battery but no assault.

Key cases

Case	Facts	Law
Constanza (1997)	D wrote 800 letters and made phone calls to V.	Written words can be an assault if they cause V to fear immediate violence.
Smith v Chief Superintendent (Woking) (1983)	D looked through V's bedroom window late at night.	Fear of what D would do next was sufficient for the *actus reus* of assault.
Tuberville v Savage (1669)	D put hand on sword and said 'Were it not assize time, I would not take such language from you'.	Words can prevent an act from being an assault, but it depends on the circumstances.
Collins v Wilcock (1984)	A police officer held a woman's arm to prevent her walking away.	Any touching may be a battery, and always is if there was physical restraint.
Wood (Fraser) v DPP (2008)	An officer took hold of W's arm to check his identity.	This was a battery by the police and W was entitled to struggle to release himself.
Fagan v MPC (1968)	D, unknowingly, stopped his car with a wheel on a policeman's foot and refused to move when requested.	The *actus reus* of assault can be an ongoing act so that the complete offence is committed when D forms the *mens rea*.
DPP v K (1990)	D put acid in a hand drier – the next person to use it was sprayed with acid.	An indirect act can be the *actus reus* of assault.
DPP v Santana-Bermudez (2003)	D failed to tell a policewoman that he had a needle in his pocket – she was injured when she searched him.	An omission is sufficient for the *actus reus* of assault.
DPP v Majewski (1976)	D, who had taken drink and drugs, attacked the landlord of a pub and police officers.	Getting drunk is a reckless course of conduct and is sufficient for the *mens rea* of assault.

Figure 9.1 Key cases chart on assault and battery

Activity

Explain whether there is an assault and/or battery in the following situations.

1. At a party Tanya sneaks up behind Wilhelm, whom she knows well, and slaps him on the back.
2. Vince throws a stone at Delyth, but misses. He picks up another stone and this time hits the edge of Delyth's coat.
3. Imram turns round quickly without realising that Harry is standing just behind him, and bumps into Harry. Harry shouts at him, 'If you were not wearing glasses, I would hit you in the face'.
4. Ramsey and Sue are having an argument. During the argument, Ramsey says, 'If you don't shut up, I'll thump you.' Sue is so annoyed at this that she gets out a penknife and waves it in front of Ramsey's face. Ramsey pushes her away.

9.1.4 *Mens rea* of assault and battery

The *mens rea* for an assault is either an intention to cause another to fear immediate unlawful personal violence, or recklessness as to whether such fear is caused. The *mens rea* for battery is either an intention to apply unlawful physical force to another or recklessness as to whether unlawful force is applied. So intention or recklessness is sufficient for both assault and battery.

The test for recklessness is subjective. For an assault, the defendant must realise there is a risk that his acts/words could cause another to fear unlawful personal violence. For a battery the defendant must realise there is a risk that his act (or omission) could cause unlawful force to be applied to another.

Assault and battery are classed as offences of basic intent. This means that if the defendant is intoxicated when he does the relevant *actus reus* he is considered as doing it recklessly. This was stated by the House of Lords in *DPP v Majewski* (1976).

DPP v Majewski (1976)

D had consumed large quantities of alcohol and drugs and then attacked the landlord of the public house where he was drinking. The landlord called the police and D also attacked the police officers who tried to arrest him. The Law Lords held that becoming intoxicated by drink and drugs was a reckless course of conduct, and recklessness is enough to constitute the necessary *mens rea* in assault cases.

This ruling can be criticised, as the point at which the drink or drugs are taken is a quite separate time to the point when the *actus reus* for the offence is committed. It is difficult to see how there is coincidence of the two. It is reasonable to say that the defendant is reckless when he takes drink or other intoxicating substances, but this does not necessarily mean that when he commits an assault or battery three or four hours later he is reckless for the purposes of the offence. The decision can be viewed as a public policy decision.

9.2 Assault occasioning actual bodily harm

We now look at assaults where an injury is caused. The lowest level of injury is referred to in the Offences Against the Person Act 1861 as 'actual bodily harm' under s 47. It is a triable either way offence. The section states:

> 'Whosoever shall be convicted of any assault occasioning actual bodily harm shall be liable ... to imprisonment for five years.'

As can be seen from this very brief section, there is no definition of 'assault' or 'actual bodily harm'. Nor is there any reference to the level of *mens rea* required. For all these points it is necessary to look at case law.

9.2.1 Definition of assault occasioning actual bodily harm

Definition

Assault occasioning actual bodily harm

An assault or battery which causes actual bodily harm, with the intention to cause the victim to fear unlawful force, or to subject unlawful force, or to be subjectively reckless as to whether the victim fears or is subjected to unlawful force.

9.2.2 *Actus reus* of s 47

It is necessary to prove that there was an assault or battery and that this caused actual bodily harm.

Actual bodily harm

In *Miller* (1954) it was said that actual bodily harm is 'any hurt or injury calculated to interfere with the health or comfort of the victim'. In *T v DPP* (2003) loss of consciousness, even momentarily, was held to be actual bodily harm.

T v DPP (2003)

D and a group of other youths chased V. V fell to the ground and saw D coming towards him. V covered his head with his arms and was kicked. He momentarily lost consciousness and remembered nothing until being woken by a police officer. D was convicted of assault occasioning actual bodily harm.

So, s 47 can be charged where there is any injury. Bruising, grazes and scratches all come within this offence.

In *T v DPP* (2003) it was held that loss of consciousness, even for a very short time, could be actual bodily harm. In *DPP v Smith (Michael)* (2006) it was held that cutting the victim's hair can amount to actual bodily harm.

DPP v Smith (Michael) (2006)

The defendant had had an argument with his girlfriend. He cut off her ponytail and some hair from the top of her head without her consent. He was charged with an offence under s 47 of the Offences Against the Person Act 1861. The magistrates found there was no case to answer as they thought that cutting hair could not amount to actual bodily harm. The prosecution appealed and the Divisional Court held that cutting off a substantial amount of hair could be actual bodily harm.

In *Smith* the court held that physical pain was not a necessary ingredient of actual bodily harm. Hair is attached to the head and this makes it a part of the body so that harm to the hair comes within the meaning of 'actual bodily harm.'

However, the court did stress that a substantial amount of hair has to be cut off for the harm to be 'actual' as opposed to trivial or insignificant harm.

Psychiatric injury is also classed as 'actual bodily harm'. This was decided by the Court of Appeal in *Chan Fook* (1994). However, they pointed out that actual bodily harm does not include 'mere emotions such as fear, distress or panic' nor does it include 'states of mind that are not themselves evidence of some identifiable clinical condition'.

This decision was approved by the House of Lords in *Burstow* (1997) where it was said that 'bodily harm' in ss 18, 20 and 47 OAPA 1861 must be interpreted so as to include recognisable psychiatric illness.

9.2.3 *Mens rea* of s 47

The section in the Act makes no reference to *mens rea* but, as the essential element is a common assault, the courts have held that the *mens rea* for a common assault is sufficient for the *mens rea* of a s 47 offence.

This means the defendant must intend or be subjectively reckless as to whether the victim fears or is subjected to unlawful force. This is the same *mens rea* as for an assault or a battery. It is important to note that there is no need for the defendant to intend or be reckless as to whether actual bodily harm is caused. This is demonstrated by the case of *Roberts* (1971).

Roberts (1971)

D, who was driving a car, made advances to the girl in the passenger seat and tried to take her coat off. She feared that he was going to commit a more serious assault and jumped from the car while it was travelling at about 30 miles per hour. As a result of this she was slightly injured. D was found guilty of assault occasioning actual bodily harm even though he had not intended any injury or realised there was a risk of injury. He had intended to apply unlawful force when he touched her as he tried to take her coat off. This satisfied the *mens rea* for a common assault and so he was guilty of an offence under s 47.

This decision was confirmed by the House of Lords in the combined appeals of *Savage* (1991) and *Parmenter* (1991).

Savage (1991)

D threw beer over another woman in a pub. In doing this the glass slipped from D's hand and V's hand was cut by the glass. D said that she had only intended to throw beer over the woman. D had not intended her to be injured, nor had she realised that there was a risk of injury. She was convicted of a s 20 offence but the Court of Appeal quashed that and substituted a conviction under s 47 (assault occasioning actual bodily harm). She appealed against this to the House of Lords. The Law Lords dismissed her appeal.

The fact that she intended to throw the beer over the other woman meant she had the intention to apply unlawful force and this was sufficient for the *mens rea* of the s 47 offence.

9.3 Malicious wounding/ inflicting grievous bodily harm

This is the next offence in seriousness. It is an offence under s 20 OAPA 1861 which gives the definition below.

Definition

Section 20 OAPA

'Whosoever shall unlawfully and maliciously wound or inflict any grievous bodily harm upon any other person, either with or without a weapon or instrument, shall be guilty of an offence and shall be liable … to imprisonment for not more than five years.'

The offence is commonly known as 'malicious wounding'. It is triable either way and the maximum sentence is five years. This is the same maximum sentence as for a s 47 offence, despite the fact that s 20 is seen as a more serious offence and requires both a higher degree of injury and *mens rea* as to an injury.

For the offence to be proved it must be shown that the defendant:

● wounded, OR
● inflicted grievous bodily harm

and that he did this:

Key facts

Offence	*Actus reus*	Consequence (injury) required	*Mens rea*
Assault	Causing V to fear immediate unlawful violence. Requires an act but can be by silent telephone calls, *Ireland* (1997) or letters, *Constanza* (1997).	None needed.	Intention of, or subjective recklessness as to, causing V to fear immediate unlawful violence.
Battery	Application of unlawful violence, even the slightest touching, *Collins v Wilcock* (1984).	None needed.	Intention of, or subjective recklessness as to, applying unlawful, force *DPP v Majewski* (1976).
NB Assault and battery are both charged under s 39 Criminal Justice Act 1988 and are known as common assault.			
Assault occasioning actual bodily harm **s 47 OAPA 1861**	Assault, ie an assault or battery.	Actual bodily harm (eg bruising). This includes: ● momentary loss of consciousness, *R(T) v DPP* (2003) ● psychiatric harm, *Chan Fook* (1994).	Intention of, or subjective recklessness as to, causing fear of unlawful force, ie the *mens rea* for an assault or battery.

Figure 9.2 Key facts chart on assault, battery and s 47

● intending some injury (but not serious injury) be caused, OR

● being reckless as to whether any injury was inflicted.

9.3.1 Wound

'Wound' means a cut or a break in the continuity of the whole skin. A cut of internal skin, such as in the cheek, is sufficient, but internal bleeding where there is no cut of the skin is not sufficient. In *JCC v Eisenhower* (1983) the victim was hit in the eye by a shotgun pellet. This did not penetrate the eye but did cause severe bleeding under the surface. As there was no cut, it was held that this was not a wound. The cut must be of the whole skin, so that a scratch is not considered a wound.

Even a broken bone is not considered a wound, unless the skin is broken as well. In the old case of *Wood* (1830) the victim's collar bone was broken but, as the skin was intact, it was held there was no wound.

9.3.2 Grievous bodily harm

It was held in *DPP v Smith* (1961) that grievous bodily harm means 'really serious harm'. The harm does not have to be life-threatening and in *Saunders* (1985) it was held that it was permissible to direct a jury that there need be 'serious harm' not including the word 'really'.

In *Bollom* (2004) it was held that the severity of the injuries should be assessed according to the victim's age and health.

Bollom (2004)

A 17-month-old child had bruising to her abdomen, both arms and left leg. D was convicted of causing grievous bodily harm. The Court of Appeal quashed his conviction and substituted a conviction for assault occasioning actual bodily harm. However, the Court of Appeal stated that bruising could amount to grievous bodily harm. Bruising of this severity would be less serious on an adult in full health, than on a very young child.

In *Burstow* (1997) where the victim of a stalker suffered a severe depressive illness as a result of his conduct, it was decided that serious psychiatric injury can be grievous bodily harm.

In *Dica* (2004) there was the first ever conviction for causing grievous bodily harm through infecting victims with the HIV virus. The defendant had had unprotected sex with two women without telling them he was HIV-positive. Both women became infected as a result. Although on appeal the defendant's conviction was quashed on the question of consent and the case sent for re-trial, there was no doubt that infecting someone with HIV was inflicting grievous bodily harm. At his re-trial the defendant was convicted.

9.3.3 Inflicting grievous bodily harm

Section 20 uses the word 'inflict'. Originally, this was taken as meaning that there had to be a technical assault or battery. Even so it allowed the section to be interpreted quite widely, as shown in *Lewis* (1974) where D shouted threats at his wife through a closed door in a second-floor flat and tried to break his way through the door. The wife was so frightened that she jumped from the window and broke both her legs. D was convicted of a s 20 offence. The threats could be considered as a technical assault.

In *Burstow* (1997) it was decided that 'inflict' does not require a technical assault or a battery.

Burstow (1997)

D carried out an eight-month campaign of harassment against a woman with whom he had had a brief relationship some three years earlier. The harassment consisted of both silent and abusive telephone calls, hate mail and stalking. This caused V to suffer from severe depression. D's conviction under s 20 OAPA 1861 was upheld by the House of Lords.

This means that it need only be shown that the defendant's actions have led to the consequence of the victim suffering grievous bodily harm. The decision also means that there now appears to be little, if any, difference in the *actus reus* of the offences under s 20 and s 18 which uses the word 'cause'. In fact, in *Burstow* (1997) Lord Hope said that for all practical purposes there was no difference between the two words.

9.3.4 *Mens rea* of s 20

The word used in the section is 'maliciously'. In *Cunningham* (1957) it was held that 'maliciously' did not require any ill will towards the person injured. It simply meant either:

- an intention to do the particular kind of harm that was in fact done, or
- recklessness as to whether such harm should occur or not (ie the accused has foreseen that the particular kind of harm might be done, and yet gone on to take the risk of it).

Cunningham (1957)

The defendant tore a gas meter from the wall of an empty house in order to steal the money in it. This caused gas to seep into the house next door where a woman was affected by it. Cunningham was not guilty of an offence against s 23 OAPA 1861 of maliciously administering a noxious thing, as he did not realise the risk of gas escaping into the next-door house. He had not intended to cause the harm, nor had he been subjectively reckless about it.

Offence	*Mens rea*	Injury
s 18	Specific intent to wound OR cause grievous bodily harm or resist arrest etc.	Wound OR grievous bodily harm.
s 20	Intention OR recklessness as to some harm.	
s 47	Intention OR recklessness as to putting V in fear of unlawful force or applying unlawful force assault.	Actual bodily harm.
Common assault		No injury.

Figure 9.3 Different levels of *mens rea* and injury for assault cases

In *Parmenter* (1991) the House of Lords confirmed that the *Cunningham* meaning of recklessness applies to all offences in which the statutory definition uses the word 'maliciously'.

So, for the *mens rea* of s 20 the prosecution can prove either that the defendant intended to cause another person some harm or that he was subjectively reckless as to whether another person suffered some harm.

This left another point which the courts had to resolve. What was meant by the particular kind of harm? Does the defendant need to realise the risk of a wound or grievous bodily harm? It was decided by the House of Lords in *Parmenter* that, although the *actus* reus of s 20 requires a wound or grievous bodily harm, there is no need for the defendant to foresee this level of serious injury.

Parmenter (1991)

D injured his three-month-old baby when he threw the child in the air and caught him. D said that he had often done this with slightly older children and did not realise that there was risk of any injury. He was convicted of an offence under s 20. The House of Lords quashed this conviction as there was no evidence that he foresaw any injury, but substituted a conviction for assault occasioning actual bodily harm under s 47.

This decision means that, although there are four offences which appear to be on a ladder in terms of seriousness, there is overlap in terms of the *mens rea*.

9.4 Wounding or causing grievous bodily harm with intent

This offence under s 18 OAPA 1861 is often referred to as 'wounding with intent'. In fact, it covers a much wider range of offences than this implies.

It is considered a much more serious offence than s 20, as can be seen from the difference in the maximum punishments. Section 20 has a maximum of five years' imprisonment whereas the maximum for s 18 is life imprisonment. Also, s 20 is triable either way but s 18 must be tried on indictment at the Crown Court. The definition in OAPA 1861 states:

Definition

S 18 OAPA

'Whosoever shall unlawfully and maliciously by any means whatsoever wound or cause any grievous bodily harm to any person, with intent to do some grievous bodily harm to any person, or with intent to resist or prevent the lawful apprehension or detainer of any person, shall be guilty of … an offence.'

9.4.1 *Actus reus* of s 18

This can be committed in two ways:

- wounding or
- causing grievous bodily harm.

The meanings of 'wound' and 'grievous bodily harm' are the same as for s 20. The word 'cause' is very wide so that it is only necessary to prove that the defendant's act was a substantial cause of the wound or grievous bodily harm.

9.4.2 *Mens rea* of s 18

This is a specific intent offence. The defendant must be proved to have intended to:

- do some grievous bodily harm or
- resist or prevent the lawful apprehension or detainer of any person.

Intent to do some grievous bodily harm

Although the word 'maliciously' appears in s 18, it has been held that this adds nothing to the *mens rea* of this section where grievous bodily harm is intended. The important point is that s 18 is a specific intent crime. Intention must be proved; recklessness is not enough for the *mens rea* of s 18. 'Intention' has the same meaning as shown in the leading cases on murder.

Key facts

Offence	*Actus reus*	Consequence (injury) required	*Mens rea*
Maliciously wounding or inflicting grievous bodily harm **s 20 OAPA 1861**	A direct or indirect act or omission: *Martin* (1881). No need to prove an assault: *Burstow* (1997).	Either a wound – a cutting of the whole skin: *JJC v Eisenhower* (1984) or Grievous bodily harm (really serious harm) which includes psychiatric harm: *Burstow* (1998).	Intention or subjective recklessness as to causing some injury (though not serious): *Parmenter* (1991).
Wounding or causing grievous bodily harm with intent **s 18 OAPA 1861**	A direct or indirect act or omission which causes V's injury.	A wound or grievous bodily harm (as above).	Specific intention to wound or to cause grievous bodily harm, or Specific intention to resist or prevent arrest plus recklessness as to causing injury: *Morrison* (1989).

Figure 9.4 Key facts chart on s 20 and s 18

So, as decided in *Moloney* (1985), foresight of consequences is not intention; it is only evidence from which intention can be inferred or found. Following the cases of *Nedrick* (1986) and *Woollin* (1998), intention cannot be found unless the harm caused was a virtual certainty as a result of the defendant's actions and the defendant realised that this was so. (See section 3.1.2 for a fuller discussion on these cases and the meaning of intention.)

Where the defendant is trying to resist or prevent arrest or detention then the level of intention regarding the injury is lower. The prosecution must prove that he had specific intention to resist or prevent arrest, but so far as the injury they need only prove that he was reckless as to whether his actions would cause a wound or injury. This was decided in *Morrison* (1989).

Morrison (1989)

A police officer seized hold of D and told him that she was arresting him. He dived through a window, dragging her with him as far as the window so that her face was badly cut by the glass. The Court of Appeal held that as the word 'maliciously' is used in respect of this part of the section it must have the same meaning as in *Cunningham* (1957). This means that the prosecution must prove that the defendant either intended injury or realised there was a risk of injury and took that risk.

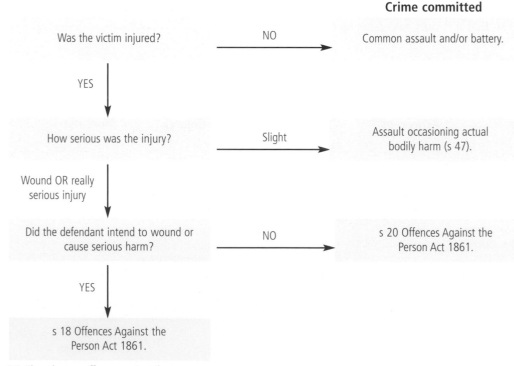

Crime committed

Was the victim injured? — NO → Common assault and/or battery.

YES ↓

How serious was the injury? — Slight → Assault occasioning actual bodily harm (s 47).

Wound OR really serious injury ↓

Did the defendant intend to wound or cause serious harm? — NO → s 20 Offences Against the Person Act 1861.

YES ↓

s 18 Offences Against the Person Act 1861.

Figure 9.5 Flow chart on offences against the person

Activity

Read the following article from the *Kent Messenger* and answer the questions below.

Thug jailed for stamping on policeman's face

'A thug has been jailed for two-and-a-half years for a vicious attack on a police officer after New Year's Eve celebrations erupted in violence.

Kevin Vidler assaulted the PC and then stamped on his face, fracturing his cheekbone, and kicked him in the head.

His brother Neil was given 240 hours' community punishment order for assaulting another man. He was ordered to pay his victim £250 compensation.

Maidstone Crown Court heard in October how the party at a working men's club in

Southborough was in full swing when the victim, a club member, intervened in a couple's heated argument. There was a 'verbal tirade' and he asked one of the men to leave.

Soon afterwards he was punched in the face by 37-year-old Neil Vidler. The police were called but the trouble continued outside.

When the PC and a fellow officer arrived, a teenager hit out at them. Kevin Vidler, aged 36, tried to help the youth, grabbing the constable by the throat and punching him in the head.

Kevin Vidler was convicted of causing grievous bodily harm with intent. Neil Vidler was convicted of assault causing actual bodily harm.'

(*Kent Messenger*, 5th December 2003)

Questions

1. What offence was Kevin Vidler convicted of?

2. Which section of the Offences Against the Person Act 1861 would this come under?

3. What are the elements which have to be proved for this section?

4. Explain what Kevin had done to make him guilty of this offence.

5. What offence was Neil Vidler convicted of?

6. Which section of the Offences Against the Person Act 1861 would this come under?

7. What are the elements which have to be proved for this section?

8. What had Neil done to make him guilty of this offence?

9. What sentences were the two brothers given?

10. Explain why they received different sentences.

9.5 The Crown Prosecution Charging Standards

When Crown Prosecutors decide on which level of offence to charge, they refer to a document called 'Charging Standards' which is issued to all Crown Prosecutors. This document sets out the matters they should consider in deciding the level to be charged. This document is not the law on the subject and it can be argued that on some occasions prosecutors choose a lower level of offence than might be strictly available under the law.

However, the Charging Standards do give some useful examples. For example, in deciding whether to charge the defendant with a common assault or with a s 47 offence, it states:

> 'Where battery results in injury, a choice of charge is available. The Code for Crown Prosecutors recognises that there will be factors which may properly lead to a decision not to prefer or continue with the gravest possible charge. Thus, although any injury that is more than transient or trifling can be classified as actual bodily harm, the appropriate charge ... will be contrary to section 39 [common assault] where

the injuries amount to no more than the following:

- grazes;
- scratches;
- abrasions;
- minor bruising;
- swellings;
- reddening of the skin;
- superficial cuts;
- a "black eye".'

Aggravating features

It is also recognised that there are features which make an assault more serious when it is appropriate to charge the highest possible level of offence. For example, the following features make it more appropriate to charge a s 47 offence even though the level of injury is within the list above:

- the nature of the assault, such as the use of a weapon, biting or kicking a victim who is on the ground;
- the vulnerability of the victim, such as when the victim is elderly, disabled or a child.

Actual bodily harm

The Crown Prosecution charging guidelines state that the following injuries should normally be prosecuted under s 47:

Activity

Explain in each of the situations below, what type of offence may have been committed.

1. In a football match Billy is kicked by Rio as Rio tries to get control of the ball. This causes bruising to Billy's leg. Billy is annoyed at this and punches Rio in the face causing a cut to his lip.
2. Anish is walking along a canal bank. Carol is in a hurry and pushes past him, knocking him into the canal. Anish hits his head on the side and suffers a fractured skull.
3. A police officer sees Jason damaging a parked car. The officer puts his hand on Jason's shoulder and says 'I am arresting you for criminal damage'. Jason punches the officer hard in the face breaking his jaw. Jason then runs off.
4. Karl waves a knife at Lily, saying 'I am going to cut that silly smile off'. Lily is very frightened and faints. She falls against Mary, who is knocked to the ground and suffers bruising.

- loss or breaking of tooth or teeth
- temporary loss of sensory functions, which may include loss of consciousness
- extensive or multiple bruising
- displaced broken nose
- minor fractures
- minor, but not merely superficial, cuts of a sort probably requiring medical treatment (eg stitches)
- psychiatric injury that is more than mere emotions such as fear, distress or panic.

Grievous bodily harm

The Crown Prosecution charging guidelines stress that grievous bodily harm means serious bodily harm and it is for the jury to decide whether the harm is serious. However, examples of what would usually amount to serious harm include:

- injury resulting in permanent disability or permanent loss of sensory function
- injury which results in more than minor permanent, visible disfigurement; broken or displaced limbs or bones, including fractured skull
- compound fractures, broken cheekbone, jaw, ribs, etc
- injuries which cause substantial loss of blood, usually necessitating a transfusion
- injuries resulting in lengthy treatment or incapacity
- psychiatric injury. As with assault occasioning actual bodily harm, appropriate expert evidence is essential to prove the injury.

The full charging standards can be found on the Internet at www.cps.gov.uk/legal

9.6 The need for reform of the law on assault

This area of the law is in need of reform, and recommendations have been made both by the Criminal Law Revision Committee and the Law Commission. The Law Commission pointed out that there are three main problems with the Offences Against the Person Act 1861:

1. It uses complicated, obscure and old-fashioned language; eg the words 'maliciously' and 'grievous'.
2. The structure of the Act is complicated.
3. Non-lawyers find the Act completely unintelligible.

In fact some of the difficulties have been resolved by judges in case decisions. For example, there was considerable debate as to whether the word 'inflict' in s 20 meant that a technical assault had to take place. This was resolved by the case of *Burstow* (1997) (see section 9.3.3) in which the House of Lords ruled that it did not.

Also, the courts have extended the meaning of 'bodily harm' to include injury to mental health so that defendants causing such injury can also be convicted.

9.6.1 Inconsistency between offences

There are inconsistencies in the Act, especially with regard to the *mens rea* required for each offence. In particular, s 47 has the same *mens rea* as for an assault or battery. It does not require the defendant to intend or even realise that there is a risk of any injury. This appears unjust.

It is also unjust that a person who causes a small cut can be charged with the more serious offence of s 20 instead of the offence of 'occasioning actual bodily harm' under s 47. This is because s 20 refers to 'wound or grievous bodily harm'. Yet clearly there are different levels of wound, and many of them do not equate with grievous bodily harm.

It is also inconsistent that a defendant who intends or foresees the risk of minor injury can be convicted of the very serious offence of s 18 if serious injury then occurs when he intends to resist arrest. This is the effect of the decision in *Morrison* (1989) (see section 9.4.2). Is it right that by intending to resist arrest, the defendant becomes liable for the same offence as someone who has intended to cause very serious injuries?

9.6.2 Law Commission's proposals

In 1993 the Law Commission proposed new law to take its place, but the Government did nothing about this until 1998 when the Home Office issued a Consultation Document, *Violence: Reforming the Offences Against the Person Act 1861*. This included a draft Bill which set out four main offences. These were intended to replace ss 18, 20, 47, and assault and battery. In order, starting with the most serious (which is in clause 1 of the draft Bill), they are:

1. Intentional serious injury where a person would be guilty if he intentionally caused serious injury to another.
2. Reckless serious injury where a person would be guilty if he recklessly caused serious injury to another.
3. Intentional or reckless injury where a person would be guilty if he intentionally or recklessly caused injury to another.
4. Assault: a person would be guilty if he intentionally or recklessly
    (a) applied force to or caused an impact on the body of another, or
    (b) caused the other to believe that any such force or impact is imminent.

In each of these the level of injury and the required *mens rea* are made clear by the wording. In addition, the draft Bill also defined the word 'injury', making it clear that both physical and mental injury were included. The word 'wounding' is not used. So this would mean that a serious cut would be considered to be a serious injury, while a small cut would be considered to be merely an injury. This would have cleared up most of the problems in the present law. Unfortunately, although the Bill was sent out for consultation in 1998, the Government has done nothing more, so the law still remains in an unsatisfactory state.

In the draft Bill, the Law Commission defined injury. It said that it included both physical and mental illness, and it gave a definition for both of these:

*   *physical* injury was defined as including pain, unconsciousness and any other impairment of a person's physical health;
*   *mental* injury was defined as any impairment of a person's mental health.

They also included disease as a physical injury for the purposes of the most serious offence. However, this would mean that it would be almost impossible to convict a defendant of infecting another person with HIV since the proposed most serious offence (the first in the list above) can only be committed where the defendant has intentionally caused serious injury. This would mean that convictions for recklessly transmitting HIV, as in the case of *Dica* (2004) (see section 9.3.2) would not be possible.

9.7 Self-defence/defence of another/prevention of crime

This covers not only actions needed to defend oneself from an attack, but also actions taken to defend another. The defences of self-defence and defence of another are common-law defences which justify the defendant's actions. In addition there is a statutory defence of prevention of crime under s 3(1) of the Criminal Law Act 1967 which states that:

> 'a person may use such force as is reasonable in the circumstances in the prevention of crime.'

9.7.1 Degree of force

The amount of force which can be used in self-defence, defence of another or in prevention of crime is now explained in the Criminal Justice and Immigration Act 2008. This states that, in deciding whether the force used is reasonable in the circumstances:

'(a) that a person acting for a legitimate purpose may not be able to weigh to a nicety the exact measure of any necessary action; and

(b) that evidence of a person's having only done what the person honestly and instinctively thought was necessary for a legitimate purpose constitutes strong evidence that only reasonable action was taken by that person for that purpose.'

This allows for the fact that a person who is facing an attack by another is under stress and cannot be expected to calculate the exact amount of force which needs to be used in the circumstances. If there is evidence that the person 'honestly and instinctively' thought the level of force he used to protect himself or another or to prevent crime was reasonable, then this provides strong evidence that the defensive action taken was reasonable in the circumstances.

However, if the force is used after all danger from the assailant is over (ie as retaliation or revenge), the defence is not available.

9.7.2 Mistaken use of force in self-defence

In looking at the circumstances, the defendant must be judged on the facts as he genuinely believed them to be. In *Williams* (1987) it was ruled that the defendant should be judged according to his genuine mistaken view of the facts, regardless of whether this mistake was reasonable or unreasonable. This allowed Williams to use the defence of protection of others.

Williams (1987)

D was on a bus when he saw what he thought was a man assaulting a youth. In fact it was a man trying to arrest the youth for mugging an old lady. D got off the bus and asked what was happening. The man said that he was a police officer arresting the youth, but when D asked him to show his police ID card he could not do so. There was then a struggle between D and the man in which the man was injured. D was convicted of assault after the judge directed them that D only had a defence if his mistake was a reasonable one.

The Court of Appeal quashed his conviction because the jury should have been told that if they thought the mistake was genuine they should judge the defendant according to his genuine mistaken view of the facts, regardless of whether this mistake was reasonable or unreasonable.

Section 76 of the Criminal Justice and Immigration Act 2008 puts the decision in *Williams* onto a statutory footing. The section states:

's 76(3) The question whether the degree of force used by D was reasonable in the circumstances is to be decided by reference to the circumstances as D believed them to be …

76(4) If D claims to have held a particular belief as regards the existence of any circumstances –

(a) the reasonableness or otherwise of that belief is relevant to the question whether D genuinely held it; but

(b) if it is determined that D did genuinely hold it, D is entitled to rely on it for the purposes of subsection (3), whether or not –

(i) it was mistaken, or
(ii) (if it was mistaken) the mistake
   was a reasonable one to have
   made.' 〞

So in each situation, the important point is to establish the facts as the defendant genuinely believed them to be. If the defendant genuinely made a mistake then he is to be judged on the facts as he believed them to be. This is so, even if the mistake was unreasonable.

Drunken mistake

Section 76(5) of the Criminal Justice and Immigration Act 2008 makes it clear that a defendant cannot rely on any mistaken belief, if that mistake is made due to the defendant being voluntarily intoxicated.

If the defendant made the mistake because he had voluntarily got drunk or taken drugs, and makes a mistake because of his intoxicated state, then he cannot rely on his mistaken belief. An example would be where a defendant had taken drugs which caused hallucinations causing him or her to believe that they were being attacked by snakes. If the defendant then assaults someone believing that that person is a snake, then the defendant cannot use the defence of self-defence. He genuinely believes he is being attacked by a snake, but this mistake has been caused by the defendant's voluntary intoxication.

9.7.3 Problems in the law on self-defence

Is force necessary?

The first point to be decided if the defence is to succeed is whether force was necessary. This is a question for the jury. In many cases it is straightforward. For example, if the facts are that the victim had a knife in his hand and came towards the defendant saying 'I'm going to slash you to pieces', it is quite clear that force is necessary in self-defence in this situation.

In other situations it is more difficult to decide if force was necessary, as the jury has to decide the position that the defendant honestly believed existed. For example, what if, while walking home in the dark, the defendant sees a large man shaking a club above his head in a threatening way coming towards him. D thinks it is necessary to defend himself and punches the man hard, knocking him to the ground. However in reality, the 'large man' was an elderly woman, and the 'shaking a club' was the woman trying to open an umbrella above her head.

The jury has to decide if D honestly believed he was being threatened. If they decide that he did, then he has the defence of self-defence. He can use force, even though there was no actual threat to him. In this situation an innocent person (the woman trying to open her umbrella) has been punched but D's behaviour is not a criminal offence.

Section 76 of the Criminal Justice and Immigration Act 2008 makes it clear that, provided the mistake was not made due to intoxication, then D can rely on his mistake. Provided the jury decides that D did believe there was a large man shaking a club at him, D has the defence of self-defence. This is so even if the mistake was not a reasonable one to make.

Pre-emptive strike

Another point is whether a person has to wait until they are attacked before they can use force. The law appears to be clear that they can act to prevent force. It is not necessary for an attack to have started. In the example above, no attack had started. D thought he was about to be attacked and reacted to save himself from being attacked. This appears to be a sensible rule, since it would be ridiculous if a person had to wait until they were stabbed or shot before being allowed to defend themselves.

In *Attorney-General's Reference (No 2 of 1983)* (1984) it was held that someone who fears an attack can make preparations to defend himself. This is so even if the preparations involve breaches of the law.

Attorney-General's Reference (No 2 of 1983) (1984)

D's shop had been attacked and damaged by rioters. Fearing further attacks, he made petrol bombs. D was charged with possessing an explosive substance in such circumstances as to give rise to a reasonable suspicion that he did not have it for a lawful object (contrary to s 4(10) of the Explosive Substances Act 1883). D pleaded self-defence and the jury acquitted him. The Attorney-General referred the point of law to the Court of Appeal which decided that it was correct that D could make preparations in self-defence.

Excessive force

A major problem is where a defendant uses excessive force in self-defence. If this is so then he cannot use self-defence as a defence. If he is charged with any assault charge, the judge can take any issues of self-defence into consideration when passing sentence. However, where such a defendant is charged with murder, he must be given a life sentence.

This was seen in the cases of *Clegg* (1995) and *Martin (Anthony)* (2002). The facts of both cases are set out in section 6.2.4.

However, the Government consultation paper, *Murder, manslaughter and infanticide: proposals for reform of the law* has a proposal for a partial defence of 'killing in response to a fear of serious violence'. This would be available to someone who overreacts to what they perceive as an imminent threat and would reduce the charge to manslaughter. If this proposal becomes law, then defendants in cases such as *Clegg* and *Martin (Anthony)* would be able to use this partial defence.

Relevance of D's characteristics

Another point is whether D's characteristics can be taken into account in deciding if D thought that he needed to defend himself.

In *Martin (Anthony)* (2002) the Court of Appeal held that psychiatric evidence that D had a condition entailing that he perceived much greater danger than the average person was *not* relevant to the question of whether D had used reasonable force. One of the reasons for this decision was that self-defence is usually raised in cases of minor assault and it would be 'wholly disproportionate to encourage medical disputes in cases of that sort'.

Also in *Cairns* (2005) the Court of Appeal followed the decision in *Martin* (2002) and held that when deciding whether D had used reasonable force in self-defence, it was not appropriate to take into account whether D was suffering from a psychiatric condition (such as paranoid schizophrenia) which may have caused him to have delusions that he was about to be attacked.

It is difficult to know whether these decisions are still effective following the passing of the Criminal Justice and Immigration Act 2008. Section 76 of that Act makes it clear that the question of whether the degree of force used by D was reasonable in the circumstances, is to be decided by reference to the circumstances as D believed them to be. The section continues that if the jury (or magistrates) decide that D did genuinely have a belief in the existence of particular circumstances, then D is entitled to rely on it.

If D's psychiatric condition makes him genuinely believe that force is necessary and the courts accept that he believed this, then surely, under the wording of the Act, D must be able to claim self-defence. However, it is doubtful that this is the interpretation the courts will use. It would have been helpful if the Act had made it clear whether a psychiatric condition which caused D to believe in the existence of circumstances was to be taken into account or not.

9.8 Consent as a defence

Consent may be a defence to battery and other offences against the person. However, it is never a defence to murder or to situations where serious injury is caused.

Consent is strictly speaking not a defence, as where the other person consents, there is no offence. For example, where the other person consents to being touched, there is no battery as there is no unlawful force. This is illustrated by *Donovan* (1934).

Donovan (1934)

D caned a 17-year-old girl for the purpose of sexual gratification. This caused bruising and he was convicted of indecent assault and a common assault. D appealed on the basis that V had consented to the act. His conviction was quashed.

A more extreme case illustrating the same point is *Slingsby* (1995) where the defendant was charged with manslaughter.

Slingsby (1995)

D was charged with involuntary manslaughter by an unlawful act. D and the victim had taken part in sexual activity which was described as 'vigorous' but which had taken place with the victim's consent. During this, a signet ring which D was wearing caused small cuts to the victim and this led to blood poisoning from which she died. The victim's consent meant that there was no battery or other form of assault and so D was held to be not guilty of manslaughter as there was no unlawful act.

Real consent

There must, however, be true consent. In *Tabassum* (2000) the defendant had persuaded women to allow him to measure their breasts for the purpose of preparing a database for sale to doctors. The women were fully aware of the nature of the acts he proposed to do, but said

they consented only because they thought that D had either medical qualifications or medical training. The Court of Appeal approved the trial judge's direction when he said:

> 'I should prefer myself to say that consent in such cases does not exist at all, because the act consented to is not the act done. Consent to a surgical operation or examination is not consent to sexual connection or indecent behaviour.'

The fact that the victim submits to the defendant's conduct through fear does not mean that the consent is real. This was shown by *Olugboja* (1982).

Olugboja (1982)

The victim had already been raped by D's companion and seen her friend raped by the same man. When D tried to have sexual intercourse with her, she submitted. D claimed that this meant she had consented. The Court of Appeal held that there was a difference between real consent and mere submission. It was for the jury to decide if the consent was real.

In *Dica* (2004), where consent was given to sexual intercourse without knowledge of the fact that the defendant was HIV positive, the Court of Appeal held that there was no consent to the risk of infection.

Dica (2004)

D, who knew he was HIV positive, had relationships with two women. They had unprotected sex with him and both became infected. They claimed that they did not know he was HIV positive and that if they had they would not have agreed to unprotected sex. D was charged with an offence under s 20 of the Offences Against the Person Act 1861. At his trial, the judge did not allow the issue of consent to go to the jury, so the Court of Appeal quashed the conviction but ordered a re-trial.

The decision in this case makes it clear that even though V has consented to sexual intercourse, D can be guilty of an offence under s 20 OAPA 1861. This overruled the decision in *Clarence* (1888), where unknown to the wife, the husband was suffering from a venereal disease and the wife became infected when they had sexual intercourse. It was held that a wife's consent to sexual intercourse with her husband meant that there was no assault.

9.8.1 Implied consent

There are situations in which the courts imply consent to minor touchings, which would otherwise be a battery. These are the everyday situations where there is a crowd of people and it is impossible not to have some contact. In *Wilson v Pringle* (1987) it was held that the ordinary 'jostlings' of everyday life were not battery. Nobody can complain of the jostling which is inevitable from his presence in, for example, a supermarket, an underground station or a busy street; nor can a person who attends a party complain if his hand is seized in friendship, or even if his back is (within reason) slapped.

This also applies to contact sports. When a person takes part in sport such as rugby or judo, he is agreeing to the contact which is part of that sport. However, if the contact goes beyond what is allowed within the rules then it is possible for an offence to be committed. For example, a rugby player consents to a tackle within the rules of the game, but he does not consent to an opposition player stamping on his head.

The breach of the rules of the sport must be a serious one. The Court of Appeal said in *Barnes* (2004) that where an injury is caused during a match, then a criminal prosecution should be reserved for those situations where the conduct was sufficiently grave to be properly categorised as criminal.

Barnes (2004)

D made a late tackle on V during an amateur football match. V suffered a serious leg injury. D's conviction of an offence under s 20 OAPA 1861 was quashed.

9.8.2 Consent to minor injuries

There have been arguments as to whether consent could be a defence to an offence under s 47 OAPA 1861. It used to be thought that consent could be a defence where the injuries were not serious. However, in *Attorney-General's Reference (No 6 of 1980)* (1981) where two young men agreed to fight in the street to settle their differences following a quarrel, the Court of Appeal held that consent could not be a defence to such an action as it was not in the public interest. They said:

> 'It is not in the public interest that people should try to cause, or should cause, each other bodily harm for no good reason. Minor struggles are another matter. So, in our judgment, it is immaterial whether the act occurs in private or public; it is an assault if actual bodily harm is intended and/or caused. This means that most fights will be unlawful regardless of consent.'

So it is now accepted that consent is not a defence to a s 47 offence, unless the situation is one of the exceptions which have been recognised by the courts. In *Attorney-General's Reference (No 6 of 1980)* the Court of Appeal gave the following list of exceptions:

> 'properly conducted games and sports, lawful chastisement or correction, reasonable surgical interference, dangerous exhibitions, etc.'

The court added 'etc' to the end of the list to show that there may be other situations where consent would be permitted to be a defence. It is a question of whether it is in the public interest or not.

In deciding what was in the public interest, the courts have come to decisions which are difficult to reconcile. In *Brown* (1993) the House of Lords held that consent was not a defence to sado-masochistic acts done by homosexuals, even though all the participants were adult and the injuries inflicted were transitory and trifling.

Brown (1993)

Five men in a group of consenting adult sado-masochists were convicted of offences of assault causing actual bodily harm (s 47 OAPA 1861) and malicious wounding (s 20 OAPA 1861). They had carried out acts which included applying stinging nettles to the genital area and inserting map pins or fish hooks into the penises of each other. All the victims had consented and none had needed medical attention. Their convictions were upheld by the House of Lords.

The Law Lords clearly made this decision as a matter of public policy. Lord Templeman actually said:

" 'The question whether the defence of consent should be extended to the consequences of sado-masochistic encounters can only be decided by consideration of policy and public interest ... Society is entitled and bound to protect itself against a cult of violence.' "

However, in *Wilson* (1996), the Court of Appeal held that where a defendant branded his initials on his wife's buttocks with a hot knife at her request, this was not an unlawful act, even though she had to seek medical attention for the burns which were caused. It held it was not in the public interest that such consensual behaviour should be criminalised. This was a situation of 'personal adornment' like having a tattoo.

9.8.3 Mistaken belief in consent

Where the defendant genuinely, but mistakenly, believes that the victim is consenting then there is a defence to an assault.

In this area the decisions of the courts are even more difficult to reconcile with the general principle that 'it is not in the public interest that people should try to cause, or should cause, each other bodily harm for no good reason'. In the following two cases the courts held that mistaken belief in consent was a defence to the offences charged.

Jones (1986)

Two schoolboys aged 14 and 15 were tossed into the air by older youths. One victim suffered a broken arm and the other a ruptured spleen. The defendants claimed they believed that the two victims consented to the activity. The Court of Appeal quashed their convictions for offences under s 20 OAPA 1861 because the judge had not allowed the issue of mistaken belief in consent to go to the jury. The court held that a genuine mistaken belief in consent to 'rough and undisciplined horseplay' could be a defence, even if that belief was unreasonable.

A similar decision was reached in *Aitken* (1992) where RAF officers poured white spirit over a colleague who was wearing a fire-resistant flying suit, but who was asleep and drunk at the time that this was done. He suffered 35 per cent burns. Their convictions under s 20 were quashed as the mistaken belief in the victim's consent should have been left to the jury.

9.8.4 Need for a defence of consent

It is important to allow a defence of consent in some situations. For example, if there was no defence of consent, then contact sports would all be illegal. This is why the Court of Appeal in *Attorney-General's Reference (No 6 of 1980)* (1981) stated that, although consent was not a defence to street fights, there were exceptions where consent was a defence.

The list of exceptions that the Court of Appeal gave in that case was 'properly conducted games and sports, lawful chastisement or correction, reasonable surgical interference, dangerous exhibitions, etc'. These exceptions are based on public policy.

If there was no defence of consent in 'properly conducted games and sports' then team games such as football, rugby and hockey could never be played. There would also be a large number of individual sports which would be prevented, eg judo, karate and boxing.

The important phrase in the judgment is 'properly conducted games and sports'. There has to be a distinction between playing within the rules and behaviour which is outside the rules. A deliberate 'off-the-ball' tackle aiming at another player's legs with the intention of causing serious injury must surely be considered as criminal behaviour. A player who is injured in this way has not consented to such behaviour.

The case of *Barnes* (2004) set out matters which were to be considered in deciding whether an assault in the course of a match was criminal. The court said that in deciding whether conduct in the course of a sport is criminal or not, the following factors should be considered:

- Intentional infliction of injury will always be criminal.
- For reckless infliction of injury, did the injury occur during actual play, or in a moment of temper or over-excitement when play had ceased?
- 'Off-the-ball' injuries are more likely to be criminal.
- The fact that the play is within the rules and practice of the game and does not go beyond it will be a firm indication that what has happened is not criminal.

By applying these factors a good balance should be achieved between allowing contact sports to be played without unnecessary restrictions on their rules and upholding the criminal law on assault. Only those who

deliberately inflict injury or who go beyond the rules of the game should be liable under the criminal law.

Medical procedures

Another exception where consent is allowed as a defence is 'reasonable surgical interference'. Clearly where the surgery is needed to save the patient's life or to improve a patient's health in some way, then consent to the operation is a defence to any charge of assault.

Mentally capable adults can consent to reasonable medical treatment or they can refuse it. If they refuse consent, then if surgery or other treatment was performed it would be a criminal act. For example, if a person refuses a blood transfusion because of their religious beliefs then such treatment cannot be given.

If a patient is unconscious so that their consent cannot be asked, medical staff will try to obtain consent from relatives. If this is not possible then, where treatment is necessary and must be performed quickly, such an operation can be performed without actual consent.

9.8.5 Problems in the law on consent

It is difficult to reconcile the decisions by the courts in cases on consent. For example compare the case of *Brown* (1994) with the case of *Wilson* (1997).

In *Brown* the House of Lords ruled that consent could not be a defence to sado-masochistic behaviour between consenting adult homosexuals. In *Wilson* the Court of Appeal ruled that consent could be a defence where a husband had branded his wife's buttocks with his initials. These decisions were made despite the fact that none of the 'victims' in *Brown* had needed medical attention whereas the wife in *Wilson* had had to receive medical attention.

This suggests that the courts are prepared to condone acts where the parties are consenting adult heterosexuals, but not where the parties are consenting adult homosexuals. Are the courts trying to impose their own moral values on the law?

There are also contradictory decisions within cases involving heterosexuals. This was shown by *Emmett* (1999).

Emmett (1999)

'High-risk' sexual activity between a man and a woman had resulted in the woman suffering haemorrhages to her eyes on one occasion and burns to her breast on another occasion. The Court of Appeal held that consent could not be a defence.

The basis for this decision was that consent cannot be a defence where the harm caused is more than 'transient or trivial' injury. Yet in *Wilson* (1997) the Court of Appeal had accepted consent as a defence even though the wife had needed medical attention.

Policy considerations

Public policy issues were important considerations in the decision of the House of Lords in *Brown*. In the judgment in *Brown* it was said that:

> 'In principle there is a difference between violence which is incidental and violence which is inflicted for the indulgence of cruelty.'

In a civilised society, cruelty should not be tolerated. This was a main reason for the House of Lords' decision that victims could not consent to injuries caused by the deliberate infliction of cruelty.

The Law Lords also felt that the violence involved the degradation of the victims. They were treated in a humiliating and uncaring way. In addition, there was also no way of knowing what injuries might result to the victim from the conduct.

All these points meant that it was in the public interest for the law to interfere with the freedom of individuals to do what they chose.

Horseplay

Another area of law where the courts are prepared to accept consent as a defence is in what is called 'horseplay'. That is where those of a similar age use 'friendly' violence to each other. This is seen in the playground of schools where boys, in particular, often push each other or trip each other up in play.

Even where such behaviour results in serious injury the courts have ruled that consent can be a defence. This is the legal basis that the aggressor does not have the *mens rea* for assault. Even more surprisingly, the courts have held that honest belief in consent provides a defence although the victim in fact has not consented.

This is shown in the two cases *Jones and another* (1986) and *Aitken* (1992). In *Jones* two schoolboys aged 14 and 15 were tossed into the air by older youths, causing them serious injuries. In *Aitken* the victim suffered 35 per cent burns when RAF officers poured white spirit over him when he was asleep and drunk. In both cases the courts accepted that the defence of consent was available, even though there was a mistaken belief in the existence of consent.

When these cases are contrasted with *Brown* (1994) and *Emmett* (1999) above, there appear to be further inconsistencies in the law. Why should consent be refused as a defence for disapproved types of sexual behaviour and yet allowed for horseplay which results in serious injury, even where the victim was not actually consenting?

9.8.6 Consent and sexual offences

There are specific problems for offences under the Sexual Offences Act 2003 as the defence of consent is not always available. One such offence is s 5 of the Act which covers the offence of rape of a child aged under 13. For the purposes of this offence a girl aged under 13 is presumed never to be able to consent to sexual intercourse. The offence is also a strict liability one.

These two facts mean that if a 15-year-old boy has consensual sex with a girl whom he genuinely believes is the same age as himself, but is in fact only 12, he will be guilty of rape of a child aged under 13.

This situation occurred in *G* (2008). At the appeal to the Court of Appeal, the court had stated that consent was relevant only to sentence. G appealed against his conviction on the basis that his human rights had been breached. The House of Lords rejected his appeal by a majority of three judges to two. The fact that two House of Lords Judges would have decided the case in favour of the defendant shows how difficult this area of law is.

9.8.7 Consent and euthanasia

There is also a problem that no one can consent to their own death. This means that if a terminally ill patient wishes to die, they must take their own life. If anyone kills them, it is murder. Even if anyone assists them to take their own life, that person is guilty of the offence of assisting suicide. This was decided in *R (on the application of Pretty) v DPP* (2001).

> ### *R (on the application of Pretty) v DPP (2001)*
>
> Mrs Pretty was suffering from motor neurone disease. As a result she was becoming more and more incapable of movement. She knew that eventually she would suffocate to death. She wanted her husband to be able to assist her to take her own life when she felt that her life had become intolerable.
>
> She applied to the courts for a judicial declaration that, if her husband assisted her to commit suicide, he would not be prosecuted. The House of Lords refused the declaration on the basis that any assistance of the husband would be a criminal act.

This decision leads to the situation where the law recognises that people are entitled to take their own life and do not commit any crime by trying to do so. But in cases where the person who wishes to commit suicide is physically incapable of doing it, then they are denied their wishes as anyone who helps them will be guilty of an offence.

Note that prior to 1961 it was a criminal offence to commit suicide, so that if the person was not successful then they would be prosecuted for attempting to commit suicide.

Key facts

Offence	Can consent be a defence?	Comment/case
Murder s 18 OAPA 1861	Never a defence to these crimes.	Not in the public interest.
s 20 OAPA 1861 s 47 OAPA 1861	Generally not a defence.	Not in public interest, eg fighting (*Attorney-General's Reference (No 6 of 1980)* (1981)) or sado-masochistic acts (*Brown* (1993)).
	BUT there are exceptions where consent is a defence.	Properly conducted sports, surgery, dangerous exhibitions (*Jones* (1986)) or personal adornment such as tattoos (*Wilson* (1996)).
Battery	Always allowed as a defence.	Consent can also be implied to the 'jostlings' of everyday life (*Wilson v Pringle* (1986)).

Figure 9.6 Key facts chart on consent as a defence

Activity

Explain whether there would be a defence available in the following situations.

1. Anwar hears Ben shouting at Carly, 'I'm going to get you'. Anwar then sees Ben running towards Carly holding something shiny in his hand. Anwar thinks this is a knife and that Ben is about to stab Carly. Anwar rugby-tackles Ben bringing him crashing down onto the pavement and causing Ben to suffer a broken jaw. In fact Ben did not have a knife, but was holding a mobile phone in his hand.

2. Ella wants to have a tattoo of her boyfriend Damien's initials on her arm. She gets the tattooing equipment from a friend and asks Damien to use it on her arm. Damien does this. Ella suffers a serious infection from the tattooing and is left with bad scars on her arm.

3. Freya is playing in a hockey match. Using her hockey stick, she tries to take the ball from Galina, a player for the opposing side. Unfortunately, this causes Galina to trip and fall over, spraining her wrist.

4. Hans has drunk six pints of beer. While he is walking home, he stumbles and nearly falls. He is saved from falling by Shivan who catches hold of him. Hans thinks that Shivan is trying to assault him and he lashes out with his fist, punching Shivan in the mouth and causing bruising.

5. Nick plays rugby for his college team. During one match Nick is tackled very hard by Dave. Nick is angry about this and makes sure that every time Dave has the ball, he (Nick) tackles Dave hard. When they are leaving the pitch at the end of the match Nick pushes Dave. What defence(s) might be available to Nick if he is charged with battery in respect of the tackles and the push?

Examination questions

1. 'The law on consent as a defence to offences against the person recognises that the causing of deliberate harm may sometimes be justified.'

Consider the truth of this statement.

(OCR, Unit 2572, January 2008)

2. Sinita and Mina share a flat. One night Sinita finds Mina kissing Sinita's boyfriend, Alberto. She picks up a glass of water, raises it in the air and shouts at Mina, 'You hussy, I'll kill you!' She tries to throw the water at Mina but the glass slips from her hand and strikes Mina in the face, cutting her forehead.

Alberto is so angry that he pushes Sinita and she falls backwards over a stool onto the floor and is knocked unconscious for a few seconds. When Sinita recovers consciousness she is still dizzy and stumbles towards Mina, knocking her onto the floor. Mina suffers a fractured arm.

Later that evening when Sinita is sleeping, Mina gets a pair of scissors and cuts off Sinita's ponytail in an act of revenge.

Discuss the potential criminal liability of Sinita, Alberto and Mina for the above incidents.

(OCR, Unit G143, January 2008)

3. Wayne is the captain of the Northport United football team. During an important match against their local rivals, Wayne is involved in a clash of heads in an incident with an opposing player, Andrew. Wayne receives a nasty bruise above his left eye and is badly concussed. Wayne insists on continuing playing after treatment with a cold sponge, but is obviously still in a very dazed condition. A few minutes later Wayne jumps wildly into a foul tackle on Andrew. Andrew is carried off in agony and x-rays later reveal that he has a broken ankle.

Evaluate the accuracy of each of the four statements A, B, C and D individually, as they apply to the facts in the above scenario.

Statement A: Andrew is liable for ABH, s 47 OAPA 1861 for the bruise suffered by Wayne.

Statement B: Wayne is liable for GBH, s 18 OAPA 1861 for the broken ankle sustained by Andrew.

Statement C: Andrew has a defence of consent for any charge brought by Wayne.

Statement D: Wayne has a defence of automatism for any charge brought by Andrew.

(OCR, Specimen Paper)

Chapter 10

Theft

Theft is defined in s 1 of the Theft Act 1968.

The Act in the next five sections helps with the meaning of the words or phrases in the definition. This is done in the order that the words or phrases appear in the definition, making it easy to remember the section numbers. They are:

- s 2 – dishonestly (part of the *mens rea*)
- s 3 – appropriates (part of the *actus reus*)
- s 4 – property (part of the *actus reus*)
- s 5 – belonging to another (part of the *actus reus*)
- s 6 – with the intention of permanently depriving the other of it (part of the *mens rea*).

Remember that the offence is in s 1. A person charged with theft is always charged with stealing 'contrary to s 1 of the Theft Act 1968'. Sections 2–6 are definition sections explaining s 1. They do not themselves create any offence.

The *actus reus* of theft is made up of the three elements in the phrase 'appropriates property belonging to another'. So, to prove the *actus reus* it has to be shown that there was appropriation by the defendant of something which is property within the definition of the Act and which, at the time of the appropriation, belonged to another.

There are two elements which must be proved for the *mens rea* of theft. These are that the appropriation of the property must be done 'dishonestly' and there must be the intention of permanently depriving the other person of it.

Figure 10.1 The elements of theft

10.1 'Appropriation'

The more obvious situations of theft involve a physical taking, for example a pickpocket taking a wallet from someone's pocket. But appropriation is much wider than this.

Section 3(1) states that:

> 'Any assumption by a person of the rights of an owner amounts to an appropriation, and this includes, where

he has come by the property (innocently or not) without stealing it, any later assumption of a right to it by keeping or dealing with it as owner.'

The important words are 'any assumption by a person of the rights of an owner amounts to appropriation'. The rights of the owner include selling the property or destroying it as well as possessing it, consuming it, using it, lending it or hiring it out. So for there to be appropriation, the thief must do something which assumes (takes over) one of the owner's rights.

Taking goods from a shelf in a supermarket and placing them in one's pocket or own shopping bag is a clear example of an appropriation. This is clearly assuming the rights of an owner. It has also been decided that the action of taking the goods from a shelf in a supermarket is of itself an appropriation. The issue of the shop's consent to this normal action of shopping is discussed at section 10.1.1.

The rights of an owner also include the right to sell property. An appropriation by assuming the right to sell is demonstrated by the case of *Pitham v Hehl* (1977).

Pitham v Hehl (1977)

D had sold furniture belonging to another person. This was held to be an appropriation. The offer to sell was an assumption of the rights of an owner and the appropriation took place at that point. It did not matter whether the furniture was removed from the house or not. Even if the owner was never deprived of the property D had still appropriated it by assuming the rights of the owner to offer the furniture for sale.

The right to destroy property is also an owner's right. This means that if D destroys property belonging to another person, D can be charged with theft, although D has also, of course, committed the offence of criminal damage.

Theft can also be charged where D does not destroy the other's property but throws it away. For example, if D threw a waterproof watch belonging to another into the sea, this could be theft. Again, only the owner has the right to do this to the property.

The wording in s 3(1) is 'any assumption by a person of *the* rights of an owner'. One question which the courts have had to deal with is whether the assumption has to be of *all* of the rights or whether it can just be of *any* of the rights. This was considered in *Morris* (1983).

Morris (1983)

D had switched the price labels of two items on the shelf in a supermarket. He had then put one of the items, which now had a lower price on it, into a basket provided by the store for shoppers and taken the item to the checkout, but had not gone through the checkout when he was arrested. His conviction for theft was upheld.

Lord Roskill in the House of Lords stated that:

'It is enough for the prosecution if they have proved … the assumption of any of the rights of the owner of the goods in question.'

So it is clear that there does not have to be an assumption of all the rights. This is a sensible decision since in many cases the defendant will not have assumed all of the rights. Quite often, only one right will have been assumed, usually the right of possession. In *Morris* the right was the owner's right to put a price label on the goods.

10.1.1 Consent to the appropriation

Can a defendant appropriate an item when it has been given to them by the owner? This is an area which has caused major problems. The Theft Act

1968 does not state that the appropriation has to be without the consent of the owner. So, what is the position where the owner has allowed the defendant to take something because the owner thought that the defendant was taking what was owed to him? This point was considered in *Lawrence* (1971).

Lawrence (1971)

An Italian student, who spoke very little English, arrived at Victoria Station and showed an address to Lawrence who was a taxi driver. The journey should have cost 50p, but Lawrence told him it was expensive. The student got out a £1 note and offered it to the driver. Lawrence said it was not enough and so the student opened his wallet and allowed Lawrence to help himself to another £6. Lawrence put forward the argument that he had not appropriated the money as the student had consented to him taking it. Both the Court of Appeal and the House of Lords rejected this argument and held that there was appropriation in this situation.

You can't have it – the House of Lords says I've appropriated it.

The issue of consent to the taking was also considered in *Morris*. This issue is important in shop cases, as the whole system of supermarket shopping relies on the customer taking goods from shelves. This means that there is an implied consent from shops operating a self-service style of shopping to customers removing items from shelves or rails.

In *Morris* Lord Roskill stated *obiter dicta* that where there is:

> 'an honest customer taking goods from a shelf to put in his or her trolley to take to the checkpoint there to pay the proper price, I am unable to see that any of these actions involves any assumption by the shopper of the rights of the supermarket.'

This does seem a common sense point of view. However, it was only *obiter* and, when the point was considered again in the case of *Gomez* (1993), the House of Lords rejected Lord Roskills's view.

The effect of the decision in *Gomez* is that any removal of goods from a shelf in a shop is an appropriation. However, the complete offence of theft will only be committed if the person appropriating the goods has the required *mens rea* for theft.

Gomez (1993)

D was the assistant manager of a shop. He persuaded the manager to sell electrical goods worth over £17,000 to an accomplice and to accept payment by two cheques, telling the manager they were as good as cash. The cheques were stolen and had no value. D was charged and convicted of theft of the goods.

The Court of Appeal quashed the conviction relying on the judgment in *Morris* (1983) that there had to be 'adverse interference' for there to be appropriation. They decided that the manager's consent to and authorisation of the transaction meant there was no appropriation at the moment of taking the goods.

The case was appealed to the House of Lords with the Court of Appeal certifying, as a point of law of general public importance, the following question:

'When theft is alleged and that which is alleged to be stolen passes to the defendant with the consent of the owner, but that has been obtained by a false representation, has:

(a) an appropriation within the meaning of s 1(1) of the Theft Act 1968 taken place, or

(b) must such a passing of property necessarily involve an element of adverse interference with or usurpation of some right of the owner?'

The House of Lords, by a majority of four to one, answered (a) 'yes'. An appropriation has taken place. They answered (b) 'no'. There was no need for adverse interference with or usurpation of some right of the owner. In other words, to be guilty of theft, the defendant need not do anything contrary to the owner's wishes. They pointed out that the decision in the case of *Lawrence* (1971) ruled that an act may be an appropriation even if it is done with the consent of the owner.

10.1.2 Consent without deception

So does the decision in *Gomez* (1993) extend to situations where a person has given property to another without any deception being made? This was the problem raised in the case of *Hinks* (2000).

Hinks (2000)

D was a 38-year-old woman who had befriended a very naïve man with a low IQ. He was, however, mentally capable of understanding the concept of ownership and of making a valid gift. Over a period of about eight months D accompanied the man on numerous occasions to his building society where he withdrew money. The total was about £60,000 and this money was deposited in D's account. The man also gave D a television set. The judge directed the jury to consider whether the man was so mentally incapable that D herself realised that ordinary and decent people would regard it as dishonest to accept a gift from him. D was convicted of theft of the money and the television set.

On appeal, it was argued that if the gift was valid, the acceptance of it could not be theft. The House of Lords dismissed the appeal by a majority of three judges to two. Four of the judges decided that, even though the property was a valid gift, there was an appropriation. Lord Hobhouse dissented, ruling that there could not be an appropriation in these circumstances. Lord Hutton, although agreeing with the majority on the point of law, dissented on whether the conduct showed dishonesty.

A major argument against the ruling in *Hinks* is that in civil law the gift was valid and the £60,000 and the television set belonged to the defendant. Lord Steyn, in the leading judgment, accepted that this was the situation but he considered it was irrelevant to the decision.

10.1.3 Appropriation at one point in time

Another effect of the decision in *Gomez* is that the appropriation is viewed as occurring at one point in time. This is illustrated by the case of *Atakpu and Abrahams* (1994).

Atakpu and Abrahams (1994).

The defendants hired cars in Germany and Belgium using false driving licences and passports. They were arrested at Dover and charged with theft. The Court of Appeal quashed their convictions because the moment of appropriation under the law in *Gomez* was when they obtained the cars. So the thefts had occurred outside the jurisdiction of the English courts and as the defendants had already stolen the cars in Germany and Belgium, keeping and driving them in England was not an appropriation.

10.1.4 A later assumption of a right

Section 3(1) makes it clear that there can also be an appropriation where the defendant acquires property without stealing it, but then later decides to keep or deal with the property as owner. The appropriation in this type of situation takes place at the point of 'keeping' or 'dealing'.

This could occur where the defendant hires a video from a shop, but instead of returning it decides to keep it. He is acting as though he is the owner with the right to keep the video.

Dealing in the property could occur where the defendant borrows a cycle (or other property) but then sells it or gives it away. This can also happen where D hires a car. If he sells it instead of returning it, then he has dealt with it as an owner.

10.2 'Property'

For there to be theft the defendant must have appropriated 'property'. Section 4 gives a very comprehensive definition of property which means that almost anything can be stolen. The definition is in s 4(1) of the Theft Act 1968:

> '"Property" includes money and all other property real or personal, including things in action and other intangible property.'

Activity

Applying the law

Discuss whether there has been an appropriation in each of the following situations.

1. Jake has an argument with his neighbour. When his neighbour is out, Jake holds an auction of the neighbour's garden tools. The neighbour returns before any of the tools are taken away.
2. Saskia goes shopping at the local supermarket and takes her five-year-old son, Tom, with her. While at the checkout Tom takes some bars of chocolate and puts them in his pocket. Saskia does not realise Tom has done this until she finds the chocolate when they get home. Saskia decides that she will not take the chocolate back to the supermarket.
3. The owner of a shop asks Parvati, who is a lorry driver, to pick up a load of computer equipment and take it to a warehouse. Parvati agrees to do this but, after collecting the equipment, she decides that she will not take it to the warehouse but will instead sell it.
4. Otto, aged 18, is infatuated with Harriet, a married woman aged 32. Otto uses his student loan to buy expensive presents for Harriet. She knows he is a student and has very little money but she accepts the gifts from him.

This section lists five types of items which are included in the definition of 'property'. These are:

- money
- real property
- personal property
- things in action
- other intangible property.

In this list money is self-explanatory. It means coins and banknotes of any currency. Personal

Key cases

Case	Law
Pitham and Hehl (1977)	Selling property of another is appropriation of that property.
Morris (1983)	Switching price labels on goods in a shop is an appropriation of those goods at that point. House of Lords: appropriation is an assumption of any of the rights of the owner.
Lawrence (1971)	Where V does not validly consent to the taking there can be an appropriation even though V apparently consented.
Gomez (1993)	Where V allowed D to take goods believing that D had paid for them, there can still be an appropriation if D has used worthless cheques so payment has not in fact been made.
Hinks (2000)	Even though there has been a gift of property from V to D, there can still be an appropriation where V suffers from mental incapacity and D is aware of it.

Figure 10.2 Case chart on appropriation

property is also straightforward as it covers all moveable items. Books, CDs, jewellery, clothes, cars are obvious examples, but it also includes very large items such as aeroplanes or tanks. It also includes very small trivial items such as a sheet of paper. It has even been held in *Kelly and Lindsay* (1998) that dead bodies and body parts can be personal property for the purposes of theft.

Kelly and Lindsay (1998)

Kelly was a sculptor who asked Lindsay to take body parts from the Royal College of Surgeons where he worked as a laboratory assistant. Kelly made casts of the parts. They were convicted of theft and appealed on the point of law that body parts were not property. The Court of Appeal held that, though a dead body was not normally property within the definition of the Theft Act 1968, the body parts were property as they had acquired 'different attributes by virtue of the application of skill, such as dissection or preservation techniques, for exhibition or teaching purposes.'

10.2.1 Real property

Real property is the legal term for land and buildings. Under s 4(1) land can be stolen, but s 4(2) states that this can only be done in three circumstances. These are where:

- a trustee or personal representative takes land in breach of his duties as a trustee or personal representative;
- someone not in possession of the land severs anything forming part of the land from the land;
- a tenant takes a fixture or structure from the land let to him.

Under the second point, it is theft to dig up turf from someone's lawn or to dismantle a wall and take the bricks. In 1972 a man was prosecuted for stealing Cleckheaton railway station by dismantling it and removing it. He was in fact acquitted by the jury as he said he was acting under a claim of right, but there was no doubt that the station could be property under the Theft Act 1968 definition.

10.2.2 Things in action

A thing in action is a right which can be enforced against another person by an action in law. The right itself is property under the definition in s 4. An example is a bank account. The bank does not keep coins or banknotes for each customer's account in a separate box! Instead the customer has a right to payment of the amount in his account. So, if D causes the bank to debit another person's account he has appropriated a thing in action. If he does this dishonestly and with the intention to permanently deprive the other of it, then D is guilty of theft.

A cheque itself is a thing in action, but it is also a piece of paper which is property which can be stolen, and it is a 'valuable security' which can also be stolen under the definition of property.

10.2.3 Other intangible property

This refers to other rights which have no physical presence but can be stolen under the Theft Act 1968. In *Attorney-General for Hong Kong v Chan Nai-Keung* (1987) an export quota for textiles was intangible property which could be stolen. A patent is also intangible property which can be stolen.

However, there are some types of intangible property which have been held not to be property within the Theft Act 1968 definition. In *Oxford v Moss* (1979) knowledge of the questions on an examination paper was held not to be property.

Oxford v Moss (1979)

D was a university student who acquired a proof of an examination paper he was due to sit. It was accepted that D did not intend to permanently deprive the university of the piece of paper on which the questions were printed. But he was charged with theft of confidential information (ie the knowledge of the questions). He was found not guilty.

10.2.4 Things which cannot be stolen

There are some things which cannot be stolen. These are set out in ss 4(3) and 4(4) of the Theft Act 1968. The first of these concerns plants and fungi growing wild.

> 'A person who picks mushrooms growing wild on any land, or who picks flowers, fruit or foliage from a plant growing wild on any land, does not (although not in possession of the land) steal what he picks, unless he does it for reward or sale or other commercial purpose.
>
> For the purposes of this subsection "mushroom" includes any fungus, and "plant" includes any shrub or tree.'

This only applies to plants etc growing wild, so it is possible to steal cultivated plants. Taking apples from trees in a farmer's orchard would be theft, but picking blackberries growing wild in the hedgerow around the field would not be theft unless it was done for sale or reward or other commercial purpose. Similarly, picking roses from someone's garden would be theft, but picking wild flowers in a field would not (unless for sale or reward). It should however be noted that it is an offence to pick, uproot or destroy certain wild plants under the Wildlife and Countryside Act 1981.

Where picking fungi, flowers, fruit or foliage is done with the intention of selling them or for reward or any commercial purpose then they are considered property which can be stolen. An example of this is picking holly to sell at Christmas time.

The other exception of personal property which is not 'property' for the purpose of theft concerns wild creatures. Section 4(4) states:

> 'Wild creatures, tamed or untamed, shall be regarded as property; but a person cannot steal a wild creature not tamed nor ordinarily kept in captivity,

Activity

Explain whether the items in each of the following situations would be property for the purposes of theft.

1. Arnie runs a market stall selling flowers. Just before Christmas, he picks a lot of holly from a wood, intending to sell it on his stall. He then digs up a small fir tree for his own use. On his way home, he sees some late flowering roses in a garden and picks them to give to his girlfriend.

2. Della discovers the examination papers she is to sit next week in the next-door office. She writes out the questions from the first paper on her own note pad. The second paper is very long, so she uses the office photocopier to take a copy, using paper already in the machine.

> or the carcase of any such creature, unless it has been reduced into possession by or on behalf of another person and possession of it has not since been lost or abandoned, or another person is in course of reducing it into possession.'

The effect of this subsection is that it is not theft if a wild creature such as a deer is taken from the grounds of a large estate (though there is an offence of poaching), but it is theft if a deer is taken from a zoo, as in this case it is ordinarily kept in captivity.

Electricity

Electricity is another sort of intangible property which cannot be stolen, but there is a separate offence under s 11 of the Theft Act 1968 of dishonestly using electricity without due authority, or dishonestly causing it to be wasted or diverted.

10.3 'Belonging to another'

In order for there to be a theft of the property, that property must 'belong to another'. However, s 5(1) of the Theft Act 1968 gives a very wide definition of what is meant by 'belonging to another'.

> 'Property shall be regarded as belonging to any person having possession or control of it, or having in it any proprietary right or interest (not being an equitable interest arising only from an agreement to transfer or grant an interest).'

From this it can be seen that possession or control of the property or any proprietary interest in it is sufficient. One reason for making it wide-ranging is so that the prosecution does not have to prove who is the legal owner.

10.3.1 Possession or control

Obviously, the owner of property normally has possession and control of it, but there are many other situations in which a person can have either possession or control of property. Someone who hires a car has both possession and control during the period of hire. If the car is stolen during this time then the thief can be charged with stealing it from the hirer. Equally, as the car hire firm still owns the car (a proprietary right), the thief could be charged with stealing it from them.

The possession or control of the item does not have to be lawful. Where B has stolen jewellery from A and subsequently C steals it from B, B is in possession or control of that jewellery and C can be charged with stealing it from B. This is useful where it is not known who the original owner is, as C can still be guilty of theft. This wide definition of 'belonging to' has led to the situation in which an owner was convicted of stealing his own car.

Turner (No 2) (1971)

D left his car at a garage for repairs. It was agreed that he would pay for the repairs when he collected the car after the repairs had been completed. When the repairs were almost finished the garage left the car parked on the roadway outside their premises. D used a spare key to take the car during the night without paying for the repairs. The Court of Appeal held that the garage was in possession or control of the car and so D could be guilty of stealing his own car.

It is possible for someone to be in possession or control of property even though they do not know it is there. This happened in *Woodman* (1974).

Woodman (1974)

A company, English China Clays, had sold all the scrap metal on its site to another company which arranged for it to be removed. Unknown to English China Clays a small amount had been left on the site. There was no doubt that they were in control of the site itself as they had put a barbed wire fence round it and had notices warning trespassers to keep out. D took the remaining scrap metal. He was convicted of theft and the Court of Appeal upheld the conviction.

10.3.2 Proprietary interest

Where the defendant owns property and is in possession and control of property, he can still be guilty of stealing it if another person has a

proprietary interest in it. This point was the key matter in the case of *Webster* (2006).

Webster (2006)

D was an army sergeant who had served in Iraq. He had been awarded a medal for his service there. By mistake the Ministry of Defence sent him a second copy of the medal. D sold this second medal on the Internet auction site eBay. He was convicted of theft of the medal. On appeal his conviction was upheld on the basis that the Ministry of Defence had retained an equitable interest in the medal. In other words the Ministry still had a proprietary interest in the medal.

Section 5 makes it clear that in certain situations a defendant can be guilty of theft even though the property may not 'belong to another'. These are situations in which the defendant is acting dishonestly and has caused a loss to another or has made a gain. These are:

- trust property, where a trustee can steal it
- property received under an obligation
- property received by another's mistake.

10.3.3 Property received under an obligation

There are many situations in which property (usually money) is handed over to D on the basis that D will keep it for the owner or will deal with it in a particular way. Subsection 5(3) of the Theft Act 1968 tries to make sure that such property is still considered to 'belong to the other' for the purposes of the law of theft. It states:

> 'Where a person receives property from or on account of another, and is under an obligation to the other to retain and deal with that property or its proceeds in a particular way, the property shall be regarded (as against him) as belonging to the other.'

Under this subsection there must be an obligation to retain and deal with the property in a particular way. So, where money is paid as a deposit to a business, the prosecution must prove that there was an obligation to retain and deal with those deposits in a particular way. If the person paying the deposit only expects it to be paid into a bank account of the business, then if that is what happens, there cannot be theft, even if all the money from the account is used for other business expenses and the client does not receive the goods or service for which he paid the deposit. This is what happened in *Hall* (1972).

Hall (1972)

D was a travel agent who received deposits from clients for air trips to America. D paid these deposits into the firm's general account but never organised any tickets and was unable to return the money. He was convicted of theft but on appeal his conviction was quashed because when D received the deposits he was not under an obligation to deal with it in a particular way. The Court of Appeal stressed that each case depended on its facts.

In *Klineberg and Marsden* (1999) there was a clear obligation to deal with deposits in a particular way.

Klineberg and Marsden (1999)

The two defendants operated a company which sold timeshare apartments in Lanzarote to customers in England. Each purchaser paid the purchase price on the understanding that the money would be held by an independent trust company until the apartment was ready for the purchaser to occupy. Over £500,000 was paid to the defendants' company but only £233 was actually paid into the trust company's account. The defendants were guilty of theft as it was clear that they were under an obligation to the

purchasers 'to retain and deal with that property or its proceeds in a particular way' and that they had not done this.

There can be an obligation in less formal situations. This was shown by *Davidge v Bunnett* (1984).

Davidge v Bunnett (1984)

D was given money by her flatmates to pay the gas bill but instead she used it to buy Christmas presents. There was a legal obligation to deal with the money in a particular way and, as she had not, she was guilty of theft.

In *Davidge v Bunnett* there was an intention to create legal relations under contract law, so the obligation was clear. However, it is not certain whether there would be a legal obligation (and so theft) if the situation happened between members of the same family. This might be considered as a domestic arrangement without the intention to create legal relations, so that there would not be theft.

10.3.4 Property received by a mistake

Section 5 also provides for situations where property has been handed over to D by another's mistake and so has become D's property. If there were no special provision in the Act then this could not be 'property belonging to another' for the purposes of the law of theft. The section states, in s 5(4):

> 'Where a person gets property by another's mistake, and is under an obligation to make restoration (in whole or in part) of the property or its proceeds or of the value thereof, then to the extent of that obligation the property or proceeds shall be regarded (as against him) as belonging to the person entitled to restoration, and an

intention not to make restoration shall be regarded accordingly as an intention to deprive that person of the property or proceeds.' "

This section was considered in *Attorney-General's Reference (No 1 of 1983) (1985)*.

Attorney-General's Reference (No 1 of 1983) (1985)

D's salary was paid into her bank account by transfer. On one occasion her employers mistakenly overpaid her by £74.74. She was charged with theft but acquitted by the jury. The prosecution asked the Court of Appeal to rule on whether a person in this situation who dishonestly decided not to repay the £74.74 would be guilty of theft. The Court of Appeal held that s 5(4) clearly provided for exactly this type of situation. The defendant was under an 'obligation to make restoration' and if there was a dishonest intention not to make restoration then all the elements of theft were present.

There must be a legal obligation to restore the property. In some situations there is no legal obligation to restore money. This is shown by *Gilks* (1972).

Gilks (1972)

D had placed a bet on a horse race. The bookmaker made a mistake about which horse D had backed and overpaid D on the bets he had placed. D realised the error and decided not to return the money. The ownership of the money had passed to D, so the only way he could be guilty of theft was if s 5(4) applied. It was held that as betting transactions are not enforceable at law s 5(4) did not apply and D was not guilty.

10.4 'Dishonestly'

The first point which needs to be proved for the *mens rea* of theft is that when the defendant appropriated the property he did it dishonestly. There is no definition of what is meant by this in the Act but s 1(2) states that:

" '… it is immaterial whether the appropriation is made with a view to gain, or is made for the thief's own benefit.' "

In other words, if all the elements of theft are present, the motive of the defendant is not relevant. This means that a modern-day Robin Hood stealing to give to the poor could be guilty of theft. The defendant does not have to gain anything from the theft.

10.4.1 Behaviour which is not dishonest

The Theft Act 1968 does not define dishonesty, though it does give three situations in which D's behaviour is not considered dishonest. Section 2 of the 1968 Act provides that a person's appropriation of property belonging to another is not to be regarded as dishonest if he appropriates the property in the belief that:

1. he has in law the right to deprive the other of it, on behalf of himself or of a third person (s 2(1)(a)); or
2. he would have the other's consent if the other knew of the appropriation and the circumstances of it (s 2(1)(b)); or
3. the person to whom the property belongs cannot be discovered by taking reasonable steps (s 2(1)(c)).

All these three situations depend on D's belief. It does not matter whether it is a correct belief or even whether it is a reasonable belief. If D has a genuine belief in one of these three then he is not guilty of theft.

Key cases

Case	Facts	Law
Turner (No 2) (1971)	D left his car for repair at a garage. He agreed he would pay for the repairs when he collected the car. He used a spare key to take the car from the garage without their knowledge.	An owner can steal his own property if another has possession and control of it.
Woodman (1974)	Site-owners had arranged for all scrap metal on the site to be removed. Unknown to them a small amount was left on the site.	A person (or company) can be in possession or control of property even though they do not know the property is on their land.
Webster (2006)	An army sergeant sold a duplicate medal on eBay.	The Ministry of Defence retained an equitable interest in the medal and so D was guilty of theft.
Hall (1972)	A travel agent received deposits from customers. He put these deposits into the firm's general account. He did not arrange the tickets for the customers and was unable to repay the money.	D was not under an obligation to deal with the deposits in a particular way under s 5(3), so he was not guilty of theft.
Klineberg and Marsden (1999)	Money was paid for timeshare apartments on the understanding that the money would be held in an independent trust. The money was instead paid into the company's general account.	Where there was a clear obligation to deal with property in a certain way, D was guilty of theft if the property was dealt with in another way.
Davidge v Bunnett (1984)	D was given money by her flatmates to pay the gas bill. She did not pay the bill but used the money to buy Christmas presents.	Even though it was an informal arrangement, there was a clear obligation to deal with property in a certain way. D was guilty of theft when the property was dealt with in another way.
Attorney-General's Reference (No 1 of 1983) (1985)	An overpayment was made by D's employers into her bank account.	By s 5(4) D was under an 'obligation to make restoration'. If she did not, then there was an appropriation of the property. Whether D was guilty of theft would depend on whether or not she acted dishonestly.
Gilks (1972)	D was overpaid for winnings on a bet. He realised the error and decided not to make repayment.	There was no legal obligation to restore the money as betting transactions are not enforceable at law. This meant that s 5(4) did not apply and D was not guilty of theft.

Figure 10.3 Case chart on belonging to another

Unreasonable belief

It has been held in two cases, *Small* (1988) and *Holden* (1991), that the fact that the belief was an unreasonable one does not prevent the defendant from relying on these sections. If the jury decide that the defendant did have a genuine belief, even though an unreasonable one, in one of the three situations then the defendant must be found not guilty.

10.4.2 Willing to pay

In some situations D may say that he is willing to pay for the property or may, on taking property, leave money to pay for it. This does not prevent D's conduct from being dishonest as s 2(2) states that 'a person's appropriation of property belonging to another may be dishonest notwithstanding that he is willing to pay for the property'.

At first this may seem severe, but it prevents D taking what he likes, regardless of the owner's wishes. For example, D likes a painting which is hanging in a friend's home. He asks the friend how much it is worth and is told that it is only a copy, worth less than £100, but it was painted by the friend's grandmother and is of sentimental value. A few days later D takes the painting without the friend's consent but leaves £200 in cash to pay for it. D's taking of the painting may be considered dishonest even though he left more than the cash value of it.

10.4 3 The *Ghosh* test

The case of *Ghosh* (1982) is the leading case on what is meant by 'dishonestly'. In this case the Court of Appeal set out the tests to be used.

Ghosh (1982)

Ghosh was a doctor acting as a locum consultant in a hospital. He claimed fees for an operation he had not carried out. He said that he was not dishonest as he was owed the same amount for consultation fees. The trial judge directed the jury that they must apply their own standards to decide if what he did was dishonest. He was convicted and appealed against the conviction.

The Court of Appeal decided that the test for dishonesty has both an objective and a subjective element to it:

- Was what was done dishonest according to the ordinary standards of reasonable and honest people?
- Did the defendant realise that what he was doing was dishonest by those standards?

The *Ghosh* test means that the jury has to start with an objective test. Was what was done dishonest by the ordinary standards of reasonable and honest people? If it was not dishonest by those standards, that is the end of the matter and the prosecution fails. The defendant is not guilty. However, if the jury decides that it was dishonest by those standards then they must consider the more subjective test of whether the defendant knew it was dishonest by those standards.

This second test is not totally subjective as the defendant is judged by what he realised ordinary standards were. This prevents a defendant from saying that, although he knew that ordinary people would regard his actions as dishonest, he did not think that those standards applied to him.

In a trial the judge will use the *Ghosh* test to direct the jury only where there is an issue about dishonesty.

10.5 'Intention of permanently depriving'

The final element which has to be proved for theft is that the defendant had the intention permanently to deprive the other of the property. In many situations there is no doubt that the defendant had such an intention; for example, where an item is taken and sold to another person or where cash is taken and spent by the defendant. This last example is true even if the defendant intends to replace the money later as was shown in *Velumyl* (1989).

Velumyl (1989)

D, a company manager, took £1,050 from the office safe. He said that he was owed money by a friend and he was going to replace the money when that friend repaid him. The Court of Appeal upheld his conviction for theft as he had the intention of permanently depriving the company of the banknotes which he had taken from the safe, even if he intended replacing them with other banknotes to the same value later.

Another situation where there is a clear intention to permanently deprive is where the defendant destroys property belonging to another. This can be charged as theft, although it is also criminal damage.

There are, however, situations where it is not so clear and, to help in these, s 6 Theft Act 1968 explains and expands the meaning of the phrase. It provides that, even though a person appropriating property belonging to another does not mean the other permanently to lose the thing itself, he can be regarded as having the intention to permanently deprive the other of it if his intention is to treat the thing as his own to dispose of, regardless of the other's rights.

The Court of Appeal has stated that the meaning of 'dispose of' should be that given by the *Shorter Oxford Dictionary*, which is: 'To deal with definitely: to get rid of; to get done with, finish. To make over by way of sale or bargain or sell'.

However, in *DPP v Lavender* (1994) the Divisional Court ruled that the dictionary definition of 'dispose of' was too narrow as a disposal could include 'dealing with' property.

DPP v Lavender (1994)

D took doors from a council property which was being repaired and used them to replace damaged doors in his girlfriend's council flat. The doors were still in the possession of the council but had been transferred without permission from one council property to another. The Divisional Court held that the question was whether he intended to treat the doors as his own, regardless of the rights of the council. The answer to this was yes, so the defendant was guilty of theft.

10.5.1 Borrowing or lending

Another difficulty with s 6 is the point at which 'borrowing or lending' comes within the definition. Normally borrowing would not be an intention to permanently deprive. Take the situation of a student taking a textbook from a fellow student's bag in order to read one small section and then replace the book. This is clearly outside the scope of s 6 and cannot be considered as an intention to permanently deprive. But what if that student also took a photocopying card, which had a limit placed on its use, used it, then returned it. The photocopy card has been returned but it is no longer as valuable as it was. So is there an intention to permanently deprive so far as the card is concerned?

Section 6 states that borrowing is not theft unless it is for a period and in circumstances making it equivalent to an outright taking or disposal. In *Lloyd* (1985) it was held that this meant borrowing the property and keeping it until 'the goodness, the virtue, the practical value ... has gone out of the article'.

Lloyd (1985)

The projectionist at a local cinema gave D a film that was showing at the cinema so that D could make an illegal copy. D returned the film in time for the next screening at the cinema. His conviction for theft was quashed because, by returning the film in its original state, it was not possible to prove an intention to permanently deprive.

From this it appears that, in the example of the photocopy card, there would an intention to permanently deprive if all the value of the card had been used up, but if it still had a reasonable value then there is no intention to permanently deprive.

Proportion of value

In *Lloyd* the film was returned undamaged so it is easy to accept that the 'goodness, the virtue, the practical value' had not gone out of it. In other situations when part of the value has gone, it can be difficult to decide whether the 'goodness' and 'practical value' have gone out of an item.

In the photocopy example, if the photocopy card had had £5 remaining when it was taken and £4.50 when it was returned, then the 'goodness' and 'practical value' would probably not have gone out of it. However, if the card had only 50 pence remaining on it when it was returned, the 'goodness' and 'practical value' would probably be held to have gone out of it. It has to be a matter of proportion.

Conditional intent

Another difficulty is where the defendant examines property to see if there is anything worth stealing. What is the position if he decides it is not worth stealing and returns it? This is what happened in *Easom* (1971). The defendant picked up a handbag in a cinema, rummaged through the contents and then replaced the handbag without having taken anything. His conviction for theft of the handbag and its contents was quashed. There was no evidence that the defendant had intended to permanently deprive the owner of the bag or items in it so he could not be guilty of theft. (See section 5.3 on the point of whether a defendant in this situation can be guilty of attempted theft.)

10.6 Problems in the law of theft

When the Theft Act 1968 was passed, the definition of 'theft' was meant to be in simple everyday language that ordinary people could understand. However, there have been some case decisions on the elements of theft which make it more difficult to understand the law. The main problems with each element are discussed below.

10.6.1 Appropriation

There are a number of problems with the concept of appropriation in the law of theft. These include:

- the width of the acts which can be considered as appropriation
- the problem of appropriation being regarded as occurring at one point in time
- the implication of the one-point concept for robbery and the conflict with decisions in robbery cases
- the difficulty of being able to appropriate even though the owner has consented to the act
- the conflict between civil and criminal law on gifts
- the reliance on dishonesty, a difficult concept of itself, to distinguish between innocent appropriations and appropriations which are theft
- the need for clarity and certainty in the law.

Width of appropriation

As already seen in section 10.1, a wide variety of acts can be considered as appropriation. They include the physical picking up of an item, destroying property, throwing items away, selling property, switching price labels on items, giving worthless cheques in payment for goods, receiving a gift, and deciding to keep an item.

All these are considered to be the assumption of the rights of an owner. This width of acts is as a result of the decision in *Morris* that what needed to be proved was the assumption of *any* of the rights of an owner.

This leads to the question of whether this is the correct test. The Theft Act 1968 uses the phrase 'any assumption of the rights of an owner'. It can be argued that by interpreting the phrase as 'the assumption of *any* of the rights' the courts have gone beyond what was intended by Parliament.

Assumption at one point in time

The decision in *Gomez* means that appropriation is considered to have occurred at one point in the whole process of theft. As seen in section 10.1.3, this led to the acquittal of the defendants in *Atakpu and Abrahams*. Yet the defendants in that case were bringing the cars into this country to sell them. Surely this was an on-going part of the theft? Why should the appropriation be regarded as only occurring when they hired the cars in Germany?

The defendants were still assuming the right of an owner by continuing to drive the cars and by bringing them into this county. It seems more sensible to say that the appropriation was continuing. This is a view taken by judges in cases of robbery.

There has to be a theft immediately before or at the time of the stealing for the offence of robbery to have been committed. One would assume that the definition of appropriation would be the same for robbery as for theft. Yet in two cases, *Hale* (1979) and *Lockley* (1995) it has been held that theft is an on-going process (see section 11.1.3).

Consent to appropriation

A major criticism of the law is that there can be an appropriation, even though the owner of the goods has consented to the act the defendant has done in relation to the goods.

This appears to be particularly odd in relation to items in shops. Lord Roskill's view of the matter that the honest shopper is only doing what the shop expects and so has not assumed any of the rights of an owner is a very strong argument.

There is also the argument that where an owner consents to the taking of property due to a false statement, then it is more appropriate to charge the defendant with an offence of fraud under the Fraud Act 2006. For cases prior to 2006 defendants could have been charged with the old offence of obtaining property by deception under s 15 of the Theft Act 1968.

If this had been done then the law on theft would not have needed to be made so complicated.

Theft of gifts

The problems caused by the decisions in *Lawrence* and *Gomez* that there could be an appropriation even though the owner consented to the taking have become even greater since the decision of the House of Lords in *Hinks* (2000) (see section 10.1.2).

In *Hinks* the owner had given the property to the defendant. It is difficult to understand how a defendant can have assumed the rights of an owner when the property has actually been given to them.

Conflict of civil and criminal law

The decision in *Hinks* also means that the civil law and criminal law are in conflict.

Lord Hobhouse, one of the judges in the case, stated that in his opinion there was no appropriation. This was because the civil law on gifts involves conduct by the owner who transfers the ownership of the gift to the donee (the person receiving the gift). Once this is done the gift is the property of the donee. The donee does not have to do anything for the gift to become their property. It is not even necessary that the donee should know of the gift. For example, money could be transferred to the donee's bank account without the donee's knowledge. In view of this Lord Hobhouse thought that it was impossible to say that there was any appropriation by the defendant.

Key facts

Section of Theft Act 1968	Definition	Comment
s 1	A person is guilty of theft if he dishonestly appropriates property belonging to another with the intention of permanently depriving the other of it.	Full definition of theft. D is charged under this section.
s 2	**Dishonesty** Not dishonest if D believes: ● he has a right in law ● he would have the other's consent ● the owner cannot be discovered. Can be dishonest even if intends paying for property.	No definition of 'dishonesty' in the Act. *Ghosh* (1982): two-part test: ● Is it dishonest by ordinary standards? ● If so, did D know it was dishonest by those standards?
s 3	**Appropriation** 'any assumption of the rights of an owner' Includes a later assumption of rights.	Held to be assumption of *any* of the rights of an owner: *Gomez* (1993). Given 'neutral' meaning, so consent irrelevant: *Lawrence* (1971), *Hinks* (2000).
s 4	**Property** Includes money and all other property real or personal, including things in action and other intangible property. Land cannot be stolen except by trustee or tenant or by severing property from land. Wild mushrooms, fruit, flowers and foliage cannot be stolen unless done for commercial purpose. Wild animals cannot be stolen unless tamed or in captivity.	
s 5	**Belonging to another** Property is regarded as belonging to any person having possession or control or any proprietary right. Property belongs to the other where it is received under an obligation to retain and deal with it in a particular way. Property belonging to the other received by a mistake where there is a legal obligation to make restoration.	Not limited to owner: *Turner (No 2)* (1972) stole own car. Must be a particular way: *Hall* (1972), *Klineberg and Marsden* (1999). *A-G's Reference (No 1 of 1983)* (1985). Must be a legal obligation: *Gilks* (1972).
s 6	**Intention to permanently deprive** Treat the thing as his own to dispose of regardless of the other's rights. Dispose of includes 'dealing with' property.	The 'goodness' or practical value must have gone from the property: *Lloyd* (1985). *DPP v Lavender* (1994).

Figure 10.4 Key facts chart on theft

Activity

In each of the following situations, explain whether all the elements of theft are present.

1. Roland works in a small factory where there are only 20 employees. One day he finds a small purse in the washroom. He opens it. It contains a £10 note and some coins. There is no name or other identification in it. Roland decides to keep the money as he does not think he can find the owner.

2. Venus comes from a country where property placed outside a shop is meant for people to take free of charge. She sees a rack of clothes on the pavement outside a shop and takes a pair of jeans from it.

3. Natalie is given a Christmas cash bonus in a sealed envelope. She has been told by her boss that the bonus would be £50. When she gets home and opens the envelope she finds there is £60 in it. She thinks her employer decided to be more generous and so keeps the money. Would your answer be different if:
   • Natalie realised there had been a mistake but did not return the money, or
   • the amount in the envelope was £200?

4. Errol is given permission by his employer to borrow some decorative lights for use at a party. Errol also takes some candles without asking permission. When putting up the lights Errol smashes one of them. He lights two of the candles so that by the end of the evening they are partly burnt down. One of the guests admires the remaining lights and asks if he can have them to use at a disco at the weekend. Errol agrees to let him take the lights.

5. John is late for work one day so he takes his neighbour's bicycle to get to work on time. His neighbour is away, but John has used the bicycle on previous occasions. He intends returning it that evening when he comes home from work. John parks the bicycle at the back of the shop where he works. When he leaves work in the evening he finds that the lamp and the pump have been taken from the bicycle and it has been damaged. He is frightened to return the bicycle in this state so he throws it into the local canal.

Reliance on dishonesty to prove theft

Because of the problems arsing from making appropriation so wide, proof of dishonesty is now the only distinguishing point between theft and an honest appropriation. This causes further difficulties as the law on dishonesty also causes problems. These are discussed in section 10.6.3.

Need for clarity and certainty in the law

It is important that all law should be as clear and certain as possible. This is especially important for the criminal law. A conviction for theft carries a social stigma. It may even lose a person their job. Yet, as we can see from the above point, the law on theft is not clear.

Remember that appropriation on its own is not enough for theft. All the other elements of theft must be present; in particular there must be dishonesty. There are many situations where there is appropriation but there is no dishonesty so that there cannot be theft. For example, all honest shoppers who place items in a basket or trolley provided by the store are appropriating the items, but because they intend to pay for them, they are not dishonest and so there is no offence of theft.

10.6.2 Property belonging to another

The word 'property' has not caused any real problems. The definition in the Act is so very wide, it includes almost everything. The Act itself sets out detailed rules on when land, animals and plants can or cannot be stolen. The decision in *Oxford v Moss* (1979), where information on examination questions was obtained, that knowledge cannot be stolen, does not normally cause any problems as most instances are covered by other offences such as copyright laws.

'Belonging to another'

The Act states that 'belonging to another' includes situations where property is in the possession or control of another, or where another person had any proprietary right or interest in the property. This wide definition of 'belonging to another' is needed since in many cases it might be difficult for the prosecution to prove that the victim was the legal owner. However, this phrase has caused some surprising decisions, in particular the decision in *Turner (No 2)* (1971).

In this case the owner of a car took it from a garage without paying for repairs. The garage clearly had a lien (a legal right to retain the car until payment was made) and it could have been held that this gave the garage control of the car. However, the judge at the trial had directed the jury to ignore any question of a lien. On appeal to the Court of Appeal the judges simply based their decision to uphold the conviction on the fact that the garage had possession and control. In fact, if the question of lien is ignored, then Turner had the right to take the car back.

10.6.3 Dishonesty

There are criticisms of the *Ghosh* test (1982) for dishonesty. The main criticism is that it leaves too much to the jury, so that there is a risk of inconsistent decisions with different juries coming to different decisions in similar situations. It has been argued that it would be better for the judge to rule on whether there was dishonesty as a point of law rather than leave it as a matter of fact for the jury. However, this overlooks the fact that members of the jury still need to decide whether they believe what the defendant says.

Another criticism of the test is that it places too much emphasis on objective views of what is dishonest rather than the defendant's intentions. The first stage of the test requires the jury to consider whether what was done was dishonest according to the ordinary standards of reasonable and honest people. This has the odd effect that if the jury thinks it is not dishonest, then the defendant will be found not guilty even though he may have thought he was being (and intended to be) dishonest.

The points above were emphasised by Professor Griew in an article he wrote in 1985. He put forward several problems with the definition of theft following the decision in *Ghosh*. As well as the points above he also pointed out that:

- the *Ghosh* test leads to longer and more difficult trials
- the idea of standards of ordinary reasonable and honest people is a fiction
- the *Ghosh* test is unsuitable in specialised cases.

Longer trials

The complicated nature of the *Ghosh* test means that trials take longer. The jury has first to decide if the defendant's behaviour is dishonest according to the ordinary standards of reasonable and honest people. This is not always a straightforward matter.

Then they have to decide if the defendant realised that what he was doing was dishonest by those standards. This is another difficult point as evidence of a state of mind is not easy to prove.

Griew also thought that the nature of the test meant that more defendants might decide to plead not guilty in the hope that a jury would decide their behaviour was not dishonest.

Fiction of community standards

Griew points out that using a test of ordinary standards of reasonable and honest people assumes that there is a common standard. In fact society is very diverse and different sections of the community may well have slightly varying standards.

Griew's view is supported by the Law

Commission in their report on the law of fraud in 2002 when they said:

> 'There is some evidence that people's moral standards are surprisingly varied.'

This creates problems when the jury have to decide on the ordinary standards. The jurors are likely to come from different backgrounds with different experiences of life. They can also vary in age from 18 to 70. All these factors may mean that the jury disagree on what the ordinary standards are.

Specialised cases

It is even more difficult to apply ordinary standards where the offence involves a specialised area such as futures trading or other complex financial dealing. The first part of the *Ghosh* test is even more unsuitable in such cases.

Ordinary people have no experience of such financial dealing, so how can they say what is 'honest' or 'not honest' in such cases?

Whether the defendant is being dishonest has become much more important in view of the ruling in *Hinks* (2000) that appropriation is a neutral word. This means that whether a theft has occurred or not is dependent on whether the appropriation was dishonest. The whole of the illegality of the act is based on the *mens rea* of the defendant.

10.6.4 Intention to permanently deprive

The first point that can be made on this part of the definition of theft is whether it is necessary to include it as part of the law of theft. If someone dishonestly takes property belonging to another, does it matter whether they intend permanently to deprive that person of the property? This would make it possible to convict of theft in situations such as *Lloyd* (1985) where a film was copied and then returned. On the present law Lloyd was not guilty, yet he had appropriated property belonging to another, was being

dishonest as the only reason for the appropriation was to take an illegal copy, and temporarily deprived the other of his property. Abolishing the need for an intention *permanently* to deprive would include this behaviour within the law of theft.

It is because of this need to prove an intention permanently to deprive another of property that the Theft Act 1968 includes a separate offence of taking vehicles without consent. It is recognised that in many cases where a car or other vehicle is taken there is no intention permanently to deprive. The taker merely wants to drive the vehicle, but will then abandon it, often not far from where it was originally parked.

The other problem is what can be called 'conditional' intention to deprive. This is where the defendant examines property to see if it is worth stealing. If he then decides it is not worth stealing and returns it, there is no theft. This happened in *Easom* (1971) where the defendant picked up a handbag, looked in it, could not find anything worth stealing and put the bag back. Easom was not guilty of theft because a conditional intention to deprive is not enough to convict the defendant of theft. Again, if in the definition of theft, the word 'permanent' were replaced with the word 'temporary', defendants behaving in this way could be convicted.

This would also bring the law into line with the law on burglary where the courts have ruled that a conditional intention to steal anything worth stealing in the building which the defendant is entering, is sufficient for the defendant to be guilty of burglary under s 9(1)(a) Theft Act 1968.

Activity

Read the following extract and answer the question below.

£2,000 stolen in cash scam

'A commuter became the latest victim of a cashpoint scam when she had nearly £2,000 stolen from her bank account after using a Paddock Wood cash machine on her way to work on December 19.

When she checked her balance on the Internet on December 27 she found that the money, which included her entire December salary, was missing from her account.

She said: "I was shocked. I thought, 'I could have sworn I had been paid,' then I saw withdrawals of £150, £200 and £250 two or three times a day.

"It didn't say the location of the banks but different ones had been used including Barclays, Alliance and Leicester, NatWest and HSBC."

She is not Paddock Wood's only victim of card "skimming", where a removable scanner is placed in the machine to copy the card details.

As reported last week a 50-year-old man from the town had money stolen from his account between December 19 and December 22 after using the NatWest machine.'

(Adapted from an article in *The Courier*, 9th January 2004)

Question

The article states that the money has been stolen from the victim's account. Define 'theft' and explain the different elements of theft in relation to this situation.

Examination questions

1. 'The relationship between dishonesty and appropriation in the offence of theft has been clearly established by statute and case law. Their meaning is now free from uncertainty.'

   Assess the truth of this statement.

   (OCR, Unit 2572, January 2005)

2. While shopping Susan places some items of food in the wire basket which is provided. She also hides a bottle of perfume in her coat pocket. She then takes a label off an expensive CD, switches it with the label from a reduced price CD and places the expensive one in the basket. She goes to the checkout and only pays for the items in the basket.

   Outside the shop Susan sees a bike which was there when she went in and which she remembers seeing there for several days. She rides home on it alongside a caravan park. She notices a personal CD player on a table inside one of the caravans. She goes inside and takes the CD player. She leaves the bike at the end of her road and goes home.

   Discuss Susan's potential criminal liability for the above incidents.

   (OCR, Unit G143, June 2008)

See also the last paragraph of question 1 and Statement B in question 2, in the examination questions at the end of Chapter 11.

Robbery and burglary

11.1 Robbery

Robbery is an offence under s 8 Theft Act 1968. In effect it is a theft which is aggravated by the use or threat of force. Section 8 states:

Definition

Robbery

'A person is guilty of robbery if he steals, and immediately before or at the time of doing so, and in order to do so, he uses force on any person or puts or seeks to put any person in fear of being then and there subjected to force.'

So the elements which must be proved for robbery are for the *actus reus*:

- theft
- force or putting or seeking to put any person in fear of force.

In addition, there are two conditions on the force and these are that it must be immediately before or at the time of the theft, and it must be in order to steal.

For the *mens rea* of robbery it must be proved that the defendant:

- had the *mens rea* for theft and
- intended to use force to steal.

11.1.1 Completed theft

There must be a completed theft for a robbery to have been committed. This means that all the elements of theft have to be present. If any one of them is missing then, just as there would be no theft, there is no robbery. For example, there is no theft in the situation where D takes a car, drives it a mile and abandons it because D has no intention permanently to deprive. Equally there is no robbery where D uses force to take that car. There is no offence of theft, so using force cannot make it into robbery.

The case of *Robinson* (1977) demonstrates that if the elements of theft are not complete then there cannot be robbery.

Robinson (1977)

D ran a clothing club and was owed £7 by V's wife. D approached V and threatened him. During a struggle the man dropped a £5 note and D took it claiming he was still owed £2. D's conviction for robbery was quashed because the trial judge had wrongly directed the jury that D had honestly to believe he was entitled to get the money in that way. In fact if D had a genuine belief that he had a right in law to the money, then his actions were not dishonest under s 2(1)(a) Theft Act 1968.

Where force is used to steal, then the moment the theft is complete there is a robbery. This is demonstrated by the case of *Corcoran v Anderton* (1980).

Corcoran v Anderton (1980)

One of the defendants hit a woman in the back and tugged at her bag. She let go of the bag and it fell to the ground. The defendants ran off without the bag (because the woman was screaming and attracting attention). It was held that the theft was complete so the defendants were guilty of robbery.

However, if the theft is not completed, for instance if the woman in the case of *Corcoran v Anderton* had not let go of the bag, then there is an attempted theft and the defendant could be charged with attempted robbery.

11.1.2 Force or threat of force

As well as theft the prosecution must prove force or the threat of force. The amount of force can be small. This is clearly shown by the case of *Dawson and James* (1976).

Dawson and James (1976)

One of the defendants pushed the victim causing him to lose his balance, which enabled the other defendant to take his wallet. They were convicted of robbery. The Court of Appeal held that 'force' was an ordinary word and it was for the jury to decide if there had been force.

This decision was confirmed in *Clouden* (1987) where the Court of Appeal held that D was guilty of robbery when he had wrenched a shopping basket from the victim's hand. The Court of Appeal held that the trial judge was right to leave the question of whether D had used force on a person to the jury.

It can be argued that using force on the bag was effectively using force on the victim as the bag was wrenched from her hand. However, if a thief pulls a shoulder bag so that it slides off the victim's shoulder, would this be considered force? Probably not. It would certainly not be force if a thief snatched a bag which was resting (not being held) on the lap of someone sitting on a park bench.

The definition of robbery makes clear that robbery is committed if D puts or seeks to put a person in fear of force. It is not necessary that the force be applied. Putting V 'in fear of being there and then subjected to force' is sufficient for robbery. This covers threatening words, such as 'I have a knife and I'll use it unless you give me your wallet', and threatening gestures, such as holding a knife in front of V.

Robbery is also committed even if the victim is not actually frightened by D's actions or words. If D seeks to put V in fear of being then and there subjected to force, this element of robbery is present. So if V is a plain clothes policeman put there to trap D and is not frightened, the fact that D sought to put V in fear is enough.

'On any person'

This means that the person threatened does not have to be the person from whom the theft occurs. An obvious example is an armed robber who enters a bank, seizes a customer and threatens to shoot that customer unless a bank official gets money out of the safe. This is putting a person in fear of being then and there subjected to force. The fact that it is not the customer's property which is being stolen does not matter.

11.1.3 Force immediately before or at the time of the theft

The force must be immediately before or at the time of stealing. This raises two problems. First, how immediate does 'immediately before' have to be? Consider the situation where a bank official is attacked at his home by a gang in order to steal keys and security codes from him. The gang then drives to the bank and steals money. The theft has taken place an hour after the use of force. Is this 'immediately before'? It would seem sensible that the gang should be convicted of robbery. But what if the time delay were longer, as could happen if the attack on the manager was on Saturday evening and the theft of the money not until 24 hours later. Does this still come within 'immediately before'? There have been no decided cases on this point.

The second problem has come in deciding the point at which a theft is completed, so that the force is not 'at the time of stealing'. This was considered in *Hale* (1979).

Hale (1979)

The two defendants knocked on the door of a house. When a woman opened the door they forced their way into the house. One defendant put his hand over her mouth to stop her screaming while the other defendant went upstairs to see what he could find to take. He took a jewellery box. Before they left the house they tied up the householder.

On appeal the defendants argued that the theft was complete as soon as the second defendant picked up the jewellery box, so the use of force in tying up the householder was not at the time of stealing. However, the Court of Appeal upheld their convictions. The Court of Appeal thought that the jury could have come to the decision that there was force immediately before the theft when one of the defendants put his hand over the householder's mouth. In addition, the Court of Appeal thought that the tying up of the householder could also be force for the purpose of robbery, as they held the theft was still ongoing.

The decision in *Hale* was followed in *Lockley* (1995).

Lockley (1995)

D was caught shoplifting cans of beer from an off-licence. He used force on the shopkeeper who tried to stop him from escaping. D appealed on the basis that the theft was complete when he used the force, but the Court of Appeal followed the decision in *Hale* (1979) and upheld his conviction for robbery.

But there must be a point when the theft is complete and so any force used after this point does not make it robbery. What if in *Lockley* the defendant had left the shop and was running down the road when a passer-by (alerted by the shouts of the shopkeeper) tried to stop him; the defendant then uses force on the passer-by to escape? Surely the theft is completed before this use of force. The force used is a separate act to the theft and does not make the theft a robbery. The force will, of course, be a separate offence of assault.

11.1.4 Force in order to steal

The force must be used in order to steal. So if the force was not used for this purpose, then any later theft will not make it into robbery. Take the situation where D has an argument with V and punches him, knocking him out. D then sees that some money has fallen out of V's pocket and decides to take it. The force was not used for the purpose of that theft and D is not guilty of robbery, but guilty of two separate offences: an assault and theft.

11.1.5 *Mens rea* for robbery

D must have the *mens rea* for theft, ie he must be dishonest and he must intend to permanently deprive the other of the property. He must also intend to use force to steal.

Activity

Read the following extract from an article in *Sevenoaks Chronicle* on 15th January 2004 and answer the questions below.

Armed raid at off-licence

'An armed raider burst into a village off-licence and demanded cash.

The man entered Unwins in The Square, Riverhead at about 6.30 pm on Sunday, and produced what appeared to be a pistol.

He threatened staff with the weapon and demanded money, which the employees handed over from the till.

The raider then fled on foot along London Road, towards Dunton Green.

None of the staff, who have not been identified, were hurt in the attack.

The incident comes less than six months after two men used knives to intimidate employees into giving them cash and cigarettes at the store.'

Questions

1. Identify the offence which was committed at the off-licence.

2. Explain what is required for the *actus reus* of that offence and identify the acts which form the *actus reus* in this particular raid.

3. Explain what has to be proved for the *mens rea* of the offence.

Activity

Explain whether or not a robbery has occurred in each of the following situations.

1. Albert holds a knife to the throat of a three-year-old girl and orders the child's mother to hand over her purse or he will 'slit the child's throat'. The mother hands over her purse.

2. Brendan threatens staff in a post office with an imitation gun. He demands that they hand over the money in the till. One of the staff presses a security button and a grill comes down in front of the counter so that the staff are safe and Brendan cannot reach the till. He leaves without taking anything.

3. Carla snatches a handbag from Delia. Delia is so surprised that she lets go of the bag and Carla runs off with it.

4. Ellie breaks into a car in a car park and takes a briefcase out of it. As she is walking away from the car, the owner arrives, realises what has happened and starts to chase after Ellie. The owner catches hold of Ellie, but she pushes him over and makes her escape.

5. Freya tells Harmid to hand over his Rolex watch and, that if he does not, Freya will send her boyfriend, Grant, round to beat Harmid up. Harmid knows that Grant is a very violent man. Harmid takes his watch off and gives it to Freya.

Key facts

Element	Law	Case
Theft	There must be a completed theft; if any element is missing there is no theft and therefore no robbery.	*Robinson* (1977)
	The moment the theft is completed (with the relevant force) there is robbery.	*Corcoran v Anderton* (1980)
Force or threat of force	The jury decides whether the acts were force, using the ordinary meaning of the word.	*Dawson and James* (1976)
	It includes wrenching a bag from V's hand.	*Clouden* (1987)
On any person	The force can be against *any* person. It does not have to be against the victim of the theft.	
Immediately before or at the time of the theft	For robbery, theft has been held to be a continuing act.	*Hale* (1979)
	Using force to escape can still be at the time of the theft.	*Lockley* (1995)
In order to steal	The force must be in order to steal. Force used for another purpose does not become robbery if D later decides to steal.	
Mens rea	*Mens rea* for theft plus an intention to use force to steal.	

Figure 11.1 Key facts chart for robbery

11.2 Burglary

This is an offence under s 9 Theft Act 1968. Section 9 provides two different ways in which burglary can be committed. Under s 9(1)(a) a person is guilty of burglary if he enters any building or part of a building as a trespasser with intent to steal, inflict grievous bodily harm, or do unlawful damage to the building or anything in it.

Under s 9(1)(b) a person is guilty of burglary if, having entered a building or part of a building as a trespasser, he steals or attempts to steal anything in the building or inflicts or attempts to inflict grievous bodily harm on any person in the building.

The following chart shows these different ways of committing burglary.

Burglary	
s 9(1)(a)	s 9(1)(b)
Enters a building or part of a building as a trespasser.	Having entered a building or part of a building as a trespasser.
With intent to: • steal • inflict grievous bodily harm • do unlawful damage.	• Steals or attempts to steal, or • inflicts or attempts to inflict grievous bodily harm.

Figure 11.2 Different ways of committing burglary

Although ss 9(1)(a) and 9(1)(b) create different ways of committing burglary, they do have common elements. There must be:

- entry
- of a building or part of a building
- as a trespasser.

The difference between the subsections is the intention at the time of entry. For s 9(1)(a) the defendant must intend to do one of the three listed offences (known as ulterior offences) at the time of entering. However, there is no need for the ulterior offence to take place or even be attempted. For s 9(1)(b) what the defendant intends on entry is irrelevant, but the prosecution must prove that he actually committed or attempted to commit theft or grievous bodily harm.

11.2.1 Entry

Entry is not defined in the Theft Act 1968, but there have been several cases on the meaning of the word. The first main case on this point was *Collins* (1972) (see section 11.2.3 for the facts of this case). In this case the Court of Appeal said that the jury had to be satisfied that D had made 'an effective and substantial entry'.

However, in *Brown* (1985) this concept of 'an effective and substantial entry' was modified to 'effective entry'.

Brown (1985)

D was standing on the ground outside but leaning in through a shop window rummaging through goods. His feet and lower part of his body were outside the shop, but the top part of his body and his arms were inside the shop. The Court of Appeal said that the word 'substantial' did not materially assist the definition of entry and his conviction for burglary was upheld as clearly in this situation his entry was effective.

However, in another case, *Ryan* (1996), the need for an 'effective' entry does not appear to have been followed.

Ryan (1996)

In this case the defendant was trapped when trying to get through a window into a house at 2.30 am. His head and right arm were inside the house but the rest of his body was outside. The fire brigade had to be called to release him. This could scarcely be said to be an 'effective' entry. However, the Court of Appeal upheld his conviction for burglary saying that there was evidence on which the jury could find that the defendant had entered.

11.2.2 Building or part of a building

The Theft Act 1968 gives an extended meaning to the word 'building' so that it includes inhabited places such as houseboats or caravans, which would otherwise not be included in the offence. However, it does not give any basic definition for 'building'. Usually there is no problem. Clearly houses, blocks of flats, offices, factories and so on are buildings. The word also includes outbuildings and sheds.

The main problems for the courts have occurred where a structure such as a portacabin has been used for storage or office work. There are two cases on whether a large storage container is a building. In these cases the court came to different decisions after looking at the facts.

- In *B and S v Leathley* (1979) a 25-foot-long freezer container had been kept in a farmyard for over two years. It was used as a storage facility. It rested on sleepers, had doors with locks and was connected to the electricity supply. This was held to be a building.
- In *Norfolk Constabulary v Seekings and Gould* (1986) a lorry trailer with wheels which had been used for over a year for storage, had steps providing access and was connected to the electricity supply, was held not to be a building. The fact that it had wheels meant that it remained a vehicle.

'Part of a building'

The phrase 'part of building' is used to cover situations in which the defendant may have permission to be in one part of the building (and therefore is not a trespasser in that part) but does not have permission to be in another part.

A case example to demonstrate this is *Walkington* (1979).

Walkington (1979)

D went into a counter area in a shop and opened a till. This area was clearly marked by a three-sided counter. D's conviction for burglary under s 9(1)(a) was upheld as he had entered part of a building (the counter area) as a trespasser with the intention of stealing.

The critical point in *Walkington* was that the counter area was not an area where customers were permitted to go. It was an area for the use of staff, so D was a trespasser.

Other examples include storerooms in shops where shoppers would not have permission to enter, or a hall of residence where one student would be a trespasser if he entered another student's room without permission.

11.2.3 'As a trespasser'

In order for D to commit burglary he must enter as a trespasser. If a person has permission to enter they are not a trespasser. This was illustrated by the unusual case of *Collins* (1972).

Collins (1972)

The defendant, having had quite a lot to drink, decided he wanted to have sexual intercourse. He saw an open window and climbed a ladder to look in. He saw there was a naked girl asleep in bed. He then went down the ladder, took off all his clothes except for his socks and climbed back up the ladder to the girl's bedroom. As he was on the window sill outside the room, she woke up, thought he was her boyfriend and helped him into the room where they had sex.

Collins was convicted of burglary under s 9(1)(a), ie that he had entered as a trespasser with intent to rape. (Note that before 2004 entering as a trespasser with intent to rape was also included under s 9(1)(a), but is now an offence under the Sexual Offences Act 2003. Also note that Collins could not be charged with rape as the girl agreed that she had consented to sex.) He appealed on the basis that he was not a trespasser as he had been invited in. The Court of Appeal quashed his conviction because there was no evidence that he was a trespasser; the girl had invited him into the room.

The court said that there could not be a conviction for entering premises 'as a trespasser' unless the person entering did so either knowing he was a trespasser or was reckless as to whether or not he was entering the premises of another without the other person's consent.

So, to succeed on a charge of burglary, the prosecution must prove that the defendant knew he was trespassing or that the defendant was subjectively reckless as to whether he was trespassing.

'Going beyond permission'

Where the defendant is given permission to enter but then goes beyond that permission, he may be considered a trespasser. This was decided in *Smith and Jones* (1976).

Smith and Jones (1976)

Smith and his friend, Jones, went to Smith's father's house in the middle of the night and took two television sets without the father's knowledge or permission. The father stated that his son would not be a trespasser in the house; he had a general permission to enter. The Court of Appeal upheld their convictions for burglary, ruling that:

'a person is a trespasser for the purpose of s 9(1)(b) of the Theft Act 1968 if he enters premises of another knowing that he is entering in excess of the permission that has been given to him to enter, or being reckless whether he is entering in excess of that permission'.

This decision is in line with the Australian case of *Barker v R* (1983) where one person who was going away asked the defendant, who was a neighbour, to keep a eye on the house and told the defendant where a key was hidden should he need to enter. The defendant used the key to enter and steal property. He was found guilty of burglary.

There are many situations where a person has permission to enter for a limited purpose. For example, someone buys a ticket to attend a concert in a concert hall, or to look round an historic building or an art collection. The ticket is a licence (or permission) to be in the building for a very specific reason and/or time. If D buys a ticket intending to steal one of the paintings from the art collection, these cases mean that he is probably guilty of burglary.

Shoppers have permission to enter a shop. It is obvious that if a person has been banned from entering a shop they will be entering as a trespasser if they go into that shop. Such a person would be guilty of burglary if he intended to steal goods (s 9(1)(a)) or if, having entered, he then stole goods (s 9(1)(b)).

The case of *Smith and Jones* (1976) takes matters further than this as it means that any person who enters a shop intending to steal is going beyond the permission to enter the shop in order to buy goods. They will be guilty of burglary under s 9(1)(a). However, it is rare for anyone to be charged with this as, unless D admits he intended to steal when he entered, it is difficult for the prosecution to prove the intent.

The law is also clear where D gains entry through fraud, such as where he claims to be a gas meter reader. There is no genuine permission to enter and D is a trespasser.

11.2.4 *Mens rea* for burglary

There are two parts to the *mens rea* in burglary. These are in respect of:

- entering as a trespasser and
- the ulterior offence.

First, for both s 9(1)(a) and s 9(1)(b) the defendant must know, or be subjectively reckless, as to whether he is trespassing. In addition, for s 9(1)(a) the defendant must have the intention to commit one of the three offences at the time of entering the building. Where D is entering intending to steal anything he can find which is worth taking, then this is called a conditional intent. This is sufficient for D to be guilty under s 9(1)(a) even if there is nothing worth taking and he does not actually steal anything.

For s 9(1)(b) the defendant must also have the *mens rea* for theft or grievous bodily harm when committing (or attempting to commit) the *actus reus* of one of these offences.

Key facts

Elements	Comment	Case/section
Entry	This has changed from: • 'effective and substantial' entry to • 'effective' entry to • evidence for the jury to find D had entered.	*Collins* (1972) *Brown* (1985) *Ryan* (1996)
Building or part of a building	Must have some permanence. Includes inhabited vehicle or vessel. Can be entry of part of a building.	*B and S v Leathley* (1979) *Norfolk Constabulary v Seekings and Gould* (1986) s 9(4) Theft Act 1968 *Walkington* (1979)
As a trespasser	If D has permission he is not a trespasser. If D goes beyond permission then he can be a trespasser.	*Collins* (1972) *Smith and Jones* (1976)
Mens rea	D must know or be subjectively reckless as to whether he is a trespasser PLUS EITHER Intention at point of entry to commit: • theft or • grievous bodily harm or • criminal damage OR *Mens rea* for theft or grievous bodily harm at point of committing or attempting to commit these offences in a building.	s 9(1)(a) Theft Act 1968 s 9(1)(b) Theft Act 1968

Figure 11.3 Key facts chart for burglary

11.3 Problems in the law on robbery and burglary

11.3.1 The element of theft in robbery

Robbery requires a theft to be completed. However, there is a difference in the way that the law on theft is applied in robbery to the way the courts have applied it in theft cases. In theft cases it has been held that appropriation occurs at one point in time (see 10.1.3).

However, in robbery in the cases of *Hale* (1979) and *Lockley* (1995) the courts have been prepared to view appropriation as a continuing act. In *Lockley* the defendant used force to escape after he had stolen. Despite the fact that the appropriation for the theft occurred before the force, the Court of Appeal still held that the defendant was guilty of robbery. This conflicts with the courts' approach in theft cases.

The theft has to be completed otherwise there is no robbery. It can be argued that a completed theft should not be necessary. This would bring the law into line with burglary. In burglary a defendant is guilty under s 9(1)(a) where he intends to steal (or do various other offences) at the moment he enters as a trespasser. Also, in

Activity

In each of the following, explain whether or not a burglary has occurred and, if so, whether it would be an offence under s 9(1)(a) or s 9(1)(b) Theft Act 1968.

1. Jonny has been banned from a local pub. One evening he goes there for a drink with a friend. While he is waiting for the friend to get the drinks at the bar, Jonny sees a handbag under one of the chairs. He picks it up and takes a £10 note from it. He then puts the handbag back under the chair.
2. Ken and his partner, Lola, have split up and Ken has moved out of the flat he shared with Lola, taking most of his belongings with him. One evening he goes back there to collect the rest of his belongings. Lola is out and he asks the neighbour to let him have the spare key which the neighbour keeps for emergencies. While Ken is packing his clothes, Lola returns. They have an argument and Ken beats up Lola causing her serious injuries.
3. Nyasha works as a shelf-filler in a DIY store. One day when he is putting packs of batteries out onto a shelf, he slips one in his pocket. He does not intend to pay for it. Later in the day he sees the manager leave her office. Nyasha goes in and takes money from the desk. The door to the office has a notice saying 'Private'.
4. Nigella, who is a pupil at the local comprehensive, goes to the school buildings late in the evening after school. She intends to damage the science lab as she hates the teacher. She gets in through a window but is caught by the caretaker before she does any damage.

s 9(1)(b) a defendant is guilty if having entered as a trespasser he attempts to steal. If it is thought to be just that a defendant can be guilty of burglary where he intends or attempts, then there seems no reason why the same rules should not have been applied to robbery. To bring the law into line with burglary, the law would need to be altered to include that a person would be guilty of robbery if he used force intending to steal or if he attempted to steal using force for that purpose.

11.3.2 Level of force in robbery

The level of force required for robbery is very low. There is also the problem that in *Dawson and James* (1976) the Court of Appeal held that 'force' was an ordinary word and it was for the jury to decide if there had been force. There are not likely to be any problems in deciding whether there had been force where higher levels of force have been used such as pointing a gun at the victim or punching them. The problems arise where the force is minimal, and different juries may come to different decisions as to whether or not there has been force.

In fact some of the decisions on the amount of force seem to contradict what was intended by the Criminal Law Revision Committee when they proposed the law. They said in their report that they would not regard 'mere snatching of property, such as a handbag, from an unresisting owner as using force for the purpose of the definition [of robbery], though it might be so if the owner resisted'. Despite this the Court of Appeal in the case *Clouden* (1987) upheld the defendant's conviction for snatching a handbag from the victim.

11.3.3 Intention in burglary

There are anomalies between the different ways of committing burglary under s 9(1)(a) and s 9(1)(b). Under s 9(1)(a) the defendant at the time of entering must have the intention to inflict grievous bodily harm, steal something from inside the building, or damage the building or anything in it. For s 9(1)(b) there is no need to prove the defendant's intention at the time of entry, but it must be shown that once in the building he stole (or attempted to) or inflicted grievous bodily harm (or attempted to).

Protecting people or property

The first point is that the defendant need only intend some damage (even slight) to be guilty under s 9(1)(a). Yet so far as injuring a person is concerned, the prosecution must prove an intention to inflict grievous bodily harm. This difference appears to be placing the protection of property above the protection of people.

Section 9(1)(a) and (1)(b)

However, under s 9(1)(b) only theft or inflicting grievous bodily harm will trigger the required elements for burglary. This has the effect that under s 9(1)(a) a defendant who enters a building as a trespasser with the intention of causing damage is guilty of burglary, while under s 9(1)(b) a defendant who enters a building as a trespasser with no particular intention and then when in the building damages it or other property, has not committed burglary.

There seems no reason why damage should not be included as one of the trigger offences for s 9(1)(b). The point of s 9(1)(b) is to catch the opportunist burglar: that is, the person who only decides to steal or cause gbh after they have entered. So it would be logical to include criminal damage as one of the 'trigger' offences under s 9(1)(b).

Another comparison between the two subsections is that it is easier to prove a s 9(1)(b) burglary than s 9(1)(a). This is because for s 9(1)(a) the defendant's intention has to be proved, while for s 9(1)(b) the commission of one of the trigger offences has to be proved. Proving a fact is easier than proving intention.

Conditional intention

As already pointed out, a defendant can be guilty of burglary based on his intention when he enters the building as a trespasser. The courts have interpreted this as including where the defendant only intends to steal if there is something worth taking, as in *Walkington* (1979) where the defendant would have stolen from the till in the shop if there had been anything in it to steal. This is known as conditional intention. It can be argued that convicting of the completed offence of burglary on conditional intention is unjust. Conditional intention does not permit a conviction for the full offence in other situations. In particular, in robbery there must be a completed theft as intention to steal is not sufficient for the offence.

Lack of definitions

The Theft Act 1968 does not define key elements of the offence of burglary. There is no definition of 'entry', 'trespasser' or 'part of a building'. 'Building' is only defined to extend its meaning to include inhabited places such as houseboats and caravans. There is no other definition of 'building'.

This lack of definitions means that the courts have had to decide what the Act was meant to cover. This has created difficulty in some cases and inconsistent decisions, especially on what is meant by 'entry'.

Entry

The law on entry has changed through the cases of *Collins*, *Brown* and *Ryan*. In *Collins* the Court of Appeal clearly stated that there had to be 'an effective and substantial entry'. However, in *Brown* the Court of Appeal discarded the 'substantial' element of entry and ruled that *Brown* was guilty of burglary as his entry was 'effective'.

In the case of *Ryan* even the need for the entry to be 'effective' was abandoned. Ryan's conviction was upheld on the basis that there was evidence on which the jury could find that the defendant had entered the house.

The decisions in these cases are inconsistent and leave the law uncertain. The problems might have been avoided if the Theft Act had given a definition of 'entry'.

Building

Generally the meaning of building has not caused problems in cases. There are only a few instances where it has been difficult to decide if the place the defendant has entered is a building or not.

The main problems have come where the place was not originally intended as a building but its use has become that of a building. This was seen in the cases of *B and S v Leathley* (1979) and *Norfolk Constabulary v Seekings and Gould* (1986). It appears from these two cases that it will depend on the exact facts of the case as to whether the court will take the view that the place is a building or not. Again, this leaves the law uncertain.

Part of a building

The Act included this phrase as it is clear that there are many situations when a defendant can be lawfully in one part of a building, but not in another part. There is no problem with most of the situations that can arise: for example, a resident in a block of flats entering a neighbouring flat and stealing property from there, or someone entering a room clearly marked 'private' or 'staff only'.

The only case in which the decision can be criticised is *Walkington*. This extended 'part of a building' to include an area which had a counter around three sides but was open on one side. There were no walls or partitions clearly separating the place out from the rest of the store floor area. The argument was that it was sufficiently clearly defined by the counter and that the counter area was intended only for staff use.

The problem arose because, as the till was empty, the defendant did not actually steal anything. This meant he could not be charged with theft. Also, at the time, it the law was that it

was impossible to be guilty of attempted theft if there was nothing to steal.

So Walkington at that time could not have been guilty of attempted theft either. This meant that unless he could be charged with burglary he would have not been guilty of any offence. However, the law on attempts has been changed by the Criminal Attempts Act 1981 and Walkington's actions would now constitute attempted theft. So this decision is really irrelevant today as there is another and, arguably, more accurate offence with which someone could now be charged.

Trespasser

The original use of the word 'trespasser' in law comes from the civil law. When the Theft Act was first passed, it was assumed that the meaning of 'trespasser' would be the same as in the civil law. This is that trespass is entry without the consent of the lawful occupier of the building.

However, in *Collins* the Court of Appeal made it clear that more than this is required. The defendant must enter 'knowing he was a trespasser or was reckless as to whether or not he was entering the premises of another without the other party's consent.'

This element of knowledge of trespassing or being reckless as to whether he is a trespasser is important in the criminal law. It is part of the *mens rea* of the offence of burglary.

The main problems on the issue of 'trespasser' come where the defendant has gone beyond the permission he was given to enter the building.

Going beyond permission

Another area of the law on burglary which can be criticised is where judges have decided that a person who is not a trespasser can become one when he goes beyond the permission given to him. In *Smith and Jones* (1976) the Court of Appeal ruled that the son of the householder was a trespasser where he had entered and stolen two television sets even though the father stated that his son would not be a trespasser in the house; he had a general permission to enter. This decision could mean that a guest at a dinner party in someone's house may become a trespasser if they go into another room, such as a bedroom, uninvited. If they then steal in that room, they could be guilty of burglary.

The concept of burglary originally was to protect people's homes and other buildings from trespassers who intended to (or did) steal etc. There is no need to extend the law on burglary to include people who have permission to be in the house, even though they have gone beyond their permission. A thief, as in *Smith and Jones* (1976),

can still be charged with theft.

This concept of going beyond the permission has also been applied to shoplifters on the basis that the permission to enter a shop is only given for legitimate shopping purposes. Where someone enters and then steals, they can be considered to have gone beyond the permission given to them when they entered.

As with the *Smith and Jones* case, there is no need to charge such a person with burglary. The obvious and correct charge for this behaviour is theft.

Examination questions

1. Ricky, a student, has no food in his cupboard. He goes to a local supermarket taking an mp3 player belonging to his flatmate, Paul, so that he can listen to some music. He enters the supermarket and goes to the chiller units. He picks up a tray of chicken breasts which he places inside his coat. He notices that another shopper is watching him. Ricky replaces the chicken breasts in the chiller unit and runs out of the store.

   Feeling cold, Ricky decides to go to the local cinema to watch a film and keep warm. On his way out he sees there is no one around so he reaches behind a counter at the kiosk in the foyer and takes some chocolate bars.

   As he is walking home, Ricky sees a wallet lying in the gutter. It contains £500 in ten-pound notes. He decides to keep the money but leaves the wallet. He gives the mp3 player back to Paul but he has cracked the display screen and erased 1,000 of Paul's favourite tracks.

   Consider what offences, if any, Ricky has committed.

   (OCR, Unit 2572, January 2008)

2. John enters a supermarket intending to steal some food. He is in the shop when he notices that the door to the manager's office is open. He goes inside hoping to find something of value. There is no one present but, as he is about to leave, he notices a wallet lying on the manager's desk. John picks the wallet up and takes a £20 note out of it. The manager, Sue, sees him leaving the office and shouts at him. John pushes Sue aside and runs out of the store.

   Evaluate the accuracy of each of the four statements A, B, C and D individually, as they apply to the facts in the above scenario.

   Statement A: John is guilty of burglary under s 9(1)(a) Theft Act 1968.

   Statement B: John is guilty of theft under s 1 Theft Act 1968

   Statement C: John is guilty of robbery under s 8 Theft Act 1968.

   Statement D: John is guilty of burglary under s 9(1)(b) Theft Act 1968.

   (OCR, Specimen Paper)

Chapter 12

Defences

When a person is charged with an offence, there are various defences that may be available to them. Some defences can be used for any offence; other defences can only be used for some offences. Normally, if a defence is used successfully the defendant is acquitted of the crime and is free. The exception to this is the defence of insanity where a special verdict of 'not guilty by reason of insanity' is given.

Figure 12.1 shows the availability of the defences. It also shows limitations on when the defences can be used.

Defence	Availability	Limitation
Insanity	All offences where *mens rea* is required.	Not available for strict liability offences where no mental element is required.
Automatism	All offences.	Not available for offences of basic intent if the automatic state is self-induced through drink or drugs.
Intoxication	Offences of specific intent including murder, s 18 OAPA, and theft if the intoxication prevents D from forming the required *mens rea*.	Not available for offences of basic intent, manslaughter, ss 20 and 47 OAPA, assault, battery.
Duress	Most offences.	Not available for murder, attempted murder or, possibly, treason.
Necessity	Possibly all offences including murder.	BUT is very rarely successful.

Figure 12.1 Availability of defences

12.1 Insanity

12.1.1 The M'Naghten Rules

The rules on insanity are based on the M'Naghten Rules (1843).

M'Naghten (1843)

D suffered from extreme paranoia. He thought he was being persecuted by the 'Tories' (the then Government). He tried to kill a member of the Government, Sir Robert Peel, but instead killed his secretary. Because of his mental state D was found not guilty of murder. In fact, he was committed to a mental hospital because of his mental state, but this was not as a result of the verdict. The fact that he could be found not guilty and need not have been sent to a mental hospital caused a public outcry, leading the judges in the House of Lords to answer a series of questions in order to clarify the law in respect of insanity. The answers to those questions have created the rules on insanity which are used in legal cases today.

The answer that the House of Lords gave in the case of *M'Naghten* (1843) created the rules on insanity. The main rule is that:

> 'in all cases every man is presumed to be sane and to possess a sufficient degree of reason to be responsible for his crimes'.

For the defence of insanity to be established, the House of Lords gave the following definition showing what a defendant must prove at the time of committing the act if the defence of insanity is to be successful.

Definition

Insanity

The defendant must be 'labouring under such a defect of reason, from disease of the mind, as not to know the nature and quality of the act he was doing, or if he did know it, that he did not know he was doing what was wrong.'

From this it can be seen that three elements need to be proved. These are:

1. a defect of reason
2. which must be the result of a disease of the mind
3. causing the defendant not to know the nature and quality of his act *or* not to know he was doing wrong.

The burden of proving insanity is on the defence, who must prove it on the balance of probabilities. Where a defendant is found to be insane, the verdict is 'not guilty by reason of insanity'.

It used to be thought that insanity was a defence to all offences. However, in *DPP v H* (1997), where the defendant was charged with driving with excess alcohol, it was held that insanity is not a defence to offences of strict liability where no mental element is required.

12.1.2 Defect of reason

This means that the defendant's powers of reasoning must be impaired. If the defendant is capable of reasoning but has failed to use those powers, then this is not a defect of reason. This was decided in *Clarke* (1972) where it was held that the defect of reason must be more than absent-mindedness or confusion.

Clarke (1972)

D went into a supermarket, picked up three items including a jar of mincemeat, put them into her own bag and then left the store without paying. She was charged with theft but claimed in her defence that she lacked the *mens rea* for theft as she had no recollection of putting the items into her bag. Indeed, she did not even want the mincemeat as neither she nor her husband ate it. She said she was suffering from absent-mindedness caused by diabetes and depression. The trial judge ruled that this amounted to a plea of insanity, so she then pleaded guilty to the theft but appealed against it.

The Court of Appeal quashed the conviction. They held that the phrase 'defect of reason' in the M'Naghten Rules applied only to 'persons who by reason of a "disease of the mind" are deprived of the power of reasoning'. The Court of Appeal also said that the rules of insanity do not apply to people who simply have moments of confusion or absent-mindedness.

12.1.3 Disease of the mind

The defect of reason must be due to a disease of the mind. This is a legal term, not a medical one. The disease can be a mental disease or a physical disease which affects the mind. An example of this is seen in *Kemp* (1956).

Kemp (1956)

D was suffering from hardening of the arteries which caused a problem with supply of the blood to the brain. This caused D to have moments of temporary loss of consciousness. During one of these he attacked his wife with a hammer causing her serious injury. He was charged with inflicting grievous bodily harm under s 20 of the Offences Against the Person Act 1861.

At his trial the question arose as to whether this condition came within the rules on insanity. D admitted that he was suffering from a 'defect of reason' but said that this was not due to a 'disease of the mind' as it was a physical illness causing the problem and not a mental illness. He was found 'not guilty by reason of insanity' and appealed against this finding. The Court of Appeal upheld this finding, stating that the law was not concerned with the brain but with the mind. Kemp's ordinary mental faculties of reason, memory and understanding had been affected and so his condition came within the rules on insanity.

In *Sullivan* (1984) the House of Lords was asked to decide whether epilepsy came within the rules of insanity.

Sullivan (1984)

D, aged 51, had suffered from epilepsy since childhood. He was known to have fits and had shown aggression to those trying to help him during a fit. He injured an 80-year-old man during a friendly visit to a neighbour's flat. The trial judge ruled that on the facts he would be directing the jury to return a verdict of 'not guilty by reason of insanity'. As a result of this, D pleaded guilty to assault occasioning actual bodily (s 47 OAPA). D then appealed. Both the Court of Appeal and the House of Lords confirmed the conviction.

The House of Lords ruled that the source of the disease was irrelevant. It could be 'organic, as in epilepsy, or functional', and it did not matter whether the impairment was 'permanent or transient and intermittent', provided that it existed at the time at which the defendant did the act.

This ruling means that for the purpose of the M'Naghten Rules, the disease can be of any part of the body provided it has an effect on the mind. In *Hennessy* (1989) high blood sugar levels because of diabetes were classed as insanity because the levels affect the mind.

Hennessy (1989)

D was a diabetic who had not taken his insulin for three days. He was seen getting into a car which had been reported stolen and driving off. He was charged with taking a motor vehicle without consent and driving while disqualified. He had no recollection of taking or driving the car. The judge ruled that on these facts D was putting forward a defence of insanity (and not non-insane automatism which the defendant wanted to use as a defence (see section 12.2 below). D then pleaded guilty, rather than have a verdict of not guilty by reason of insanity. He appealed on the basis that he should have been allowed to put forward the defence of non-insane automatism.

The Court of Appeal held that the correct defence was insanity as the disease of diabetes was affecting his mind. Thus diabetes was brought within the definition of insanity.

Another case in which it was held that the correct defence was insanity was *Burgess* (1991). In this case it was decided that, in some instances, sleep-walking was within the legal definition of insanity.

Burgess (1991)

D and his girlfriend had been watching videos. They fell asleep and in his sleep D attacked the girl. There was no evidence of any external cause for the sleep-walking and a doctor at the trial gave evidence that in this instance it was due to an internal cause: a sleep disorder. The judge ruled that this was evidence of insanity and the defendant was found 'not guilty by reason of insanity'. The Court of Appeal upheld the finding.

However, if the sleep-walking is due to an external cause, such as a blow to the head, then it is not insanity but will allow the defendant the defence of automatism (see section 12.2).

External factors

Where the cause of the defendant being in a state where he does not know what he is doing is not a disease but an external cause, then this is not insanity.

Quick (1973)

D was a diabetic who had taken his insulin but then not eaten enough. This causes low blood sugar levels which can affect the brain. In this state D, who was a nurse at a mental hospital, assaulted a patient. The Court of Appeal ruled that his condition did not come within the definition of insanity. It was caused by an external matter, in this case the drug insulin. This meant that D could rely on the defence of automatism (see section 12.2) and was entitled to be acquitted of the charge.

The decisions in *Hennessy* (1989) and *Quick* (1973) highlight the problems with the law. People with diabetes can go into an automatic state in which they do not know what they are doing. This state can be caused by:

- the disease itself which causes high levels of blood sugar (hyperglycaemia), or
- the drug, insulin, which is used to control the levels of blood sugar. If, after taking insulin, D fails to eat, the blood sugar level will become too low (hypoglycaemia).

If it is the disease which causes the automatic state then, as shown in *Hennessy* (1989), the defendant is considered to come within the rules of insanity as it is an internal cause. If it is the drug which causes the automatic state then, as shown in *Quick* (1973), they are not within the rules on insanity but can rely on the defence of automatism.

It seems ridiculous that a physical disease such as diabetes is classed as insanity, but it is even more ridiculous that diabetics have to rely on different defences available according to whether it was the drug or the disease itself which caused the automatic state.

12.1.4 Not knowing the nature and quality of the act

Nature and quality refer to the physical character of the act. There are two ways in which the defendant may not know the nature and quality of the act. These are:

- because he is in a state of unconsciousness or impaired consciousness, or
- when he is conscious but due to his mental condition he does not understand or know what he is doing.

If the defendant can show that either of these states applied to him at the time he did the act, then he satisfies this part of the M'Naghten Rules.

An example of not knowing the nature and quality of the act is where a nurse threw a baby onto a fire believing it to be piece of wood.

Where the defendant knows the nature and quality of the act he still can use the defence of insanity if he does not know that what he did was wrong. Wrong, in this sense, means legally wrong not morally wrong. If the defendant knows the nature and quality of the act and that it is legally wrong, he cannot use the defence of insanity. This is so even if the defendant is suffering from a mental illness.

Windle (1952)

D's wife constantly spoke of committing suicide. One day the defendant killed her by giving her 100 aspirins. He gave himself up to the police and said 'I suppose they will hang me for this'. He was suffering from mental illness, but these words showed that he knew what he had done was legally wrong. As a result he could not use the defence of insanity and was found guilty of murder.

Note that this case was in 1952 and the special defence of diminished responsibility to a charge of murder did not exist. That defence was only created in 1957, so Windle could not use it.

The case of *Windle* was followed more recently in *Johnson* (2007).

Johnson (2007)

D forced his way into a neighbour's flat and stabbed him. D was charged with wounding with intent (s 20 OAPA 1861). At his trial two psychiatrists gave evidence that he was suffering from paranoid schizophrenia and suffering from hallucinations. However, they both agreed that, despite this, D knew the nature and quality of his acts and that they were legally wrong. One psychiatrist was of the view that D did not consider that what he had done was wrong in the moral sense. The judge ruled that the defence of insanity was not available to D and D was convicted of wounding with intent.

The Court of Appeal upheld the judge's ruling that insanity was not available as D knew the nature and quality of his acts and that they were legally wrong. They followed the decision in *Windle* (1952) where the court had held that the word 'wrong' meant knowing that the act was contrary to law.

In their judgment in *Johnson*, the Court of Appeal pointed out that there had been an Australian case in which the Australian courts had refused to follow *Windle* (1952). The view of the Australian court was that if a defendant believed his act to be right according to the ordinary standard of reasonable men, then he was entitled to be acquitted even if he knew that it was legally wrong.

The Court of Appeal felt they were obliged to follow *Windle* (1952), but they did express the opinion that the Australian case contained 'illuminating passages indicating the difficulties and internal inconsistencies which can arise from the application of the M'Naghten Rules if the decision in *Windle* is correct'.

12.1.5 The special verdict

When a defendant successfully proves insanity, then the jury must return a verdict of 'not guilty by reason of insanity'. Up to 1991 the judge then had to send the defendant to a mental hospital regardless of the cause of the insanity or the offence committed. This was clearly not suitable for cases where the defendant suffered from diabetes, epilepsy or hardening of the arteries. So, in 1991 the Criminal Procedure (Insanity and Unfitness to Plead) Act was passed to extend the options for the judge.

The judge can now impose:

- a hospital order (with or without restrictions as to when the defendant may be released)
- a supervision order
- an absolute discharge.

If the defendant is charged with murder then the judge must impose an indefinite hospital order. This means that the hospital can only release the defendant from the hospital if the Home Secretary gives consent.

12.1.6 Problems with the law of insanity

The first major problem is that the definition of insanity was set by the M'Naghten Rules in 1843.

At that time medical knowledge of mental disorders was very limited. Much more is known today about mental disorders and a more modern definition should be used.

The definition needs to be updated in the light of modern understanding of mental illness. The only area which Parliament has reformed is the options available to judges when dealing with those found not guilty by reason of insanity.

At least this wider range of options has stopped the injustice of epileptics and diabetics having to be sent to a mental hospital. Prior to the Criminal Procedure (Insanity and Unfitness to Plead) Act 1991 the only course available to a judge was to send the defendant to a mental hospital. Judges can now instead put the defendant on a supervision order or give an absolute discharge.

Legal definition of insanity

Another major problem is that the definition has become a legal one rather than a medical one. This causes two problems.

1. People suffering from certain mental disorders do not come within the definition, for example those suffering from irresistible impulses and who are psychopaths such as *Byrne* (1960). They do not come within the M'Naghten Rules as they know what they are doing and that it is wrong. However, they cannot prevent themselves from acting and have a recognised mental disorder.
2. On the other hand those suffering from physical illnesses such as diabetes (*Hennessy* (1989)), brain tumours or hardening of the arteries (*Kemp* (1957)) are considered to be legally insane. Even a sleep-walker has come within the definition (*Burgess* (1991)). The justification for this is that there is an internal cause of their actions: the behaviour may recur and it may be possible to treat it.

Key facts

	Law	Case
Definition	D must be labouring under a defect of reason, from disease of the mind; and must either not know the nature and quality of the act he was doing, or not know he was doing wrong.	*M'Naghten* (1843)
Defect of reason	D's powers of reasoning must be impaired. Absent-mindedness is not enough.	*Clarke* (1972)
Disease of the mind	This is a legal term NOT a medical one. There must be an internal cause. It need not be permanent; it can be 'transient and intermittent'. An external cause is not sufficient.	*Kemp* (1956) *Sullivan* (1984) *Quick* (1973)
Not know nature and quality of act OR Not know he is doing wrong	This means that D must not know it is legally wrong: if he does he cannot rely on the defence of insanity.	*Windle* (1952) *Johnson* (2007)
Special verdict	Not guilty by reason of insanity. Judge can impose: • a hospital order • a guardianship order • a supervision and treatment order • an absolute discharge.	Criminal Procedure (Insanity and Unfitness to Plead) Act 1991

Figure 12.2 Key facts chart on insanity

The overlap with automatism

Insanity overlaps with automatism. It is necessary to decide whether the defendant's automatic state is due to a mental illness or due to external factors. The courts have decided that those suffering from any illness, mental or physical, which affects their mind or puts them into an automatic state amounts to insanity. This means that the defence of non-insane automatism has been removed from such people as epileptics and diabetics.

This has serious consequences, as those successfully using the defence of automatism are entitled to a complete acquittal. Whereas, on a finding of not guilty by reason of insanity, the judge has to impose some order on the defendant.

It may be argued that the reason the courts are reluctant to allow defendants to use the full defence of automatism is because it will lead to an acquittal and the defendant will be free from any order or supervision. There is the argument that, even though the cause of the erratic behaviour may be a physical illness, there is still the risk that such a person may commit further offences. Extending insanity to cover those who commit an offence because of a physical illness means that these people can be supervised.

Decision in *Windle* (1952)

Following the decision in *Windle* (1952), a defendant who is suffering from a serious recognised mental illness and who does not know that his act is morally wrong cannot have a defence of insanity when he knows that his act is legally wrong. An Australian case refused to follow this decision. In *Johnson* (2007) the Court of Appeal clearly thought that the Australian case had some merit, but they were obliged to follow *Windle*.

Social stigma

Even the use of the word 'insanity' is unfortunate. It carries a social stigma. It is bad enough to apply it to people who are suffering from mental disorders, but it is entirely inappropriate to apply it to those suffering from such diseases as epilepsy or diabetes.

Proof of insanity

The defendant has to prove that he is insane. This places the burden of proof on him. It is possible that this is in breach of Article 6 of the European Convention on Human Rights, which states that the defendant is innocent until proven guilty.

There is also the point that the jury is required to decide if the defendant is insane or not. This is not an appropriate function for a jury. It is a matter which should be decided by medical experts. Where there is dispute, the jury has to listen to medical evidence and try to understand technical and complex psychiatric issues.

The role of the jury

As jurors have to decide if the verdict should be not guilty by reason of insanity, it means that ordinary people with no medical knowledge have to make what is, in effect, a medical decision. This means there is potential for jurors to be confused over the medical evidence due to the technical terminology of psychiatric medicine.

There is also the possibility that jurors may be so revolted by the crimes committed by the person that they will refuse to return the verdict of not guilty by reason of insanity. Especially in murder cases, jurors may disregard the medical evidence and, instead of returning the special verdict, find the defendant guilty of murder.

This actually happened in the case of Peter Sutcliffe, the 'Yorkshire Ripper', in 1981 where the defendant was charged with the murder of several women. All the doctors giving evidence agreed that the defendant was suffering from paranoid schizophrenia, a recognised serious mental illness. Despite this the jury found Sutcliffe guilty of murder.

Overlap with diminished responsibility

Since 1957, for defendants with mental illness charged with murder, there has been an alternative defence of diminished responsibility. If successful in this defence the charge of murder is reduced to manslaughter. This allows the judge a wider range of sentencing options.

Diminished responsibility covers a wider range of mental illnesses than insanity. It is much more likely to be used as a defence to a murder charge than insanity. In the 1990s there were on average about 50 cases per year where the defendant relied successfully on the defence of diminished responsibility. In contrast there were only on average about five cases a year where the defendant relied on the defence of insanity.

These figures show that for murder, insanity is not particularly important as a defence. There is a better alternative which does not carry the stigma of insanity.

Interestingly, the use of both defences has gone down in the last nine or ten years. There have been only about 20 cases each year where the defendant relied on diminished responsibility and only one or two cases where the defence relied on the defence of insanity.

12.1.7 Proposals for reform

There have been several proposals for reform of the law on insanity. In 1953, the Royal Commission on Capital Punishment suggested that the M'Naghten Rules should be extended so that a defendant would be considered insane if he 'was incapable of preventing himself' from committing the offence. If this had been acted upon, then those suffering from 'irresistible impulses' would have come within the definition of insanity.

However, instead of making this reform, the Government introduced the defence of diminished responsibility. This gives a special defence to those charged with murder (see section 7.1). It does not give a defence to any other offence, but judges have discretion on sentencing for all other offences.

In 1975, the Butler Committee suggested that

Key cases

Case	Facts	Law
M'Naghten (1843)	Suffering from paranoia, shot Sir Robert Peel's secretary. Acquitted but House of Lords asked to clarify the law on insanity.	D must be labouring under a defect of reason, from disease of the mind; and must either not know the nature and quality of the act he was doing, or not know he was doing wrong.
Clarke (1972)	Absent-mindedly took items from a supermarket.	Mere absent-mindedness or confusion is not insanity.
Kemp (1956)	Suffering from hardening of the arteries which caused blackouts.	Was within the rules of insanity as his condition affected his mental reasoning, memory and understanding.
Sullivan (1984)	Injured friend during epileptic fit.	Insanity included any organic or functional disease. It also applied even where it was temporary.
Hennessy (1989)	Diabetic who took a car after failing to take his insulin.	If the disease affects the mind then it is within the definition of insanity.
Burgess (1991)	Injured his girlfriend while he was asleep.	If the cause of sleep-walking is internal, it is a disease within the definition of insanity.
Quick (1973)	Diabetic who failed to eat after taking his insulin.	This was an external cause (the effect of the drug) and so not insanity.
Windle (1952)	Was suffering from a mental disorder and killed his wife, who had constantly spoken of committing suicide.	Because he knew what he had done was legally wrong, he was not insane by the *M'Naghten* Rules.
Johnson (2007)	D, who was suffering from paranoid schizophrenia and hallucinations, stabbed his neighbour.	Because he knew what he had done was legally wrong, he was not insane by the *M'Naghten* Rules.

Figure 12.3 Key cases on insanity

the verdict of not guilty by reason of insanity should be replaced by a verdict of not guilty on evidence of mental disorder.

In 1989, the Law Commission's Draft Criminal Code proposed that a defendant should be not guilty on evidence of severe mental disorder or severe mental handicap.

None of these proposals have been made law. However, changes to the ways in which judges can deal with a defendant after they are found not guilty by reason of insanity, has improved matters. As explained in section 12.1.5, a judge can now make a supervision and treatment order or even give an absolute discharge where that is suitable.

12.2 Automatism

In *Bratty v Attorney-General for Northern Ireland* (1963) automatism was clearly defined.

Definition

Automatism

An act done by the muscles without any control by the mind, such as a spasm, a reflex action or a convulsion; or an act done by a person who is not conscious of what he is doing such as an act done whilst suffering from concussion or whilst sleep-walking.

In fact this definition covers two types of automatism:

1. **Insane automatism**
   This is where the cause of the automatism is a disease of the mind within the M'Naghten Rules. In such a case the defence is insanity and the verdict not guilty by reason of insanity. The law on insanity is set out in section 12.1 of this chapter.
2. **Non-insane automatism**
   This is where the cause is an external one. Where such a defence succeeds, it is a complete defence and the defendant is not guilty.

12.2.1 Non-insane automatism

This is a defence because the *actus reus* done by the defendant is not voluntary. In addition the defendant does not have the required *mens rea* for the offence.

The cause of the automatism must be external. Examples of external causes include:

- a blow to the head
- an attack by a swarm of bees
- sneezing
- hypnotism
- the effect of a drug.

This concept of no fault when the defendant was in an automatic state through an external cause was approved in *Hill v Baxter* (1958).

Hill v Baxter (1958)

D drove through a halt sign without stopping, and collided with another car. He was charged with dangerous driving but acquitted by the magistrates who accepted that he remembered nothing from some distance before reaching the halt sign. The Divisional Court allowed the prosecution's appeal and remitted the case back to the magistrates with a direction to convict as there was no evidence to support a defence of automatism.

The court approved the judgment in the earlier case of *Kay v Butterworth* (1945) where the judge said:

'A person should not be made liable at the criminal law who, through no fault of his own, becomes unconscious when driving, as, for example, a person who has been struck by a stone or overcome by a sudden illness, or when the car has been put temporarily out of his control owing to his being attacked by a swarm of bees.'

In *T* (1990) it was accepted that exceptional stress can be an external factor which may cause automatism.

T (1990)

D was raped. Three days later she took part in a robbery and an assault. She claimed that at the time she was suffering from post-traumatic stress disorder as a result of the rape and that she had acted in a dream-like state. The trial judge allowed the defence of automatism to go to the jury, but D was convicted.

Reduced or partial control of one's actions is not sufficient to constitute non-insane automatism. In *Attorney-General's Reference (No 2 of 1992)* (1993) the Court of Appeal held that there must be 'total destruction of voluntary control'.

Attorney-General's Reference (No 2 of 1992) (1993)

D was a lorry driver, who after driving for several hours, drove along the hard shoulder of a motorway for about half a mile. He hit a broken-down car which was stationary on the hard shoulder, killing two people. He said that he was suffering from the condition 'driving without awareness' which puts a driver into a trance-like state. It may be brought on by driving for long distances on motorways. The jury acquitted him. The Attorney-General referred the point of law to the Court of Appeal who ruled that because this condition only causes partial loss of control it did not amount to automatism.

12.2.2 Self-induced automatism

This is where the defendant knows that his conduct is likely to bring on an automatic state. Examples include a diabetic, who knows the risk of failing to eat after taking insulin, or a person who drinks after taking medication when he has

been told by his doctor that he must not take alcohol while on that medication. This law comes from the case of *Bailey* (1983).

Bailey (1983)

D was a diabetic who had failed to eat enough after taking his insulin to control the diabetes. He became aggressive and hit someone over the head with an iron bar. The trial judge ruled that the defence of automatism was not available. The Court of Appeal held that this ruling was wrong but upheld D's conviction as there was insufficient evidence in the case to raise the defence of automatism.

Although the appeal was dismissed in *Bailey*, the Court of Appeal set out the rules on self-induced automatism. The first point was that there is a difference in the way the defence applies to specific intent offence and basic intent offences.

Specific intent offences

If the offence charged is one of specific intent, then self-induced automatism can be a defence. This is because the defendant lacks the required *mens rea* for the offence.

Basic intent offences

If the offence charged is one of basic intent then the law is more complicated. The main rule is that the defendant cannot use the defence of automatism if he has brought about the automatic state by being reckless. The law set out in *Bailey* (1983) states:

1. If the defendant has been reckless in getting into a state of automatism, self-induced automatism cannot be a defence. Subjective recklessness is sufficient for the *mens rea* of crimes of basic intent.
2. Where the self-induced automatic state is caused through drink or illegal drugs or other intoxicating substances, the defendant cannot

use the defence of automatism. This is because *DPP v Majewski* (1977) decided that becoming voluntarily intoxicated is a reckless course of conduct (see section 12.3).

3. Where the defendant does not know that his actions are likely to lead to a self-induced automatic state in which he may commit an offence, he has not been reckless and can use the defence of automatism.

This third situation was seen in *Hardie* (1984).

Hardie (1984)

D was depressed because his girlfriend had told him to move out of their flat. He took some Valium tablets which had been prescribed for his former girlfriend. She encouraged him to take the tablets, stating that it would calm him down. He then set fire to a wardrobe in the flat. He said he did not know what he was doing because of the Valium. The trial judge directed the jury to ignore the effect of the tablets and he was convicted of arson.

The Court of Appeal quashed his conviction as the defendant had taken the drug because he thought it would calm him down. This is the normal effect of Valium. So the defendant had not been reckless and the defence of automatism should have been left to the jury.

12.2.3 Problems in the law on automatism

The main problem is that in each case it has to be decided whether the situation is one of insane automatism or non-insane automatism. This is very important as the effect of these two types of automatism as a defence is so different.

Situations which would seem to the non-lawyer to be ones of non-insane automatism, such as a diabetic being in a high blood sugar state, or someone sleep-walking, may at law be considered to be insane automatism.

12.2.4 Proposals for reform in the law on automatism

In the Draft Criminal Code (1989) the following definition was suggested:

> 'A person is not guilty of an offence if –
>
> 1. he acts in a state of automatism, that is, his act
> 2. is a reflex, spasm or convulsion; or
> 3. occurs while he is in a condition (whether of sleep, unconsciousness, impaired consciousness or otherwise) depriving him of effective control of his act; and
> 4. the act or condition is the result neither of anything done or omitted with the fault required for the offence nor of voluntary intoxication.'

This definition would include those who act during an epileptic convulsion, so that cases such as *Sullivan* (1984) would be able to use the defence of non-insane automatism instead of insanity. This would be a welcome improvement to the law.

Also cases of sleep-walking would come under this defence. This would have given *Burgess* (1991) the defence of non-insane automatism. Under the present law he was found not guilty by reason of insanity. In both these cases the defendants under the proposals for reform would have had a full defence.

On the other hand, the present system allows a judge to order medical treatment for those who are found not guilty by reason of insanity. Should there be some way of making sure that those who commit dangerous offences while in an automatic state, and who would benefit from treatment, do in fact receive treatment? It can be argued that a complete acquittal leaves a possibly dangerous person (although not intentionally) to do the same thing again.

Activity

Read the following extract from a newspaper article and answer the questions below.

Jury in rape trial accepts the defence of sleep-walking

'A man accused of raping a female friend three times in a matter of minutes was cleared yesterday after claiming that he had been sleep-walking.

After hearing his unusual defence, the jury took less than three hours to clear him of three rape charges.

York Crown Court heard that he had let the 22-year-old friend sleep in his bed when they returned to his flat after a night out with other friends.

He fell asleep on the sofa and insisted that the next thing he knew was waking up as the "victim" was leaving the flat. She claimed she had fallen asleep and woken up to find him having sex with her.

He said nothing during the alleged rapes and afterwards climbed over her and went back to the sofa.

He said he could not deny having sex with the woman but had no recollection of doing so.

He told the police he had suffered from sleep-walking since he was 13 and had a family history of the condition. "It's the only explanation I can come up with for this," he said.'

(*Daily Mail,* 20th December 2005)

Questions

1. What two defences may be used where the defendant did something while sleep-walking?
2. If these defences are successful, what verdicts will be given by the jury?
3. In the case in this article, the defendant was found not guilty. Which of the two defences did the defendant claim?
4. Name a decided case on this defence.
5. Explain how the defence operates.

Insanity	Automatism
For defence to prove, on the balance of probabilities.	For defendant to raise, the prosecution must then disprove.
Must have a defect of reason due to disease of the mind: M'Naghten Rules.	Must be caused by an external factor.
Example: Diabetic affected by disease: *Hennessey* (1989).	Example: Diabetic affected by (drug) insulin: *Quick* (1973).
Verdict: not guilty by reason of insanity.	Verdict: not guilty.
Judge must make one of the following four orders: ● a hospital order (with or without restrictions as to when the defendant may be released) ● a guardianship order ● a supervision and treatment order ● an absolute discharge.	Defendant is free.

Figure 12.4 Comparison of insanity and automatism as defences

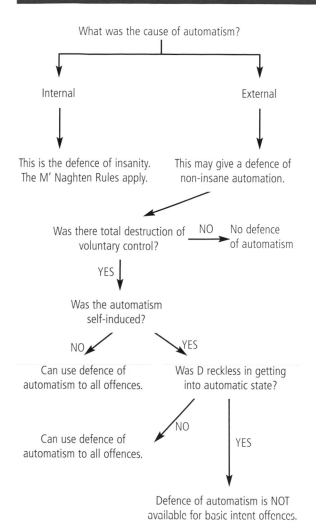

Figure 12.5 Flow chart on automatism

12.3 Intoxication

This covers intoxication by alcohol, drugs or other substances, such as glue-sniffing. Intoxication does not provide a defence as such, but is relevant as to whether or not the defendant has the required *mens rea* for the offence. If he does not have the required *mens rea* because of his intoxicated state, he may be not guilty.

Whether the defendant is guilty or not depends on:

1. whether the intoxication was voluntary or involuntary, and

2. whether the offence charged is one of specific or basic intent.

Specific intent offences are generally those which require specific intention for their *mens rea*. The specific intent offences on the OCR A2 specification are murder, s 18 OAPA 1861, theft, robbery and burglary.

Basic intent offences are generally those for which recklessness is sufficient for the *mens rea*. The basic intent offences on the OCR A2 specification are manslaughter, ss 20 and 47 OAPA 1861, assault and battery.

12.3.1 Voluntary intoxication

Voluntary intoxication is where the defendant has chosen to take an intoxicating substance. This can be by taking alcohol, illegal drugs or other intoxicants such as through sniffing glue. It can also occur where the defendant knows that the effect of a prescribed drug will be to make him intoxicated.

Voluntary intoxication and specific intent offences

Voluntary intoxication can negate the *mens rea* for a specific intent offence. If the defendant is so intoxicated that he has not formed the *mens rea* for the offence, he is not guilty. This rule comes from *DPP v Beard* (1920).

DPP v Beard (1920)

Beard had been charged with murder and had put forward as his defence the fact that he was too intoxicated to have formed the *mens rea* for murder. He was convicted but on appeal, Lord Birkenhead considered previous decisions and stated:

'Where a specific intent is an essential element in the offence, evidence of a state of drunkenness rendering the accused incapable of forming such an intent should be taken into consideration in order to determine whether he had in fact formed the intent necessary to constitute the particular crime.'

Lord Birkenhead then stated the rule which still stands today:

'If he was so drunk that he was incapable of forming the intent required, he could not be convicted of a crime which was committed only if the intent was proved.'

An example of where it was found that the defendants were so drunk that they did not have the *mens rea* for murder is *Sheehan and Moore* (1975). The defendants were very drunk when they threw petrol over a tramp and set fire to him. They were too drunk to have formed any intent to kill or cause grievous bodily harm. It was held that because they did not have the *mens rea* for murder, their intoxication was a defence to that offence. However, they were found guilty of manslaughter as that is a basic intent offence.

Where the defendant has the necessary *mens rea* despite his intoxicated state, then he is guilty of the offence. The intoxication does not provide a defence. It has been held that a drunken intent is still an intent. This was shown by *A-G for Northern Ireland v Gallagher* (1963).

Gallagher (1963)

D decided to kill his wife. He bought a knife to do the killing and also a bottle of whisky. He drank a large amount of the whisky before killing his wife. His conviction for murder was upheld.

Voluntary intoxication and basic intent offences

Where the offence charged is one of basic intent then intoxication is not a defence. This is because voluntarily becoming intoxicated is considered a reckless course of conduct, and recklessness is enough to constitute the necessary *mens rea*. The leading case on this is *DPP v Majweski* (1977).

DPP v Majweski (1977)

D had taken both alcohol and drugs. In a very intoxicated state he then attacked people in a public house and also the police officers who tried to arrest him. He was convicted of three offences of assault occasioning actual bodily harm (s 47 OAPA) and three of assaulting a police officer in the execution of his duty. The House of Lords upheld all these convictions. His intoxicated state was not a defence as the House of Lords said:

'It is a reckless course of conduct and recklessness is enough to constitute the necessary *mens rea*.'

12.3.2 Involuntary intoxication

Involuntary intoxication covers situations where the defendant did not know he was taking an intoxicating substance. This may be where, for example, a soft drink has been 'laced' with alcohol or drugs. It also covers situations where prescribed drugs have the unexpected effect of making the defendant intoxicated.

The test is, did the defendant have the necessary *mens rea* when he committed the offence? If so, it was decided in *Kingston* (1994) that he will be guilty. The involuntary intoxication will not provide a defence. This is so even though the defendant would not have committed the offence without the intoxication lowering his resistance to committing the offence.

Kingston (1994)

The defendant's coffee was drugged by someone who wanted to blackmail him. He was then shown a 15-year-old boy who was asleep and invited to abuse him. The defendant did so and was photographed by the blackmailer. The House of Lords upheld his conviction for indecent assault. They held that if a defendant had formed the *mens rea* for an offence then the involuntary intoxication was not a defence.

Where, however, the defendant did not have the necessary intent he will be not guilty. He has no *mens rea* and so cannot be guilty of a specific intent offence. Neither can he be guilty of a basic intent offence. This is because the defendant has not been reckless in getting intoxicated. An example of this is *Hardie* (1985) (see section 12.2.2) where the defendant took Valium tablets not knowing they could make his behaviour unpredictable.

12.3.3 Intoxicated mistake

If the defendant is mistaken about a key fact because he is intoxicated, then it depends on what the mistake was about as to whether he has a defence or not.

Where the mistake is about something which means that the defendant did not have the necessary *mens rea* for the offence, then for specific intent offence he has a defence. However, where the offence is one of basic intent then the defendant has no defence. An example of this was the case of *Lipman* (1970).

Lipman (1970)

D and his girlfriend had taken the drug LSD before falling asleep at her flat. LSD causes people to have hallucinations. D thought that he was at the centre of the earth and being attacked by snakes. When he awoke he found his girlfriend was dead. He had strangled her and stuffed a sheet into her mouth believing she was a snake attacking him. His conviction for manslaughter was upheld.

Lipman did not have the specific intention for murder as he thought he was killing a snake. He did not intend to kill or cause grievous bodily

harm to any human being. However, he was guilty of manslaughter because he had voluntarily taken the drug LSD. This was 'a reckless course of conduct' and so was guilty of manslaughter.

If the mistake is about another aspect, for example the amount of force needed in self-defence, the defendant will not have a defence. This was stated in *O'Grady* (1987) and confirmed in *Hatton* (2005).

O'Grady (1987)

After D and V, who was a friend, had been drinking heavily, they fell asleep in D's flat. D claimed that he awoke to find V hitting him. D picked up a glass ashtray and hit V with it, and then went back to sleep. When he woke the next morning, he found that V was dead. D was charged with murder but was convicted of manslaughter. The Court of Appeal upheld this conviction.

O'Grady was convicted of manslaughter which is a basic intent offence. This is clearly in line with the decision in *DPP v Majewski* (1977) as getting drunk is a 'reckless course of conduct' and recklessness is sufficient for a basic intent offence such as manslaughter.

The interesting point in the case was that the Lord Chief Justice, Lord Lane, also stated that an intoxicated mistake as to the amount of force needed in self-defence was not a defence to a specific intent offence. This has been confirmed by *Hatton* (2005).

Hatton (2005)

D had drunk over 20 pints of beer. He and another man (V) went back to D's flat. In the morning D claimed he found V dead from injuries caused by a sledgehammer. D said he could not really remember what had happened but thought V had hit him with a five-foot-long stick and he had defended the attack. D was convicted of murder. The Court of Appeal held that the decision in *O'Grady* (1987) was not limited to basic intent crimes, but also applied to specific intent crimes. A drunken mistake about the amount of force required in self-defence was not a defence.

Criminal Justice and Immigration Act 2008

Statute law now makes it clear that a mistaken belief caused through the defendant's voluntary intoxication cannot give a defence of self-defence, defence of another or prevention of crime.

Section 76 of the Criminal Justice and Immigration Act 2008 states that reasonable force may be used for purposes of self-defence, defence of another or prevention of crime. However, s 76(5) says that this 'does not enable D to rely on any mistaken belief attributable to intoxication that was voluntarily induced'.

Exception

An exception to the rule on intoxicated mistake is *Jaggard v Dickinson* (1980).

Jaggard v Dickinson (1980)

D, who was drunk, went to what she thought was a friend's house. There was no one in and so she broke a window to get in as she believed (accurately) her friend would consent to this. Unfortunately in her drunken state she had mistaken the house and had actually broken into the house of another person.

The Divisional Court quashed her conviction holding that she could rely on her intoxicated belief as Parliament had 'specifically required the court to consider the defendant's actual state of belief, not the state of belief which ought to have existed'.

This exception is because s 5 of the Criminal Damage Act 1971 allows an honest belief that the person to whom the property belonged would have consented to the damage or destruction as a lawful excuse to a charge of criminal damage, whether or not the belief is justified. This has been interpreted as giving a defendant a defence even where the mistake was made through intoxication.

12.3.4 Public policy issues

The law on intoxication as a defence is largely policy based. This is because of two main reasons:

1. Intoxication is a major factor in the commission of many crimes; many offences are committed when D is in an intoxicated state.
2. There is a need to balance the rights of the defendant and the victim; if intoxication were always to be a defence, then victims' rights would not be protected.

There is conflict between public policy and legal principles. Public policy is based on public protection and the encouragement of good behaviour. Legal principles impose liability where there is fault. The fault must be voluntarily assumed or there must be the deliberate taking of a risk.

Key facts

	Specific intent crimes	Basic intent crimes
Voluntary intoxication	If defendant has *mens rea* he is guilty: *Gallagher* (1963). If defendant has no *mens rea* he is not guilty.	Becoming intoxicated is a reckless course of conduct: *Majewski* (1977). The defendant is guilty of the offence.
Involuntary intoxication	If defendant has *mens rea* he is guilty: *Kingston* (1994). If defendant has no *mens rea* he is not guilty: *Hardie* (1984).	The defendant has not been reckless in becoming intoxicated, so not guilty: *Hardie* (1984).
Drunken mistake	If the mistake negates *mens rea* the defendant is not guilty. If the mistake is about the need to defend oneself, it is not a defence. The defendant will be guilty. This is so for both specific and basic intent offences: *O'Grady* (1987), *Hatton* (2005). For self-defence, defence of another or prevention of crime, s 76(5) Criminal Justice and Immigration Act 2008 does not allow D to rely on 'any mistaken belief attributable to intoxication that was voluntarily induced'.	This is a reckless course of conduct, so the defendant is guilty.

Figure 12.6 Key facts chart on intoxication as a defence

The law on intoxication has endeavoured to balance these opposing points of view, but over the past 30 or so years it can be argued that public policy has become the main theme.

Public policy can be clearly seen in the law on self-defence, defence of another and prevention of crime. Parliament has enacted (in s 76(5) Criminal Justice and Immigration Act 2008) that D cannot rely on 'any mistaken belief attributable to intoxication that was voluntarily induced' when claiming any of these defences.

Mens rea

Some areas of the law on intoxication appear to be contrary to the normal rules on *mens rea* and *actus reus*. In particular this is seen in the decision in *DPP v Majewski* (1977). The decision in this case, that the defendant is guilty of a basic intent offence because getting drunk is a 'reckless course of conduct', ignores the principle that *mens rea* and *actus reus* must coincide. The decision to drink may be several hours before the defendant commits the *actus reus* of any offence. For example, in *O'Grady* (1987), the defendant had fallen asleep and only committed the act of hitting his friend some hours afterwards.

In addition, the recklessness in becoming intoxicated means that the defendant takes a general risk of doing something 'stupid' when drunk. At the time of becoming intoxicated the defendant has no idea that he will actually commit an offence. Normally, for offences where recklessness is sufficient for the *mens rea* of an offence, it has to be proved that D knew there was a risk of the specific offence being committed.

This point was considered by the Law Commission in a consultation paper in 1993. They said in that paper that the *Majewski* rule was arbitrary and unfair. However, the Law Commission's proposals for changing the law were severely criticised and by the time they published firm proposals for reform of the law in 1995 they had changed their opinion. By this time they thought that the present law operated 'fairly, on the whole, and without undue difficulty'.

Specific intent/basic intent

Where a defendant is charged with murder or a s 18 assault he can use intoxication as a defence. However, because intoxication is not a defence to a basic intent offence, such a defendant can be found guilty of a lower level offence. These are manslaughter where murder is charged, or an offence under s 20 OAPA 1861 where a s 18 offence has been charged.

However, for other crimes, there is often no 'fall-back' offence. If a defendant is charged with theft and successfully claims that he did not form the *mens rea* for theft because he was too intoxicated, he will be not guilty of any offence.

Involuntary intoxication

A final point where the law could be thought to be in need of reform is where the defendant's inhibitions are broken down by being made intoxicated involuntarily. The decision in *Kingston* (1994) makes such a defendant guilty if he formed the necessary *mens rea*. This ignores the fact that the defendant was not to blame for the intoxication. Such a defendant would be not guilty of a basic intent offence where the prosecution relied on recklessness (as in *Hardie* (1984)). This appears to be unfair to defendants in Kingston's situation.

12.3.5 Proposals for reform

There have been several proposals for reform of the law on intoxication. In 1975 the Butler

Committee proposed the creation of a new offence of 'dangerous intoxication'.

The idea was that this proposed offence would be used where the defendant was acquitted of a dangerous offence on the basis that he was intoxicated. Following the acquittal on the main offence, the defendant could then be convicted of 'dangerous intoxication'. It was proposed that such an offence would carry a maximum sentence of one year's imprisonment for a first offence and a maximum of three years' imprisonment for any further offences.

This aimed at balancing public protection against the defendant's rights. The defendant would not be liable for the serious main offence and a possible lengthy prison sentence, but could still be imprisoned for a relatively short period for the proposed offence.

However, this proposal was rejected. The main arguments against it were that it did not distinguish how serious the original offence was. This meant that those who had killed would have been treated in the same way as those who had committed an assault.

In 1993 the Law Commission proposed that evidence of voluntary intoxication should be available for all offences on the issue of *mens rea*. This would allow a defendant to be acquitted if he did not have the necessary *mens rea*. Like the Butler Committee, they also proposed a separate offence, this time of 'criminal intoxication'.

The idea was abandoned and the 1995 report of the Law Commission proposed codifying the law as it then stood with just some minor amendments. This included the rule in *Majewski* as already discussed in section 12.3.4.

Following this report the Government in 1998 issued a draft Offences Against the Person Bill. This supported the rule in *Majewski* by including the provision that a defendant who was intoxicated could not rely on evidence of intoxication to negative recklessness.

However, this draft Bill was never enacted so the law remains as developed by the case law.

Activity

Explain whether there would be a defence available in the following situations.

1. Alice took some illegal drugs. She is told that while she was under the influence of the drugs, witnesses saw her hit Peter in the face with a saucepan, breaking his jaw. Alice cannot remember doing this. What defence(s) might be available to her if she is charged with offences under s 18 and s 20 OAPA 1861?
2. Courtney is a diabetic. One morning he gets up late and in his rush to get to work he forgets to take his insulin. As a result he becomes violent later in the day and punches Jemima in the face. What defence(s) might be available to him if he is charged with an offence under s 47 OAPA 1861?
3. Zahir is hit on the head by a slate which accidentally falls off a building. He loses consciousness briefly but is then able to walk home. Later that day he attacks his partner, Lynne, causing serious injuries to her. He has no recollection of doing this. What defence(s) might be available to him if he is charged with offences under s 18 and s 20 OAPA 1861?

12.4 Duress

Duress is a defence based on the fact that the defendant has been effectively forced to commit the crime. The defendant has committed the offence because he has been threatened with death or serious injury. The law therefore allows a defence. The defendant has to choose between being himself killed or seriously injured, or committing a crime. In such a situation there is no real choice. The defendant can be considered as so terrified that he ceases 'to be an independent actor'. However, despite this the defendant knowingly does the *actus reus* for the offence and has the required *mens rea*. So, if the law did not allow the defence, he would be liable for the offence.

Duress can be either through a direct threat by another (duress by threats) or through external circumstances (duress of circumstances). Duress of circumstances overlaps with the defence of necessity.

12.4.1 For which crimes is duress available?

Duress can be used as defence to all crimes, except murder, attempted murder and, possibly, treason.

Murder

It was originally held in *DPP for Northern Ireland v Lynch* (1975) that the defence of duress was available to a secondary party on a charge of murder. This meant it was available for defendants who had participated in a murder, such as a get-away driver, but had not actually performed the act of killing. However in *Howe* (1987) the House of Lords ruled that the defence was not available to anyone charged with murder, even if they were only a secondary party and had not done the killing themselves.

Howe (1987)

D, with others, took part in torturing and abusing a man who was then strangled by one of the others. On a second occasion another man was tortured, abused and then strangled by D. D claimed that he took part in the killings because of threats to him. The trial judge ruled that duress was available to D for the first killing where D was only a secondary party to the killing, but that it was not available for the second killing where D was a principal offender, ie had carried out the actual killing. The Court of

Appeal ruled that this was correct but the House of Lords held that duress was not available as a defence for either type of defendant on a murder charge.

The reason why duress was held not to be a defence was explained by Lord Hailsham when he said in the judgment:

> 'I do not at all accept in relation to the defence of murder it is either good morals, good policy or good law to suggest … that the ordinary man of reasonable fortitude is not to be supposed to be capable of heroism if he is asked to take an innocent life rather than sacrifice his own.'

The rule that duress cannot be a defence to murder applies even where the defendant is young and less able to resist pressure. This was confirmed in *Wilson* (2007).

Wilson (2007)

D, who was aged 13, and his father were charged with the murder of D's mother. D stated that he had helped his father with the murder because he was too frightened to disobey his father. The Court of Appeal held that D did not have a defence as the rule that duress provided no defence to murder applied however susceptible D might be to duress.

Attempted murder

In the case of *Howe* (1987) the House of Lords said they thought the defence should not be available on a charge of attempted murder. This was an *obiter dicta* statement and so not binding. However, in *Gotts* (1992) the Court of Appeal decided to follow this *obiter* statement.

Gotts (1992)

D was a 16-year-old boy whose parents were separated. D was threatened with violence by his father unless he agreed to stab his mother. D attacked his mother but did not kill her. He was convicted of attempted murder. The Court of Appeal upheld his conviction on the basis that the defence of duress was not available to him.

12.4.2 Duress by threats

Duress by threats is where a person's will is overborne by threats of death or serious injury, so that he commits an act which he would not otherwise do. So, where another person threatens the defendant with serious violence unless the defendant commits an offence, and the defendant then commits the offence, he is acting under duress. For example, if an armed man pointed a gun at the defendant, gave him a fake credit card, and ordered him to use it in a cashpoint machine to get money, the defendant is stealing the money but he is only doing it because of the threat.

The threat of violence is directed at the defendant by another person who demands that the defendant commit a specific crime or else he will be shot.

Seriousness of the threat

The threat must be of death or serious injury; lesser threats do not provide a defence. For example, a threat to disclose a previous conviction is not sufficient for duress. However, provided there are serious threats, then the cumulative effect of the threats can be considered. This was decided in *Valderrama-Vega* (1985).

Valderrama-Vega (1985)

The defendant illegally imported cocaine. He claimed he had done this because of death threats made by a mafia-type organisation involved in drug-smuggling and also because of threats to disclose his homosexuality and because of financial pressures. The trial judge said that the defence was only available to him if the death threats were the sole reason for his committing the offence. The Court of Appeal quashed his conviction as the jury was entitled to look at the cumulative effects of all the threats.

If there had not been a threat of death, then the other threats in this case would not be enough on which to base a defence of duress. But as there had been a threat of death the jury was entitled to consider the whole of the threats.

Threat to whom?

It used to be thought that the threat had to be to the defendant himself. But in an Australian case in 1967 it was accepted that threats to kill or seriously injure the defendant's common-law wife were sufficient.

In recent cases in England it has been accepted that threats to family or even to friends can be a basis for the defence of duress. In *Martin* (1989) in a case of duress of circumstances the wife of the defendant threatened to commit suicide unless he drove while disqualified (see section 12.4.9). This was held to be sufficient. In *Conway* (1988) the threats were to a passenger in the defendant's car. These were accepted as forming the basis for the defence of duress (see section 12.4.9).

There has been no decision on whether a threat to a complete stranger would be enough to give a defence of duress, but it seems likely that the courts would now allow this. Supposing an armed man seizes hold of someone you do not know, and then orders you to firebomb a particular building and cause severe damage to it or else he will kill the stranger. If you do damage to the building, can you use the defence of duress? You would be able to if the threat was to a member of your family or, under *Conway* (1988), to a friend. So, it would be reasonable to say that you should have a defence if you choose to commit a crime rather than let an innocent stranger die. In fact, the draft Criminal Code proposed that this should be the law.

12.4.3 Subjective and objective tests

In deciding if the defence should succeed the jury must consider a two-stage test. This involves both subjective and objective tests. These are:

- Was the defendant compelled to act as he did because he reasonably believed he had good cause to fear serious injury or death? (a mainly subjective test) and
- If so, would a sober person of reasonable firmness, sharing the characteristics of the accused, have responded in the same way? (an objective test).

These tests were laid down by the Court of Appeal in *Graham* (1982) and approved by the House of Lords in *Howe* (1987).

Graham (1982)

D was a homosexual who lived with his wife and another homosexual man, K. K was violent and bullied D. After both D and K had been drinking heavily, K put a flex around the wife's neck and told D to pull the other end of the flex. D did this for about a minute. The wife died. D claimed he had only held the flex because of his fear of K. D's conviction for murder was upheld.

Subjective test

The first part of the test is based on whether the defendant did the offence because of the threats he believed had been made. This is subjective, but it was thought that this had to be a reasonable belief in the sense that an ordinary person would have believed it. This made it a partially objective test.

However, in *Martin (DP)* (2000), the Court of Appeal interpreted this part of the two stage-test as being whether the defendant may have reasonably feared for his safety. So, in considering this test, the jury could take into account any special characteristic of the defendant which may have made him more likely to believe the threats.

Martin (DP) (2000)

The defendant suffered from a condition known as schizoid-affective state, which would lead him to regard things said to him as threatening and to believe that such threats would be carried out. He claimed he had been forced to carry out two robberies by two men who lived on the same estate. The judge ruled that the schizoid-affective disorder was irrelevant to the first part of the test, although it was a characteristic which could be included in the second part of the test.

The defendant appealed, saying that the correct test should have been whether, in view of his condition, he may have reasonably feared for his own or his mother's safety.

The Court of Appeal allowed the appeal and quashed his conviction. They held that duress and self-defence should be treated in the same way in regard to belief of the circumstances. In self-defence a mistaken belief by the defendant can be a defence provided it is a genuine mistake. The same applies to duress and so the defendant's mental condition is relevant in deciding whether he reasonably believed that his (or his family's) safety was at risk.

This decision is now in doubt following the House of Lords' decision in *Hasan (formerly Z)* (2005) (see section 12.4.8), which confirmed the decision in *Graham* (1982) that the defendant's belief in the threats must be reasonable and genuine.

Objective test

The second part of the test is based on whether the reasonable man would have responded in the same way. However, the jury is allowed to take certain of the defendant's characteristics into account, as the reasonable man is regarded as sharing the relevant characteristics of the defendant.

What characteristics can be taken into account was decided in *Bowen* (1996). In this case the defendant had a low IQ of 68 and he obtained goods by deception for two men who had told him they would petrol-bomb him and his family. It was held that this was irrelevant in deciding whether the defendant found it more difficult to resist any threats. The relevant characteristics must go to the ability to resist pressure and threats. In *Bowen* it was accepted that the following could be relevant:

- Age: very young people and the very old could be more susceptible to threats.
- Pregnancy: there is the additional fear for the safety of the unborn child.
- Serious physical disability: this could make it more difficult for the defendant to protect himself.
- Recognised mental illness or psychiatric disorder: this could include post-traumatic stress disorder or any other disorder which meant that a person might be more susceptible to threats. This did not include a low IQ.
- Gender: although the Court of Appeal thought that many women might have as much moral courage as men.

12.4.4 No safe avenue of escape

Duress can only be used as a defence if the defendant is placed in a situation where he has no safe avenue of escape. In *Gill* (1963) the defendant claimed that he and his wife had been threatened unless he stole a lorry. However, there was a period of time during which he was left alone and so could have raised the alarm. As he had a 'safe avenue of escape' he could not rely on the defence of duress.

It has also been held that if police protection is possible then the defendant cannot rely on duress. However, in the case of *Hudson and Taylor* (1971) it was accepted that police protection might not always be effective.

Hudson and Taylor (1971)

The defendants were two girls, aged 17 and 19, who were prosecution witnesses in a case against a man called Wright who was charged with wounding another man. When giving evidence in court they lied and said they could not identify Wright as the attacker. They were then charged with perjury (lying in court under oath). In their defence at their trial for perjury they said they lied because a man called Farrell, who had a reputation for violence, had told Hudson that if she gave evidence against the attacker, he would cut her up. They were convicted and appealed. The Court of Appeal quashed their conviction.

At the appeal the prosecution argued that the girls could have sought police protection. On this point the Court of Appeal pointed out that there were cases in which the police could not provide effective protection. They said that in deciding whether going to the police for protection was a realistic course, the jury should consider the age of the defendant, the circumstances of the threats and any risks which might be involved in trying to rely on police protection.

However, the decision in *Hudson and Taylor* was criticised by the House of Lords in *Hasan (formerly Z)* (2005) (see section 12.4.8). It is now doubtful that a defendant could use the defence of duress where there was opportunity to go to the police.

12.4.5 Imminence of threat

The threat must be effective at the moment the crime is committed, but this does not mean that the threats need to be able to be carried out immediately. In *Hudson and Taylor* (1971) the trial judge in their perjury case ruled that the defence of duress was not available to the two girls. This was because the threat could not be immediately put into effect while the girls were giving evidence, so there was no reason for them not to

have given truthful evidence.

On this point the Court of Appeal said that the threat had to be a 'present' threat but that this was in the sense that it was effective to neutralise the will of the defendant at the time of committing the offence. If the threat is hanging over the defendant at the time he or she commits the offence, then the defence of duress is available.

This was further considered in *Abdul-Hussain* (1999), a case on duress of circumstances.

Abdul-Hussain (1999)

The defendants, who were Shi'ite Muslims, had fled to Sudan from Iraq because of the risk of punishment and execution because of their religion. They feared that they would be sent back to Iraq and so they hijacked a plane. The plane eventually landed in the UK. The defendants were charged with hijacking and pleaded duress. The trial judge decided that the danger they were in was not sufficiently 'close and immediate' as to give rise to a 'virtually spontaneous reaction' and he ruled that the defence of duress could not be considered by the jury. The defendants were convicted and appealed.

The Court of Appeal quashed their convictions holding that the threat need not be immediate but it had to be imminent in the sense that it was hanging over them.

The Court of Appeal in *Abdul-Hussain* (1999) ruled that:

- There must be imminent peril of death or serious injury to the defendant, or to those for whom he has responsibility.
- The peril must operate on the defendant's mind at the time of committing the otherwise criminal act, so as to overbear his will; this is a matter for the jury.
- Execution of the threat need not be immediately in prospect.

The Court of Appeal also backed their ruling by giving a hypothetical example based on the history of Anne Frank, whose family hid from the Nazis for a long period of time during the Second World War because they knew they would be sent to a concentration camp if discovered. Anne Frank and all the members of her family were eventually caught and died in a concentration camp, except her father who survived. The Court of Appeal said:

> 'If Anne Frank had stolen a car to escape from Amsterdam and been charged with theft, the English law would not, in our judgment, have denied her a defence of duress of circumstances, on the ground that she should have waited for the Gestapo's knock on the door.'

12.4.6 Threat to make defendant commit a specific offence

The defendant can only use the defence if the threats are in order to make him commit a specific offence.

Cole (1994)

D claimed that he and his girlfriend and child had been threatened (and he had been actually hit with a baseball bat) in order to make him repay money he owed. As he did not have the money, D carried out two robberies at building societies to get sufficient money to repay the debt. D said he only did this because of the threats of violence to him and his family.

His conviction was upheld because he had not been told to commit the robberies. The threats to him were directed at getting repayment and not directed at making him commit a robbery. This meant there was not a sufficient connection between the threats and the crimes he committed, so the defence of duress was not available to him.

This applies only to duress by threats. In duress of circumstances the defence may be used for any offence which is an appropriate response to the danger posed by the circumstances. As seen in *Abdul-Hussain* (1999) above, the danger was of torture and execution, and the offence committed was hijacking which enabled them to get to a safe venue.

12.4.7 Intoxication and duress

If the defendant becomes voluntarily intoxicated and mistakenly believes he is being threatened, he cannot use duress as a defence. A mistake in these circumstances is unreasonable. However, if there is no mistake and the intoxication is irrelevant to the duress, the defendant can use the defence of duress. This could be, for example, where he is threatened by a man with a gun. In this situation there is duress and it is irrelevant whether the defendant is intoxicated or not.

12.4.8 Self-induced duress

This is where the defendant has brought the duress on himself through his own actions. For example, a defendant voluntarily joins a criminal gang and commits some offences, but then is forced under duress to commit other crimes which he did not want to do.

The normal rule is that where the defendant is aware that he may be put under duress to commit offences, he cannot use the defence. This has been held to apply to the following situations:

- The defendant joins a criminal gang which he knows is likely to use violence.
- The defendant puts himself in a position where he knows that he is likely to be subjected to threats of violence or actual violence. This could be by being involved in criminal activity although not part of a gang, or by becoming indebted to a drug dealer.

These situations can be illustrated by specific cases.

Key cases

Duress can be by threats or circumstances.
Duress is not available for murder (*Howe* (1987)) or attempted murder (*Gotts* (1992)).

Case	Facts	Law
Valderrama-Vega (1985)	Smuggled cocaine because of death threats and threats to disclose homosexuality.	Must be a threat of death or serious injury but can consider cumulative effect of threats.
Graham (1982)	Helped kill his wife because he was threatened by his homosexual lover.	Two-stage test: • Was D compelled to act as he did because he reasonably believed he had good cause to fear serious injury or death? • If so, would a sober person of reasonable firmness, sharing the characteristics of the accused have responded in the same way?
Martin (DP) (2000)	Suffered from a schizoid-affective state which would make him see things as threatening and believe the threats would be carried out.	Correct test should have been whether, in view of his condition, he may have reasonably feared for his own or his mother's safety.
Bowen (1996)	Had a low IQ (68). Obtained goods by deception for two men because of petrol-bomb threat.	Cannot take low IQ into account. Can consider: • age • pregnancy • recognised mental illness • gender.
Gill (1963)	Threatened so he stole a lorry, but had time to escape and raise the alarm.	Cannot use duress if has a 'safe avenue of escape'.
Hudson and Taylor (1971)	Two girls lied on oath because of threats to cut them up.	The threat need not be capable of being carried out immediately. Also recognised that police protection cannot always be effective. Take into account age and gender.
Hasan (2005) (see section 12.4.8)	D tried to burgle a safe after he was threatened by a drug-dealer associate.	Criticised *Hudson and Taylor* (1971) saying that D should seek police protection.
Abdul-Hussain (1999)	Hijacked plane to escape from persecution in Iraq.	Threat must be 'imminent' and operating on D's mind when he commits the offence.

Figure 12.7 Key cases on general principles of duress

Sharp (1987)

D joined a gang who carried out robberies. D claimed that he had wanted to withdraw from the robberies before the last one where a sub-postmaster was shot dead. The Court of Appeal ruled that he could not use duress as a defence. D knew when he joined the gang that they were likely to use violence, so he could not claim duress when they threatened him with violence.

A contrasting case to *Sharp* is the case of *Shepherd* (1987).

Shepherd (1987)

D had joined an organised gang of shoplifters. A group of them would enter a shop and while one of them distracted the shopkeeper, the others would steal as much as they could, usually boxes of cigarettes. This activity, although criminal, was non-violent. D said he wanted to stop taking part but was then threatened with violence unless he continued. The Court of Appeal allowed his appeal and quashed his conviction. If he had no knowledge that the gang was likely to use violence then the defence of duress was available to him.

The rule that duress is not available where it is self-induced has been extended to situations where the defendant associates with violent criminals. For example, in *Heath* (2000) the defendant owed money to a drug dealer. He was then threatened and made to help in the supply of cannabis. He could not use the defence of duress as he knew that by becoming indebted to a drugs dealer he was putting himself at risk of being threatened or having violence used on him.

However, in other cases, the courts had allowed a defendant who associated with violent people to use the defence of duress. This conflict of whether self-induced duress could be a defence was resolved in *Hasan (formerly Z)* (2005).

Hasan (formerly Z) (2005)

D associated with a violent drug dealer. This drug dealer told D to burgle a house in order to steal a large amount of money that was in a safe there. The dealer threatened that if D did not do this then D and his family would be harmed. D, carrying a knife, broke into the house but was unable to open the safe. He was convicted of aggravated burglary. The Court of Appeal quashed the conviction but certified the following question for the consideration of the House of Lords:

'Whether the defence of duress is excluded when as a result of the accused's voluntary association with others:

1. he foresaw (or possibly should have foreseen) the risk of being then and there subjected to any compulsion by threats of violence; or
2. only when he foresaw (or should have foreseen) the risk of being subjected to compulsion to commit criminal offences; and, if the latter
3. only if the offences foreseen (or which should have been foreseen) were of the same type (or possibly the same type and gravity) as that ultimately committed.'

The House of Lords reinstated his conviction. They took the view that option (i) in the certified question correctly states the law. The defence of duress is excluded where D voluntarily associates with others who are engaged in criminal activity and he foresaw or ought reasonably to have foreseen the risk of being subjected to any compulsion by threats of violence.

So self-induced duress is no longer available where a defendant realises or ought to have realised that he may be threatened with violence and compelled to commit an offence.

Key facts

	Law	Case
Availability	All offences EXCEPT: ● murder ● attempted murder ● treason (possibly).	*Howe* (1987) *Gotts* (1992)
Seriousness of threat	Must be of death or serious injury BUT can consider cumulative effect of other threats with threat of injury.	*Valderrama-Vega* (1985)
Subjective and objective tests	There are two tests: ● Was D compelled to act because he feared serious injury or death? (subjective) ● Would a sober person of reasonable firmness have responded in the same way? (objective). Some of D's characteristics can be taken into account, especially: ● age ● pregnancy ● serious physical disability ● recognised mental illness.	*Graham* (1982) *Bowen* (1996)
Avenue of escape	Duress is NOT available as a defence if there is a safe avenue of escape.	*Gill* (1963)
Imminence of threat	The threat need not be immediate but it must be imminent.	*Hudson and Taylor* (1971), *Abdul-Hussain* (1999)
Self-induced duress	Duress is NOT available where: ● D joins a criminal gang which he knows is violent ● D puts himself in a position where he foresaw (or should have foreseen) the risk of being subjected to compulsion.	*Sharp* (1987) *Hasan* (2005).

Figure 12.8 Key facts chart on duress by threats

12.4.9 Duress of circumstances

Although duress by threats has been recognised as a defence for a long time, it is only recently that the courts have recognised that a defendant may be forced to act because of surrounding circumstances. This is known as duress of circumstances.

The first case in which this was recognised was *Willer* (1986).

Willer (1986)

D and a passenger were driving down a narrow alley when the car was surrounded by a gang of youths who threatened them. D realised that the only way to get away from the gang was by driving on the pavement. He did this quite slowly (about 10 mph) and having made his escape he drove to the police station to report the gang. The police charged him with reckless driving for having driven on the pavement and he was convicted.

He appealed and the Court of Appeal said that the jury should have been allowed to consider whether the defendant drove 'under that form of compulsion, that is, under duress'.

This case was followed by *Conway* (1988).

Conway (1988)

A passenger in D's car had been shot at by two men a few weeks earlier. The car was stationary when the passenger saw two men running towards the car. He thought they were the two men who were after him (in fact they were plain clothes policemen) and he yelled at D to drive off. D did so very fast and was charged with reckless driving. The trial judge refused to leave duress for the jury to consider and D was convicted. On appeal the Court of Appeal quashed his conviction and ruled that a defence of duress of circumstances was available if, on an objective standpoint, the defendant was acting in order to avoid a threat of death or serious injury.

There was then a third case involving a driving offence. This was *Martin* (1989).

Martin (1989)

D's wife became hysterical and threatened suicide unless he drove her son (who was late and at risk of losing his job) to work. The defendant was disqualified from driving but he eventually agreed to do this. He was convicted of driving while disqualified. On appeal it was ruled that duress of circumstances could be available as a defence and the same two-stage test put

forward in *Graham* (1982) for duress by threats applied. So the tests were:

- Was the defendant compelled to act as he did because he reasonably believed he had good cause to fear serious injury or death? and
- If so, would a sober person of reasonable firmness, sharing the characteristics of the accused have responded in the same way?

Although these cases established that there was a defence of duress of circumstances, all the cases involved driving offences. It was not until the decision in *Pommell* (1995) that it became clear that duress of circumstances could be a defence to all crimes except murder and attempted murder and some forms of treason.

Pommell (1995)

D was found by police at 8 am lying in bed with a loaded sub-machine gun against his leg. He told police that at about 1 am he had taken it off another man who was going to use it 'to do some people some damage'. D said he had intended getting his brother to hand the gun in to the police that morning. At his trial for possessing a prohibited weapon the judge ruled that his failure to go to the police straight away prevented him having any defence. D was convicted. He appealed to the Court of Appeal who held that the defence of duress of circumstances was available for all offences except murder and attempted murder and some forms of treason. They quashed D's conviction and sent the case for retrial.

In *Cairns* (1999) the court had to consider whether there had to be a real threat to the defendant or whether the defence was available where the defendant reasonably perceived a threat of serious physical injury or death, even though there was no actual threat.

Cairns (1999)

V threw himself across the bonnet and windscreen of D's car. Several of V's friends were nearby shouting and D felt threatened. D drove off with V on his bonnet and some of V's friends following. These friends were in fact trying to help rather then threaten D. When D braked for a speed hump, V fell under the car and was seriously injured. At the trial the judge directed the jury that they had to consider whether D's actions were 'actually necessary'. D's conviction was quashed as he reasonably perceived a threat of serious physical injury or death.

It is sufficient for the defendant to show that he acted as he did because he reasonably perceived a threat of serious physical injury or death. He is not required to prove that the threat was an actual or real threat.

12.4.10 Problems in the law of duress

Unavailability for murder

The ruling in *Howe* (1987) that duress is not available on a charge of murder ignores situations such as a woman motorist being hijacked and forced to act as getaway driver. Lord Griffiths simply dismissed such examples on the basis that it was inconceivable that such a person would be prosecuted. However, it is possible that such a person might be prosecuted and would have no defence.

What if a young mother's car is hijacked and she is told her two young children will be killed unless she helps terrorists to plant a bomb? Lord Hailsham thought that the ordinary person should be capable of heroism if he is asked to take an innocent life rather than sacrifice his own. But in this situation the mother is being asked to sacrifice her two children, yet she would have no defence.

The age and/or susceptibility of a defendant to duress are also ignored as shown by the case of

Wilson (2007), where a 13-year-old boy was convicted of murder when he helped his father in the murder of his mother. The Court of Appeal in that case accepted that there might be grounds for criticising a principle of law that did not allow a 13-year-old any defence to a charge of murder, even though he was only doing what his father told him as he was too frightened to refuse to obey his father.

The law also creates an anomaly in that duress is not available for murder but is available for a charge under s 18 OAPA 1861. The *mens rea* of intention to cause grievous bodily harm can be the same as for murder.

There is an additional problem where a defendant is charged with murder, as this offence carries a mandatory life sentence. The judge has to send the defendant to prison for life, and cannot take the duress into account when passing sentence. Where the defendant is charged with attempted murder, the judge has some discretion in sentencing. For example, in the case of the 16-year-old defendant in *Gotts* (1992), the judge placed him on probation.

The Law Commission in its report, *Legislating the Criminal Code: Offences Against the Person and General Principles* (1993), proposed that the defence of duress should be available for all crimes. In 2006, the Law Commission's report *Murder, Manslaughter and Infanticide* proposed that duress should be allowed as a defence to murder.

No allowances for low IQ

In *Bowen* (1996) the Court of Appeal refused to allow the fact that the defendant had a very low IQ to be taken into account in deciding whether the defendant found it more difficult to resist any threats. This decision may be seen as harsh. A very low IQ can mean that the person fails to understand the true nature of matters. It should be taken into account.

Police protection

In *Hudson and Taylor* (1971) the Court of Appeal accepted that police protection could not be

Activity

Explain whether a defence of duress would be available in the following situations.

1. Clancy is threatened by Neil, a fellow employee, who tells Clancy that he will tell their boss about Clancy's previous convictions for theft. Neil says that Clancy has to help him shoplift from a small corner shop by distracting the counter-staff while Neil does the stealing. Clancy feels obliged to do this as he does not want to lose his job.
2. Joseph, who is of a timid nature and low intelligence, is told by Katya that she will beat him up unless he obtains goods for her from a shop using a stolen credit card. He does this and obtains a DVD player for her.
3. Natasha's boyfriend, Ross, is a drug dealer. She also knows that he has convictions for violence. He threatens to beat her 'senseless' unless she agrees to take some drugs to one of his 'customers'. She is caught by the police and charged with possessing drugs with intent to supply.
4. Sanjeet's wife has tried to commit suicide previously. She is very depressed because they are heavily in debt. She tells Sanjeet that she will throw herself under a train unless he can get the money to pay off their debts. Sanjeet obtains the money by robbing a local off-licence.
5. Tamara is due to give evidence against Alexia's boyfriend who is facing a trial for attempted murder. A week before the trial is due to take place, Alexia sends Tamara a text message saying that Tamara will be killed if she gives evidence. Tamara attends the court but lies in evidence saying, untruthfully, that the man she saw was much shorter than Alexia's boyfriend.

completely fool-proof. Even where a defendant had the opportunity to go to the police and tell them of the duress, many people might be so afraid of the consequences that they would not go to the police.

Unfortunately the decision in *Hudson and Taylor* (1971) has been called into question by the House of Lords' judgment in *Hasan* (2005). This leaves the law uncertain as to whether a person threatened with duress, who does not take an available opportunity to go to the police, can rely on the defence of duress.

12.5 Necessity

This is where circumstances force a person to act in order to prevent a worse evil from occurring. The defence has similarities with the defence of duress of circumstances, yet the courts have been reluctant to recognise necessity as a defence in its own right. The leading case is *Dudley and Stephens* (1884).

Dudley and Stephens (1884)

The two defendants were shipwrecked with another man and V, a 17-year-old cabin boy, in a small boat about 1,600 miles from land. After drifting for 20 days, and having been nine days without food and seven days without water, the two defendants killed and ate the cabin boy. Four days later they were picked up by a passing ship and on their return to England were convicted of murder. Their claim of necessity to save themselves from dying was rejected.

It is interesting to note that although Dudley and Stephens were convicted of murder and sentenced to be hung, their sentence was commuted to a mere six months' imprisonment.

In this case the charge was of murder, so it can be argued that the law on necessity is in line with the law on duress, as duress is not available on a charge of murder. However, in the case of *Buckoke v Greater London Council* (1971) Lord Denning stated *obiter* that he thought the defence of necessity would not be available to emergency service drivers (fire-fighters or ambulance drivers) if they broke traffic laws in an attempt to arrive at an emergency quickly. He said that such a driver should be congratulated for their action and he hoped that anyone in that situation would not be prosecuted. Nevertheless, the law seems to be that such a person could be prosecuted and would not have a defence of necessity.

As there is no general defence of necessity, the traffic laws have now been changed to give emergency service drivers a special defence in certain circumstances.

12.5.1 Recognition of the defence

It is interesting that the defence has been recognised by the courts when making an order in some civil cases. An example of this is *Re F (Mental Patient: Sterilisation)* (1990).

> ### Re F (Mental Patient: Sterilisation) (1990)
>
> A health authority applied for a declaration that it was lawful to sterilise a girl who had a very severe mental disability. The girl had formed a sexual relationship with another patient, putting her at risk of becoming pregnant. Doctors said that she would not be able to understand pregnancy and it could be disastrous for her precarious mental health. The girl's mother supported the application, but the Official Solicitor, who was acting on behalf of the girl as she was unable to give consent to an operation herself, thought that performing such an operation would be illegal.
>
> The House of Lords granted the application and Lord Brandon stated:

> 'In many cases … it will not only be lawful for doctors, on the ground of necessity, to operate on or give other medical treatment to adult patients disabled from giving their consent, it will also be the common duty to do so.'

Another case in which doctors sought a declaration that it would be lawful for them to operate was *Re A (Conjoined twins)* (2000). In this case the defence of necessity was considered and held to be available as a defence even to a potential charge of murder.

> ### Re A (Conjoined twins) (2000)
>
> Conjoined twins were born with one of them having no proper heart or lungs. She was being kept alive by the other twin, whose heart circulated blood for both of them. Their parents refused to consent to an operation to separate them. Doctors applied for a declaration that it was lawful to operate to separate the twins, even though the weaker twin would certainly die. The Court of Appeal gave the declaration. The three judges gave very different reasons for why the operation would be lawful, but one of them, Brooke LJ said that the defence of necessity would be available to the doctors were they to be charged with murder of the weaker twin. He approved the following four principles of the defence of necessity as set out in Stephen's *Digest of Criminal Law*, 1883:
>
> 1. The act was done only in order to avoid consequences which could not otherwise be avoided.
> 2. Those consequences, if they had happened, would have inflicted inevitable and irreparable evil.
> 3. No more was done than was reasonably necessary for that purpose.
> 4. The evil inflicted by it was not disproportionate to the evil avoided.

Necessity was also considered in the case of *Shayler* (2001). In this case the defendant was a former member of the British Security Service (MI5). He was charged with disclosing confidential documents in breach of the Official Secrets Act 1989. He claimed the defence of necessity. His conviction was upheld by both the Court of Appeal and the House of Lords. The Court of Appeal discussed the defences of necessity and duress of circumstances, and concluded that they were in effect the same defence. Lord Woolf stated:

> 'The distinction between duress of circumstances and necessity has, correctly been by and large ignored or blurred by the courts. Apart from some of the medical cases like *Re F* (1990), the law has tended to be treat duress of circumstances and necessity as one and the same.'

The Court of Appeal held that the tests for duress of circumstances and/or necessity were as follows:

- The act must be done only to prevent an act of greater evil.
- The evil must be directed towards the defendant or a person or persons for whom he was responsible.
- The act must be reasonable and proportionate to the evil avoided.

It can be seen that these tests are very similar to those for necessity, but there are, however, differences. The important one is that the evil must be directed towards the defendant or a person or persons for whom he was responsible. This demonstrates that it is wrong to treat necessity as being the same as duress of circumstances. In 'pure' necessity situations there is no requirement for this. In the case of *Re A (Conjoined twins)* (2000), the evil was not directed at the doctors, nor were they responsible for the twins; the parents maintained responsibility for them.

The other major difference between duress of circumstances and necessity is that duress of circumstances cannot be used as a defence to murder, yet in *Re A (Conjoined twins)* (2000) it was accepted that necessity could be a defence to the murder of the weaker twin. In that case, performing an operation which the doctors knew would kill the weaker twin, was an act which would prevent the greater evil of both twins dying.

12.5.2 The role of necessity in other defences

Even though there are doubts as to whether necessity exists as a defence in its own right, necessity effectively forms the basis of other defences. These include self-defence and special statutory defences.

Self-defence

The essence of this defence is that the defendant is claiming that he acted as he did because it was necessary for his protection.

Special statutory defences

An example is s 5(2)(b) of the Criminal Damage Act 1971, where it is a defence to a charge of criminal damage that other property was at risk and in need of immediate protection, provided that what the defendant did was reasonable in all the circumstances.

Key facts

	Law	Case
Definition	Circumstances force a person to act in order to prevent a worse evil from occurring.	
Existence	Only recognised as duress of circumstances in criminal cases. Civil cases have recognised the defence of necessity.	*Dudley and Stephens* (1884) *Re F (Mental Patient: Sterilisation)* (1990), *Re A (Conjoined twins)* (2000)
Tests	These were set out in Stephen's *Digest of Criminal Law* and approved in *Re A (Conjoined twins)* (2000): <ul><li>Act was done only to avoid consequences which could not otherwise be avoided.</li><li>Those consequences would have inflicted inevitable and irreparable harm.</li><li>No more was done than was necessary.</li><li>The evil inflicted was proportionate to the evil avoided.</li></ul>	*Re A (Conjoined twins)* (2000)

Figure 12.9 Key facts chart on necessity

Examination questions

1. Discuss whether the rules governing insanity as a defence in criminal law are in a satisfactory condition.

(OCR, Specimen Paper)

2. 'The law relating to the availability and effect of intoxication as a defence to a criminal charge has been shaped more by considerations of public policy than by sound legal principles.'

Evaluate this statement about the defence of intoxication.

(OCR, Unit 2572, January 2008)

3. 'Duress by threats is an important defence. It makes concessions to human frailty but it must not become an excuse for criminals, gang leaders and terrorists.'

Discuss whether the limitations which the courts have placed on the availability of the defence of duress by threats supports the above statement.

(OCR, Unit 2572, June 2007)

4. Carol and Diana decide to go out for the night. They meet at Carol's house and begin the evening by sharing half a bottle of vodka. They then go out and have some more drinks in a pub and they each take an ecstasy tablet. As they are leaving the pub, Carol takes a leather jacket from the back of a chair mistaking it for her own very similar jacket which she has, in fact, left at home.

By the time they arrive at a nightclub, both girls are suffering from hallucinations. The doorman, Barry, asks them for identity. Diana, who thinks Barry is an alien who wants to transport them to another planet, pokes him in the eye with her finger and then hits him over the head with her umbrella, knocking him unconscious. Carol picks up the wallet which has fallen onto the pavement from Barry's pocket and they both run off.

Consider the offences that Carol and Diana may have committed and advise them of any defences they may have available to them.

(OCR, Specimen Paper)

The OCR two-module A2

The A2 modules for the Criminal Law option are:

- Criminal Law Unit G153 – worth 60 per cent of the A2, and
- Criminal Law Special Study Unit G154 – worth 40 per cent of the A2.

The full specification, specimen papers and mark schemes can be found online at www.ocr.org.uk

A1.1 Assessment objectives

Answers to all questions are marked on the basis of three assessment objectives. These are used in marking all the units of A Level law. They are:

1. AO1 **Demonstrate knowledge and understanding**
   Demonstrate knowledge and understanding of legal rules and principles by selecting and explaining relevant information and illustrating with examples and citation.
2. AO2 **Analysis, Evaluation and Application**
   Analyse legal material, issues and situations, and evaluate and apply the appropriate legal rules and principles.
3. AO3 **Communication and Presentation**
   Present a logical and coherent argument, and communicate relevant material in a clear and effective manner, using appropriate legal terminology.

The proportion of the assessment objectives used for each question varies. Details are given for questions on Unit G153 later in this appendix and for questions on Unit G154 in Appendix 2.

A1.2 Criminal Law Unit G153

This examines all of the content area of the new specification. The question paper will have three sections:

- Section A: **essays** in which candidates are required to answer one essay from a choice of three.
- Section B: **problems** in which candidates are required to answer one problem from a choice of three.
- Section C: **dilemma boards** (evaluation of statements) in which candidates are required to answer one from a choice of two.

The examination is two hours long.

A1.3 Essay questions

On Unit G153 these can be based on any area or areas of the substantive criminal law studied for the A2 option. There are 50 marks available for each essay. These are allocated to the assessment objectives as follows:

- AO1 – maximum 25 marks
- AO2 – maximum 20 marks
- AO3 – maximum 5 marks.

These show that it is important both to know the law in question and to be able to analyse and evaluate it.

The questions in the specimen papers show that the style of essay questions will remain the same as those set for the previous six-module specification. All essay-style examination questions at the end of chapters in this book are taken from the specimen paper or past OCR papers, so they can be used as practice for the current specification.

A1.4 Problem questions

On Unit G153 these can also be based on any area or areas of the substantive criminal law studied for the A2 option. For these, knowledge and understanding of the law (AO1) together with identification of the relevant issues and application of the law (AO2) are required. Each question is worth 50 marks, and the allocation of assessment objectives is the same as for essay questions:

- AO1 – maximum 25 marks
- AO2 – maximum 20 marks
- AO3 – maximum 5 marks.

The questions in the specimen papers show that the style of problem questions will remain the same as those set for the previous six-module specification. As with the essay questions, all problem-style examination questions at the end of chapters in this book are taken from the specimen paper or past OCR papers. They can be used as practice for the current specification.

However, it should be remembered that there may be a wider mix of topics than in the examinations between 2000 and 2008, where areas of criminal law were examined separately in two separate criminal law modules. It is now possible for an examiner to create problem questions that include, for example, murder and assaults, or murder and defences such as duress

or automatism. An example is given below of a question taken from Unit G143 in June 2008.

Question

Alex and Barry are on the pavement arguing about a debt. Alex, who has been drinking excessively, suddenly lashes out at Barry with his fist, breaking Barry's nose. Barry runs into the road where he is struck by a motorcycle. Barry suffers a large wound to his leg. Barry is bleeding heavily from a severed artery in his leg and is rushed to hospital. Barry refuses to have a blood transfusion because of his religious beliefs even though it would probably save his life. He dies later that day from loss of blood.

Discuss the potential criminal liability of Alex for the above incidents.

Potential answer

For problem questions it is necessary to:

- **I**dentify the relevant areas of law
- **D**efine the law on those areas
- **E**xplain the law further with cases
- **A**pply the law.

So don't forget the **IDEA**.

In this question it is necessary to deal with the assault situation and the death situation separately. Then for both the assault and the death it is necessary to consider the defence of intoxication.

For the assault consider what category of assault this could be. How serious is it? The important points are:

- what is the injury, and
- what is the *mens rea* of Alex?

Is a broken nose actual bodily harm or grievous bodily harm? Probably actual bodily harm, s 47 Offences Against the Person Act 1861. What about the wound to Barry's leg? A wound can be charged under s 20 or s 18 Offences Against the Person Act 1861.

For ss 18 and 20, Alex's *mens rea* is the important factor. Did he intend to cause serious harm? If he did not, then the offence could be under s 20. If he did intend serous harm, then the offence could be one under s 18.

Now consider the effect of intoxication on the assault situation. Don't forget that a drunken intent is still an intent. So discuss whether Alex intended to assault Barry or whether he was so drunk he did not know what he was doing. He has, in any event, been reckless in getting drunk, so he cannot use intoxication as a defence to either a s 47 or s 20 offence (*Majewski*).

For the death, consider if it is:

- murder, or
- manslaughter.

Did Alex intend to cause grievous bodily harm? If so then murder must be considered, but on the facts it is very unlikely.

For manslaughter you should identify that this could be unlawful act manslaughter. The assault is clearly an unlawful and dangerous act. Remember that the *Church* test only requires that the sober and reasonable person would recognise that Alex's punch would subject the victim to some harm, not necessarily serious harm.

Now you have to explain causation. Apply the principles:

- is Alex's misconduct the factual cause of Barry's death? – *White*
- is Alex's misconduct is still an operative cause of death? – *Smith*
- were Barry's actions 'reasonably foreseeable?' – *Pagett.*

The mark scheme for this question can be found on the OCR website – www.ocr.org.uk

A1.5 Dilemma boards/evaluating statements

The final style of questions on Unit 3A of the four-module A level examinations is known as a dilemma board or evaluating statements. This is a new style of question in which students are faced with a scenario and then four statements about it which they have to evaluate. Each dilemma board carries 20 marks. This means that you should spend considerably less time on this than on the other two questions.

For assessment, the marks are all for AO2. This means you must concentrate on analysis and application of the law to the statements.

An example of such a question is given below. It is taken from OCR Unit G143, January 2008.

Question

Gary is in debt. Darren's wife owes Gary £20. Gary sees Darren in the street and threatens to beat him up unless he gives him £20. Darren hands over the money. Gary sees an old lady, Dorothy, in the street. He tries to snatch a bag from her grip. He grabs the handle of the bag but she resists and the bag falls to the ground. Gary runs off.

Evaluate the accuracy of each of the four statements A, B, C, and D individually, as they apply to the facts in the above scenario.

Statement A: Gary is not liable for theft because Darren gives him the £20.

Statement B: Gary is liable for robbery when Darren gives him the £20.

Statement C: Gary is not liable for the theft of Dorothy's bag.

Statement D: Gary is guilty of robbery when he grabs Dorothy's bag.

Potential answer

It is necessary to deal with each statement separately. For each one, explain whether it is a correct statement or not. Let's look at Statement A. The important points are what the scenario states that Gary did and the law on theft and robbery.

For these type of questions you can answer using bullet points.

Statement A

Points to be made are:

- appropriation can occur even where the owner of the property consents to it
- Darren's consent is not a true consent because it is induced by a threat
- consider whether Gary may have had an honest belief in a legal right to the £20, so may not dishonest
- conclude whether Gary is liable or not for theft.

Statement B

Points to be made are:

- the offence of robbery involves the use or threat of force in order to steal
- Gary has used a threat of force
- consider whether he honestly believes that he has a legal right to demand the money
- conclude that Gary may or may not be guilty of robbery.

Statement C

Points to be made are:

- appropriation is any assumption of the rights of an owner
- a theft occurs when Gary touches Dorothy's bag with a dishonest intention to permanently deprive her of it
- conclude that Gary is guilty of theft even though it falls to the ground.

Statement D

Points to be made are:

- robbery involves the use of force in order to steal
- force has been used on Dorothy's bag and this is sufficient for a robbery
- conclude that Gary is liable for robbery even though the bag falls to the ground and he runs off empty handed.

The mark scheme for this question can be found on the OCR website – www.org.or.uk

Gary is not liable for theft because Darren gives him the £20	Gary is liable for robbery when Darren gives him the £20
Gary is not liable for the theft. of Dorothy's bag	Gary is guilty of robbery when he grabs Dorothy's bag

Gary is in debt. Darren's wife owes Gary £20. Gary sees Darren in the street and threatens to beat him up unless he gives him £20. Darren hands over the money. Gary sees an old lady, Dorothy, in the street. He tries to snatch a bag from her grip. He grabs the handle of the bag but she resists and the bag falls to the ground. Gary runs off.

In the above dilemma board use the four spaces surrounding the four statements to consider whether each is or is not appropriate to the situation outlined in the central box.

Criminal Law Special Study Unit G154

The special study paper is based on the Special Study Materials pre-released by OCR. This source material is reproduced in section A2.1 below. Booklets containing this source material are available from OCR for use in preparing for the examination. In addition, in the examination each candidate will be given a clean copy of the booklet for reference purposes within the examination room.

This material will also be used in the examination sessions for January 2010 and June 2010. As this source material forms the basis of the questions on the examination paper, it is essential that all students study it carefully. The assessment objectives are the same as those set out in Appendix 1 at section A1.1 for Criminal Law Unit G153.

A2.1 Source materials

Source 1

Extracts from the Offences Against the Person Act 1861

Section 18 Shooting or attempting to shoot, or wounding, with intent to do grievous bodily harm, or to resist apprehension

Whosoever shall unlawfully and maliciously by any means whatsoever wound or cause grievous bodily harm to any person with intent to do some grievous bodily harm to any person, or with intent to resist or prevent the lawful apprehension or detainer of any person, shall be guilty of felony, and being convicted thereof shall be liable to be kept in penal servitude for life.

Section 20 Inflicting bodily injury, with or without weapon

Whosoever shall unlawfully and maliciously wound or inflict any grievous bodily harm upon any other person, either with or without any weapon or instrument, shall be guilty of a misdemeanour, and being convicted thereof shall be liable to be kept in penal servitude [for not more than five years].

Section 47 Assault occasioning bodily harm
Whosoever shall be convicted upon an indictment of any assault occasioning actual bodily harm shall be liable ... to be kept in penal servitude [for not more than five years].

Extract from the Criminal Justice Act 1988
Section 39 Common Assault
Common assault and battery shall be summary offences and a person guilty of either of them shall be liable to a fine not exceeding level 5 on the standard scale, to imprisonment for a term not exceeding six months.

Source 2

Extract adapted from the judgment in *Collins v Wilcock* [1984] 1 WLR 1172
ROBERT GOFF LJ:
We are here primarily concerned with battery. The fundamental principle, plain and incontestable, is that every person's body is inviolate. It has long been established that any touching of another person, however slight, might amount to a battery. The effect is that everybody is protected not only against physical injury but against any form of physical molestation.

But so widely drawn a principle must inevitably be subject to some exceptions. For example, ... people may be subjected to the lawful exercise of the power of arrest; and reasonable force may be used in self-defence ... Generally speaking, consent is a defence to battery; and most of the physical contacts of everyday life are not battery because they are impliedly consented to ... Among such forms of conduct long held to be acceptable is touching a person for the purpose of engaging his attention ... A police officer may wish to engage a man's attention ... to question him. But if ... his use of physical contact in the face of non-cooperation persists beyond generally accepted standards of conduct, his action will become unlawful; and if a police officer restrains a man, for example by gripping his arm or his shoulder, then his action will also be unlawful, unless he is lawfully exercising his powers of arrest.

... the respondent took hold of the appellant by the left arm to restrain her. She was not proceeding to arrest [her] ... her action constituted a battery ... and was therefore unlawful. ... the appeal must be allowed ...

Source 3

Extract adapted from the judgment in *R v Ireland; R v Burstow* [1997] 4 All ER 225
House of Lords
LORD STEYN:
Harassment of women by repeated silent telephone calls, accompanied on occasions by heavy breathing, is apparently a significant social problem. That the criminal law should be able to deal with this problem, and so far as is practicable, afford effective protection to victims is self-evident.

It is to the provisions of the Offences Against the Person Act 1861 that one must turn to examine whether our law provides effective criminal sanctions for this type of case.

An ingredient of each of the offences is 'bodily harm' to a person. In respect of each section the threshold question is therefore whether a psychiatric illness, as testified to by a psychiatrist, can amount to 'bodily harm'. If ... the answer to the question is yes, it will be necessary to consider whether the persistent silent caller, who terrifies his victim and causes her to suffer a psychiatric illness, can be criminally liable...

The correct approach is simply to consider whether the words of the 1861 Act considered in the light of contemporary knowledge cover a recognisable psychiatric injury...

The proposition that the Victorian legislator when enacting ss 18, 20 and 47 of the 1861 Act, would not have had in mind psychiatric illness is no doubt correct. Psychiatry was in its infancy. But the subjective intention of the draftsman is immaterial. The only relevant inquiry is as to the sense of the words in the context in which they are used.

[Accordingly] 'bodily harm' must be interpreted so as to include recognisable psychiatric illness.

[In] *Burstow* … counsel laid stress on the difference between 'causing' grievous bodily harm in s 18 and 'inflicting' grievous bodily harm in s 20 [and] submitted that it is inherent in the word 'inflict' that there must be a direct or indirect application of force to the body…

…The question is whether as a matter of current usage the contextual interpretation of 'inflict' can embrace the idea of one person inflicting psychiatric injury on another. One can without straining the language in any way answer … in the affirmative…

… It is now necessary to consider whether the making of silent telephone calls causing psychiatric injury is capable of constituting an assault under s 47…

It is necessary to consider the two forms which an assault may take. The first is battery, which involves the unlawful application of force… The second form of assault is an act causing the victim to apprehend an immediate application of force upon her…

The proposition that a gesture may amount to an assault, but that words can never suffice, is unrealistic and indefensible … There is no reason why something said should be incapable of causing an apprehension of immediate personal violence … I would, therefore, reject the proposition that an assault can never be committed by words.

That brings me to the critical question whether a silent caller may be guilty of an assault. The answer to this question seems to me to be 'yes, depending on the facts'. It depends on questions of fact within the province of the jury. After all, there is no reason why a telephone caller who says to a woman in a menacing way 'I will be at your door in a minute or two' may not be guilty of an assault if he causes his victim to apprehend immediate personal violence. Take now the case of the silent caller. He intends by his silence to cause fear and so he is understood. The victim … may fear the *possibility* of immediate personal violence. As a matter of law the caller may be guilty of an assault, whether he is or not will depend on the circumstance and in particular on the impact of the caller's potentially menacing call

or calls on the victim. Such a prosecution case under s 47 may be fit to leave to the jury. I conclude that an assault may be committed in the particular factual circumstances which I have envisaged. For this reason I reject the submission that as a matter of law a silent telephone caller cannot ever be guilty of an offence under s 47.

Source 4

Extract adapted from the judgment in *JCC (a minor) v Eisenhower* [1983] 3 All ER 230 QBD

ROBERT GOFF LJ:

In my judgment, that conclusion (of the magistrates) was not in accordance with the law. It is not enough that there has been a rupturing of blood vessels internally for there to be a wound under the statute because it is impossible for a court to conclude from that evidence alone whether or not there has been any break in the continuity of the whole skin. There may have simply been internal bleeding of some kind or another, the cause of which is not established. Furthermore, even if there had been a break in some internal skin, there may not have been a break in the whole skin.

In these circumstances, the evidence is not enough, in my judgment, to establish a wound within the statute. In my judgment, the magistrates erred in their conclusion on the evidence before them.

Source 5

Extracts adapted from *Criminal Law*. Michael Jefferson. 8th Edition (2007) Pearson Publishing, pp 552-3 and 556

For many years there has been debate as to the width of the word 'inflict' under s 20 [Offences Against the Person Act 1861]. These issues were raised in *Ireland; Burstow* [[1997] 4 All ER 225] … The first issue was whether or not s 20 required an assault (in the sense of a battery). The authorities were divided. Lord Steyn stated that s 20 does not require an assault on the basis that, if it did, words would have to be read into s 20 ('inflict *by assault* any grievous bodily harm') whereas s 20 'works perfectly satisfactorily without any such implication'.

There is a problem arising from [*R v*] *Wilson (Clarence)* [1984] AC 242 HL]. Lord Roskill apparently believed that 'inflict' required the direct application of force to the victim or the doing of an act which directly resulted in force being applied to the victim's body. What is said is *dictum*. On this approach, to take an old example, if one dug a pit for the victim to fall into, one would be guilty under s 20 because, although one has not directly applied force to the victim, one has done an act which directly resulted in force being applied. One will have caused GBH within s 18 because 'cause' does not require the direct application of force. On the facts of *Martin* [(1881) 8 QBD 54] … the accused would be guilty of the more serious offence, s 18, and guilty of the less serious offence, s 20, for the same reason, but one is not guilty in the poisoning example because no force is used. The result is absurd. It could have been avoided by having the same verb in ss 18 and 20 or by the House of Lords in *Wilson* deciding that 'cause' and 'inflict' covered the same ground. The House of Lords took the point further: not just did 'inflict' require direct application force, but so did assault occasioning actual bodily harm and common assault. Therefore, a person could be guilty of the most serious non-fatal assault but not of the lesser assaults! It is about time that the meaning of 'inflict' was settled. …

Another issue was whether s 20 required the direct or indirect application of force. The Lords [in *Ireland; Burstow*] held that no direct physical violence was necessary. Lord Steyn said:

The problem is one of construction. The question is whether as a matter of current usage the contextual interpretation of 'inflict' can embrace the idea of one person inflicting psychiatric injury on another. One can without straining the language in any way answer that question in the affirmative. I am not saying that the words cause and inflict are exactly synonymous. They are not. What I am saying is that in the context of the Act of 1861 one can

nowadays quite naturally speak of inflicting psychiatric injury.

… Lord Steyn thought that it would be 'absurd' if 'cause' and 'inflict' were of different width. This interpretation was consistent with the hierarchy of non-fatal offences. …

In both ss 18 and 20 the mental element is stated to be 'maliciously'. Section 18 requires proof of a further state of mind: 'with intent to do some grievous bodily harm'. Coleridge CJ said in *Martin* that 'maliciously' did not mean spitefully. It normally means in a statute 'intentionally or recklessly'. Negligence is insufficient. Yet one can be guilty of a more serious offence, manslaughter by gross negligence. …

Because s 18 is expressed in terms of 'cause GBH with intent to do GBH', the Court of Appeal in *Mowatt* [[1968] 1 QB 421] opined that the term 'maliciously' was superfluous. The thinking is that if one intends GBH, one must foresee GBH as a probable or possible outcome. If, however, the indictment is based upon GBH with intent to resist arrest, 'maliciously' is not superfluous. …

Criminal law should work in practice. Clarkson and Keating 'Codification: Offences against the person under the draft Criminal Code' (1986) 50 JCL 405 at 415, wrote:

Each of the non-fatal offences against the person is, to varying degrees, confused and uncertain … in relation to each other, they are incoherent and fail to represent a hierarchy of seriousness.

… It is possible to substitute all the terms in the sections and thereby produce an authoritative modern version of the crimes which gets rid of all the difficult and case-encrusted phraseology. The definition of concepts such as 'wound', 'cause', 'inflict', 'actual bodily harm' and 'grievous bodily harm' have to be gathered from the cases. The OAPA was a consolidation statute with no attempt made to grade the offences or fit them together … it is easy to see why modern judges find difficulty fitting modern methods into the 1861 statute.

Source 6

Extract adapted from 'Consent: public policy or legal moralism?', Susan Nash, *New Law Journal*, March 15 1996

In *R v Wilson* [[1996] 2 Cr App R 241] the Court of Appeal held that consensual activity between a husband and wife in the privacy of the matrimonial home was not a proper matter for a criminal prosecution. The defendant had been charged with assault occasioning actual bodily harm contrary to s 47 of the Offences Against the Person Act 1861. The 'activity' involved the defendant burning his initials onto his wife's right buttock with a hot knife because 'she had wanted his name on her body'. This decision rekindles the debate regarding the extent to which the criminal law should be concerned with the consensual activities of adults in private. In *R v Brown* [[1994] 1 AC 212] the House of Lords upheld convictions under ss 20 and 47 of the Offences Against the Person Act notwithstanding that the victims had given their consent. This decision has been described as 'unprincipled and incoherent'.

The trial judge in *Wilson* had ruled that consent was no defence to an assault occasioning actual bodily harm. In arriving at this conclusion he stated that he felt bound by … *R v Brown*. The Court of Appeal considered it misdirection for the judge to say these cases constrained him to rule that consent was no defence.

The majority of the House of Lords in *Brown* held that it was not in the public interest that a person should wound or cause actual bodily harm to another for no good reason. Thus, in the absence of a good reason the victim's consent would not amount to a defence to a charge under s 47 or s 20 of the 1861 Act.

The defendants had taken part in consensual acts of violence for the purpose of sexual gratification which had resulted in varying degrees of injury. The court was of the opinion that the satisfying of sado-masochistic desires could not be classed as a good reason and dismissed the appeals. Lord Templeman considered that in some circumstances the accused would be entitled to an acquittal although the activity resulted in the infliction of some injury.

'Surgery involves intentional violence resulting in actual or sometimes serious bodily harm but surgery is a lawful activity. Other activities carried on with consent by or on behalf of the injured person have been accepted as lawful notwithstanding that they involve actual bodily harm or may cause serious harm. Ritual circumcision, tattooing, ear-piercing and violent sports including boxing are lawful activities.' This reference to tattooing has now assumed significance. Lords Templeman and Jauncy referred to it as being an activity which, if carried out with the consent of an adult, did not involve an offence under s 47. Wilson had been engaged in an activity which in principle was no more dangerous than professional tattooing. Thus, the Court of Appeal was of the opinion that it was not in the public interest that his activities should amount to criminal behaviour.

The Court of Appeal has now declared that *Brown* is not authority for the proposition that consent is no defence to a charge under s 47 of the 1861 Act *in all circumstances* where actual bodily harm is deliberately inflicted upon a person. Public policy and public interest considerations will become increasingly important in deciding whether it is appropriate to criminalise consensual activity, giving rise to even greater uncertainty in the area.

A2.2 The style of questions

There will be three questions on the exam paper and candidates have to answer all three. The questions will always be in the same format. They are:

- Question 1 – A case study based on one of the cases in the special study materials.
- Question 2 – An essay on a specific area of law in the special study materials.
- Question 3 – An application question in which candidates have to apply the law to different scenarios.

There are 80 marks in total for the paper. The examination is 1½ hours long.

A2.3 The case study question

Question 1 is always on a case in the source material. The question in the specimen material carries 16 marks, and you should spend about 18 minutes on this question. 12 marks are given for Assessment Objective 2 (analysis and evaluation) and 4 marks for AO3. The source material will provide a good starting point for your answer, but you must use the information in the source to analyse and evaluate.

A2.4 The essay question

Question 2 can be on any area of criminal law in the Special Study Material. The question on the specimen paper is worth 34 marks, and you should spend about 36 minutes on this question.

Both AO1 and AO2 are tested in this question, with 15 marks available for each. For AO1, you will need to bring in extra knowledge, not merely rely on the source material. For AO2, the level of analysis and evaluation is the important aspect. There are also 4 marks for AO3.

A2.5 The application question

There will usually be three mini-scenarios, each of which will raise different points of law. On the specimen paper each mini-scenario is worth 10 marks. Overall on this question you should spend about 36 minutes.

A2.6 Using the source materials

If you want to refer to the source material, this can be done by giving the source page and line reference. Do not copy out large amounts of the source: this will earn little or no credit for you. The important points are showing an understanding of arguments in the source, being able to explain them in your own words and to use them in discussion.

Source material for G144 (legacy paper)

The following is the source material for resit candidates only.

A3.1 Source materials

Source 1

Adapted from the judgment of Lord Lane, Lord Chief Justice, in *R v Graham* (1982) 74 Cr App R 235 (Court of Appeal, Criminal Division).

'The law requires a defendant to have the self-control reasonably to be expected of the ordinary citizen in his situation. It should likewise expect him to have the steadfastness reasonably to be expected of the ordinary citizen in his situation …

'… the correct approach on the facts of this case would have been as follows: (1) Was the defendant, or may he have been, impelled to act as he did because, as a result of what he reasonably believed King had said or done, he had good cause to fear that if he did not so act, King would kill him or cause … him serious physical injury? (2) If so, have the prosecution made the jury sure that a sober person of reasonable firmness, sharing the characteristics of the defendant, would not have responded … by taking part in the killing?'

Source 2

Adapted from the judgment of Lord Hailsham, LC, in *R v Howe* [1987] 1 AC 417.

'… some degree of proportionality between the threat and the offence must, at least to some extent, be a prerequisite of the defence under the existing law. Few would resist threats to the life of a loved one if the alternative were driving across the red lights or in excess of 70 mph on the motorway. But it would take rather more than the threat of a slap on the wrist or even moderate pain or injury to discharge the evidential burden even in the case of a fairly serious assault. In such a case the "concession to human frailty" is no more than to say that in such circumstances a reasonable man of average courage is entitled to embrace as a matter of choice the alternative which a reasonable man could regard as the lesser of two evils. Other considerations necessarily arise where the choice is between the threat of death or … serious injury and deliberately taking an innocent life. In such a case a reasonable man might reflect that one innocent human life is at least as valuable as his own or that of his loved one. In such a case a man cannot claim that he is choosing the lesser of two evils. Instead he is embracing the cognate but morally disreputable principle that the end justifies the means.'

Source 3

Adapted from the judgment of Lord Griffiths in *R v Howe* [1987] 1 AC 417, HL.

'As I can find no fair and certain basis on which to differentiate between participants to a murder and as I am firmly convinced that the law should not be extended to the killer, I would depart from the decision of this House in *DPP for Northern Ireland v Lynch* and declare the law to be that duress is not available as a defence to a charge of murder, or to attempted murder.'

Source 4

Adapted from the judgment of Lord Jauncey in *R v Gotts* [1992] 2 AC 412, HL.

'… I share the view of Lord Griffiths that "it would have been better had [the development of the defence of duress] not taken place and that duress had been regarded as a factor to be taken into account in mitigation …(*R v Howe*)" … While it is not now possible for this House to restrict the availability of the defence of duress in those cases where it has been recognised to exist, I feel constrained to express the personal view that given the climate of violence and terrorism which ordinary law-abiding citizens now have to face, Parliament might do well to consider whether the defence should continue to be available in the case of all very serious crimes … The reason why duress has for so long been stated not to be available as a defence to a murder charge is that the law regards the sanctity of human life and the protection thereof as of paramount importance. Does that reason apply to attempted murder as well as to murder? As Lord Griffiths points out [in *Howe*] … intent to kill

must be proved in the case of attempted murder but not necessarily in the case of murder. Is there logic in affording the defence to one who intends to kill but fails and denying it to one who mistakenly kills intending only to injure …?

'… withholding the defence in any circumstances will create some anomalies but I would agree with Lord Griffiths (*R v Howe*) that nothing should be done to undermine in any way the highest duty of the law to protect the freedom and lives of those who live under it. I can therefore see no justification in logic, morality or law in affording to an attempted murderer the defence which is withheld from a murderer.'

Source 5

Adapted from Clarkson and Keating, *Criminal Law Text and Materials* (Sweet & Maxwell, 1998), pp 328–29 and 335–36.

'In *Valderrama-Vega* the defendant was threatened with the disclosure of his homosexuality, was under financial pressure and received threats of death or serious harm. The first two are incapable of amounting to duress but the court held that the jury was entitled to look at the cumulative effects of all of the threats. It was wrong to direct the jury that the threat of death or serious injury had to be the sole reason for him committing the crime.

'In *Cole* the defendant robbed two building societies and claimed that he had done so to pay off a debt to moneylenders who had hit him with a baseball bat and had threatened him and his family. The Court of Appeal held that the defence of duress is only available if the threats are directed at the offence committed. In this case the moneylenders had not stipulated that he commit robbery … to meet their demands [so] there was … insufficient nexus between the threat and the offence.

'In *Hudson and Taylor* the threats could have been reported to the police, but the two young girls, aged 17 and 19, were convinced that the police protection would be ineffective. Are we to blame them for their failure to seek official protection? It would appear that their response was typical of the response of most ordinary girls of that age faced with such a predicament. It would surely be ludicrous to assert that the defence of duress would only be available to them if there had been a sniper sitting in the court ready to execute his threats immediately. These views were echoed by Lord Griffiths in *Howe*:

> 'if duress is introduced as a merciful concession to human frailty it seems hard to deny it to a man who knows full well that any official protection he may seek will not be effective'.

'The Draft Criminal Law Bill 1993 has, however, not responded to these calls …'

Source 6

Adapted from Duncan Bloy and Philip Parry, *Principles of Criminal Law* (Cavendish, 2000), pp 259–60.

'The defence is likely to be denied if the accused has voluntarily joined a criminal organisation, because he has put himself into a position where he may expect others to use force to exert their will over him, particularly if he should try to resile from their operations. The leading case is *Sharp* (1987) where Lord Lane CJ stated the principle thus:

> "Where a person has voluntarily, and with knowledge of its nature, joined a criminal organisation or gang which he knew might bring pressure on him to commit an offence and was an active member when he was put under such pressure, he cannot avail himself of the defence of duress."

'[In] *Shepherd* (1987) a number of men would enter the shop, some would distract the shopkeeper while the others took the goods. S claimed that after the first expedition he wanted to withdraw but was threatened by other gang members with violence to him and his family and so he felt compelled to carry on. The trial judge

ruled that duress was not available. The appeal was allowed. This case can be distinguished from [*Sharp*] on the basis that the defendant was not at the outset joining a gang with a known propensity for violence and who could anticipate what might happen if his nerve failed. In this case there would be no immediate assumption that should he wish to withdraw then he might be faced with serious violence. As the court said:

> " … there are certain kinds of criminal enterprises the joining of which, in the absence of any knowledge or propensity to violence on the part of one member, would not lead another to suspect that a decision to think better of the whole affair might lead him into serious trouble. In such cases, if trouble materialises unexpectedly and puts the defendant into a dilemma in which a reasonable man might have chosen to act as he did, the concession to human frailty is available to the defendant."'

Source 7

Adapted from Michael Jefferson, *Criminal Law* (Pitman, 1997), pp 236–39.

'Looking at the law one might expect that necessity should be made consistent with duress by affording a defence in similar circumstances.

'Surely there must be some kind of a defence in circumstances such as those which occurred in *Kitson* (1955), which is one of the more ludicrous cases in post-war English law. The passenger in a car, having taken drink, fell asleep. He awoke to find the driver gone and the car coasting downhill. He grabbed hold of the steering-wheel and in doing so prevented a crash. Surely he should be congratulated not prosecuted. [And] if prosecuted … he should have a defence.

'Recently – and the law is not yet settled – the courts have shown themselves more amenable than previously in creating a defence. The Court of Appeal in *Conway* established a defence called "duress of circumstances". The defendant … said that he had driven recklessly because he feared that two men who approached his car were going to kill his passenger. The court allowed his appeal. The judges held that the facts amounted to duress of circumstances; that duress was an example of necessity; and that whether duress of circumstances was called duress or necessity did not matter.

'The court in *Conway* believed themselves bound by their decision in *Willer* (1986) [where] the term "duress of circumstances" was not used.

'These two cases were followed in *Martin* where the Court of Appeal drew the boundaries of the defence. There had to be a fear of death or serious bodily harm, and a question to be asked was whether a person of reasonable firmness sharing the defendant's characteristics would have responded as the accused did.'

Source 8

Adapted from the judgment of Lord Justice Kennedy in *Pommell* [1995] 2 Cr App R 607.

'The strength of the argument that a person ought to be permitted to breach the letter of the criminal law in order to prevent a greater evil [to] himself or others has long been recognised … but has, in English law, not given rise to a general defence of necessity, and … to … murder, the defence has been specifically held not to exist (see *Dudley and Stephens*) … Even in relation to other offences there are powerful arguments against recognising the general defence …

'However, that does not really deal with the situation where someone commendably infringes a regulation in order to prevent another person from committing what everyone would accept as being a greater evil with a gun. In that situation it cannot be satisfactory to leave it to the prosecuting authority not to prosecute …

'… in the present case the defence was open to the appellant … [but] a person who has taken possession of a gun in circumstances where he has the defence of duress of circumstances must "desist from committing the crime as soon as he reasonably can" …'

Source 9

Adapted from Clarkson and Keating, *Criminal Law Text and Materials* (Sweet & Maxwell, 1998), pp 357–58.

'In 1974 the Law Commission proposed that a general defence of necessity be introduced into English law. However, three years later it rejected the idea, going so far as to say that if a defence of necessity already existed at common law it should be abolished. It felt that allowing such a defence to a charge of murder could effectively legalise euthanasia in England. The Law Commission felt that specific statutory provisions already covered those areas where the defence might be most needed. For minor offences it argued that prosecutions were unlikely and, in any event, the sentencing policy of the English courts was such that people convicted in these situations would probably receive a minimal sentence, say, an absolute or conditional discharge.

'… at the same time as making these "totally negative" proposals, the Law Commission was recommending that duress be extended to *all* crimes. The absurdity of this position was exposed by the … Criminal Code Bill [which] emphasised that it was unacceptable to rely on prosecutorial discretion [and] instead proposed a defence of necessity called "duress of circumstances".

'… it is unfortunate that the Draft Bill perpetuates the terminology of "duress of circumstances". Perhaps it was introduced in *Willer* and *Conway* because the threats there came from other persons rather than from objective circumstances. However, *Martin* was a classic case of necessity and should be recognised as such.

'The courts have come a long way in a short time in recognising that blame is inappropriate in circumstances of necessity.'

Source 10

Adapted from the judgment of Lord Justice Ward in *Re A (Conjoined Twins)* [2000] NLJ Law Reports, 6th October 2000, pp 1453–54.

'J and M were conjoined twins … J was capable of independent existence, but an operation to separate the twins would inevitably have resulted in the death of M who was alive only because a common artery enabled her sister to circulate oxygenated blood for both of them. If there was no such operation they would both die … The parents would not consent …, but the doctors were convinced that they could carry out the operation so as to give J a life that would be worthwhile. The Trust therefore sought a declaration confirming the lawfulness of the proposed operation.

'Ward LJ: The judge was plainly right to conclude that the operation would be in J's best interest. The question was whether it would be in M's best interest. It could not be. It would bring her life to an end before its natural span. It denied her inherent right to life.

'A balance had to be struck … The best interests of the twins was to give the chance of life to the twin whose actual bodily condition was capable of accepting the chance to her advantage even if that had to be at the cost of the sacrifice of the life which was so unnaturally supported. This was, however, subject to whether what was proposed to be done could be lawfully done.

'The crucial question was whether the law should confer in any circumstances, however extreme, the right to choose that one innocent person should be killed rather than another.

'… the doctors could not be denied a right of choice if they were under a duty to choose. They were under a duty to M not to operate because it would kill M, but they were under a duty to J to operate because not to do so would kill her. It was important to stress that it made no difference whether the killing was by act or omission.

'In those circumstances the law had to allow an escape through choosing the lesser of the two evils. Faced as they were with an apparently irreconcilable conflict the doctors should be in no different position from that in which the court itself was placed … giving the sanctity of life principle its place in the balancing exercise that had to be undertaken. For the same reasons that led to the conclusion that consent should be given to operate, the conclusion had to be that the carrying out of the operation would be

justified as the lesser evil and no unlawful act would be committed.'

Source 11

Adapted from Christopher F Sharp QC, *The Manchester Conjoined Twins Case*, New Law Journal, 6th October 2000, pp. 1460–62.

'The issue for the court was whether an act by the doctors which, while saving Jodie's life, and although not primarily intended to kill Mary, would have that inevitable effect, would be unlawful or could be justified … This led finally to a detailed consideration of the doctrine of necessity.

'The Court's approach was to accept that the doctrine of necessity, which in its related form of duress has been rejected by the House of Lords in *Howe* … as a defence to murder, … could nevertheless in the unique circumstances of this case be extended to cover the doctors' intended action … Robert Walker LJ concluded that in the absence of Parliamentary intervention the law as to the defence is going to have to develop on a case by case basis … and this was an appropriate case to extend it, if necessary.

'Ward LJ having identified the rationale of the rejection of the defence of necessity as one based on the sanctity of life, and having identified as the crucial question in this case the question posed by Lord Mackay in *Howe* whether the circumstances could ever be extreme enough for the law to confer a right to choose that one innocent person should be killed rather than another, held that … the law should allow an escape by permitting the doctors to choose the lesser of two evils.

'Brooke LJ carried out an exhaustive review of the jurisprudence … From … Stephen, he derived three necessary requirements for the application of the doctrine:

1. the act is needed to avoid inevitable and irreparable evil;
2. no more should be done than is reasonably necessary for the purpose to be achieved;
3. the evil inflicted must not be disproportionate to the evil avoided.

'Given that the … law pointed irresistibly to the conclusion that the interests of Jodie must be preferred to the conflicting interests of Mary, he considered that all three of these requirements were satisfied in this case.'

Extract from the Law Commission Report, *Murder, Manslaughter and Infanticide,* 2006

An overview of the structure that we are recommending

1.63 We recommend that there should be a new Homicide Act for England and Wales. The new Act should replace the Homicide Act 1957. The new Act should, for the first time, provide clear and comprehensive definitions of the homicide offences and the partial defences. In addition, the new Act should extend the full defence of duress to the offences of first degree and second degree murder and attempted murder, and improve the

procedure for dealing with infanticide cases.

1.64 In structuring the general homicide offences we have been guided by a key principle: the 'ladder' principle. Individual offences of homicide should exist within a graduated system or hierarchy of offences. This system or hierarchy should reflect the offence's degree of seriousness, without too much overlap between individual offences. The main reason for adopting the 'ladder' principle is as Lord Bingham has recently put it (in a slightly different context): The interests of justice are not served if a defendant who has committed a lesser offence is either convicted of a greater offence, exposing him to greater punishment than his crime deserves, or acquitted altogether, enabling him to escape the measure of punishment which his crime deserves. The objective must be that defendants are neither over-convicted nor under-convicted … .

1.65 The 'ladder' principle also applies to sentencing. The mandatory life sentence should be confined to the most serious kinds of killing. A discretionary life sentence should be available for less serious (but still highly blameworthy) killings.

1.66 Partial defences currently only affect the verdict of murder. This is because a verdict of murder carries a mandatory sentence. That sentence is not appropriate where there are exceptional mitigating circumstances of the kind involved in the partial defences. These mitigating circumstances necessitate a greater degree of judicial discretion in sentencing. The law creates this discretion by means of the partial defences which reduce what would otherwise be a verdict of murder, which carries a mandatory sentence, to manslaughter, which does not. Therefore, our recommended scheme does not extend the application of the partial defences to second degree murder or manslaughter. These offences would permit the trial judge discretion in sentencing and they therefore lack the primary justification for having partial defences.

The structure of offences

1.67 We believe that the following structure would make the law of homicide more coherent and comprehensible, whilst respecting the principles just set out above:

1. **First degree murder** (mandatory life penalty)
   (a) Killing intentionally.
   (b) Killing where there was an intention to do serious injury, coupled with an awareness of a serious risk of causing death.

2. **Second degree murder** (discretionary life maximum penalty)
   (a) Killing where the offender intended to do serious injury.

   (b) Killing where the offender intended to cause some injury or a fear or risk of injury, and was aware of a serious risk of causing death.
   (c) Killing in which there is a partial defence to what would otherwise be first degree murder.

3. **Manslaughter** (discretionary life maximum penalty)
   (a) Killing through gross negligence as to a risk of causing death.
   (b) Killing through a criminal act:
      (i) intended to cause injury; or
      (ii) where there was an awareness that the act involved a serious risk of causing injury.
   (c) Participating in a joint criminal venture in the course of which another participant commits first or second degree murder, in circumstances where it should have been obvious that first or second degree murder might be committed by another participant.

Partial defences reducing first degree murder to second degree murder

1.68 The following partial defences would reduce first degree murder to second degree murder:

1. provocation (gross provocation or fear of serious violence);
2. diminished responsibility;
3. participation in a suicide pact.

Other specific homicide offences

1.69 There will remain a number of specific homicide offences, such as infanticide, assisting suicide and causing death by dangerous driving.

Conclusion

1.70 The Criminal Justice Act 2003 ('the 2003 Act'), one of the most important pieces of legislation in the history of criminal justice reform, brought in a new sentencing regime for murder. However, the radical reforms effected by the 2003 Act stand upon shaky foundations because the offence of murder, and the partial defences to it, do not have defensible definitions or a rational structure. Unfortunately, although twentieth-century legislation on murder brought many valuable reforms, the definitions of murder and the partial defences remain misleading, out-of-date, unfit for purpose, or all of these. Quite simply, they are not up to the task of providing the kind of robust legal support upon which the viability of the 2003 Act depends.

Index